MORE PRAISE FOR

WE'LL ALWAYS HAVE *Casablanca*

"Fascinating . . . [and] profoundly relevant."

—Rebecca Prime, *Los Angeles Times*

"Observant and astute . . . Isenberg makes some insightful contributions to *Casablanca* lore."

—Gerald Bartell, *Washington Post*

"An insightful, revelatory new book."

—Paul Teetor, *Los Angeles Weekly*

"Hugely entertaining."

—David Mikics, *Tablet*

"Four out of four stars. . . . Isenberg's great contribution is tying together the production [of *Casablanca*] and its legacy."

—Bill Desowitz, *USA Today*

"Noah Isenberg brings an appropriate passion to his pop analysis of [*Casablanca*], along with a delight of details and some savvy reassessments."

—John Anderson, *Newsday*

"Isenberg gives us . . . a rich miscellany of material that will delight fans of both the film and Hollywood's golden era. His research is clearly second to none."

—Lucy Scholes, *Times Literary Supplement*

"[A] rich account of this most beloved movie's origins."

—Kerri Jarema, *Bustle*

"Isenberg does a great job of reminding us how great [*Casablanca*] is and exploring how and why it has endured."

—David Pitt, *Chronicle Herald*

"An insightful, highly entertaining film history."

—*National Book Review*

"[Isenberg is] an industrious and sensitive writer."

—Robert Fulford, *National Post*

"Isenberg provides a story worthy of its own film. He also explores how the film's message . . . remains urgent."

—Reid Mitenbuler, *Quartz*

"As Noah Isenberg details in his excellent new book, *We'll Always Have Casablanca*, the 1942 film is a case study of how history gets depicted for popular entertainment, but it is also a powerful example of how the Hollywood machine produced work that intersected with political commitment while still holding fast to its romantic conventions."

—Michael S. Roth, *Chronicle of Higher Education*

"Immensely delightful and engaging, *We'll Always Have Casablanca* pursues the story of the Moby-Dick of movies with the passion, acumen, and dexterity of a seasoned historian in dazzling command of the narrative craft."

—Yunte Huang, author of *Charlie Chan: The Untold Story of the Honorable Detective and His Rendezvous with American History*

"As befits its subject, *We'll Always Have Casablanca* is sparkling and effervescent, rich and gimlet-eyed, and, most of all, utterly addicting. By offering a telescopic view of the beloved film's production history, reception, historical context, and ongoing allure, Noah Isenberg's superb book both expands our understanding of the movie's history and place in our cultural history and reminds us, fervently, why we fell in love with it in the first place."

—Megan Abbott, best-selling author of *You Will Know Me*

"Noah Isenberg's lively investigation of how *Casablanca* got made and why it has had such singular influence is far more than a nostalgic journey. He makes clear how *Casablanca*'s themes of war and exile and romantic self-sacrifice distilled the brutal realities of 1942, and mirrored the personal experiences of many of the film's makers, to create an entertainment of profound and enduring emotional resonance."

—Geoffrey O'Brien, author of *Sonata for Jukebox*

"Here's looking at you, Noah Isenberg! Never has *Casablanca* and the world it remakes with every screening been better loved or more meticulously illuminated."

—David Michaelis, author of *Schulz and Peanuts: A Biography*

"Somehow both scholarly and sprightly, Noah Isenberg's prismatic portrait of *Casablanca* manages to inform even as it delights. This rigorous, rollicking book shows us the ways that familiar tale has continued to shift in meaning and expand in scope as time goes by." —Dana Stevens, *Slate* film critic

"Noah Isenberg's thoroughly researched and well-written book brings new perspectives to the one movie that is on every American's playlist. This book is the perfect companion for the viewing experience."

—Jeanine Basinger, author of *The Star Machine*

ALSO BY NOAH ISENBERG

Edgar G. Ulmer:
A Filmmaker at the Margins

Weimar Cinema:
An Essential Guide to Classic Films of the Era (editor)

Detour

Between Redemption and Doom:
The Strains of German-Jewish Modernism

WE'LL ALWAYS HAVE *Casablanca*

THE LIFE, LEGEND, AND AFTERLIFE OF HOLLYWOOD'S MOST BELOVED MOVIE

NOAH ISENBERG

W. W. NORTON & COMPANY
INDEPENDENT PUBLISHERS SINCE 1923
NEW YORK | LONDON

To Melanie, Jules, and Bruno

Printed in the United States of America
First published as a Norton paperback 2018

Manufacturing by LSC Communications Harrisonburg
Book design by Chris Welch
Production manager: Anna Oler

Library of Congress Cataloging-in-Publication Data

Names: Isenberg, Noah William author.
Title: We'll always have Casablanca : the life, legend, and afterlife of Hollywood's most beloved movie / Noah Isenberg.
Description: New York : W. W. Norton & Company, 2017. |
Includes bibliographical references and index.
Identifiers: LCCN 2016045205 | ISBN 9780393243123 (hardcover)
Subjects: LCSH: Casablanca (Motion picture)
Classification: LCC PN1997.C352 I84 2017 | DDC 791.43/72—dc23
LC record available at https://lccn.loc.gov/2016045205

ISBN: 978-0-393-35566-6 pbk.

W. W. Norton & Company, Inc.
500 Fifth Avenue, New York, N.Y. 10110
www.wwnorton.com

W. W. Norton & Company Ltd.
15 Carlisle Street, London W1D 3BS

1 2 3 4 5 6 7 8 9 0

I feel about Casablanca *that it has a life of its own. There is something mystical about it. It seems to have filled a need, a need that was there before the film, a need that the film filled.*

—INGRID BERGMAN

Contents

Introduction

When *Casablanca* premiered in 1942, in the middle of the war and just two weeks after the city of Casablanca itself had surrendered to General Patton's troops, even the most optimistic of Tinseltown dreamers could hardly have predicted that it would go on to become perhaps the most beloved of all Hollywood movies. And yet this "picture that makes the spine tingle and the heart take a leap," as the *New York Times* critic Bosley Crowther called it at the time, would go on not only to win Oscars for best picture, best director, and best adapted screenplay but to enjoy more revival screenings than any other film in the history of cinema. Seventy years after the film's release, the Academy of Motion Pictures Arts and Sciences selected *Casablanca* to inaugurate its "Oscar Outdoors" series at its new open-air theater in the heart of Hollywood. As Umberto Eco once said, *Casablanca* is "not *one* movie; it is '*movies*.'"

Like so many other fans, I was reminded of the movie's indelible place in our cultural lexicon in the spring of 2016, when news arrived that cast member Madeleine Lebeau had passed away in a small Spanish town on the Costa del Sol. Not yet twenty when the film was made, the French-born Lebeau turned in a spirited performance as Yvonne, the young woman who gets snubbed by Humphrey Bogart in the film's first act, only to return defiantly to Rick's Café—shifting her allegiances with the speed of a Vichy opportunist—on the arm of a Nazi officer. She ultimately reveals her true colors by singing a vigorous rendition of "La Marseillaise" during the pivotal scene in which the café patrons sing the French national anthem with increasing fervor to drown out the competing Nazi chorus of "Die Wacht am Rhein." Tears stream down her trembling cheeks, shot in luminous close-up, as she cries out, *"Vive la France!"* and *"Vive la démocratie!"* Three decades after the film was released, Leonid Kinskey, the Russian-born actor who played Sascha the barman, remarked, "I think it was the most moving patriotic scene ever played in any picture." Without Yvonne, without her inimitable voice and her tears, the scene is unthinkable.

In the obituaries published in newspapers and posted on websites across the globe, Lebeau's age was given as ninety-two, and she was widely presumed to have been the last surviving cast member. A striking shot of her taken from the "Marseillaise" scene accompanied many of the death notices, and, in an official statement delivered soon afterward, French Culture Minister Audrey Azoulay said of Lebeau: "She will forever be the face of the French resistance."

Yvonne (Madeleine Lebeau) singing "La Marseillaise."

That sentiment encapsulates the magic of *Casablanca*: a scene from a film that was first brought to life in the dream factories of Southern California in the summer of 1942 is still, some seven and a half decades later, considered representative of a real political and historical epoch. During my research for this book, I spoke with dozens of people—filmmakers and family members, film critics and fans—who, like Minister Azoulay, felt that a specific scene or a specific character, or even the film as a whole, had come to mean something much larger with each passing decade.

We'll Always Have Casablanca is an attempt to capture the story of not just how this most remarkable movie was made—and of the indispensable role that refugees from Hitler's Europe had in making it—but to explore how and why *Casablanca* continues to live on in our collective consciousness, as affecting to our hearts and minds now as it was from the start.

Like all movies, *Casablanca* is not without its imperfections. There are undeniably corny lines and a healthy dose of Hollywood "hokum," in the parlance of the day. But its spectacular achievement, whether it's the result of the "genius of the system," as the great French critic André Bazin once termed it, or the good fortune of historical timing, prodigious talent, and a host of factors that often elude classification, remains indisputable. As Paul Whitington observed in the *Belfast Telegraph* weeks after Lebeau's death, "Maybe there are better films than *Casablanca*, but there are probably none better loved." It flickers, as bravely and beautifully as ever, in the glorious black-and-white shadows of our imagination.

WE'LL ALWAYS HAVE

Casablanca

Chapter 1

EVERYBODY COMES TO RICK'S

Casablanca began its fabled career as a modest, unproduced, three-act stage play, *Everybody Comes to Rick's*, written in 1940 by Murray Burnett and Joan Alison. An English teacher at Central Commercial High School in midtown Manhattan, Burnett was at the start of his career as a playwright. He'd only recently finished his undergraduate degree at Cornell University, and reserved his skills as a dramatist mostly for nights and weekends. A few years before, based on his experiences at his day job, he'd finished a draft of a play he called *An Apple for the Teacher*, which would later be known as *Hickory Stick*. Cowritten with Fredrick Stephani, it would eventually earn an abbreviated run on Broadway—five days total at the Mansfield Theatre—in May 1944. Sometime in the late 1930s, Burnett met his writing partner Alison at the Atlantic Beach Club, one of the many cabana-lined enclaves that dot the South Shore of Long Island, which they both frequented in summer. They quickly began a happy collaboration that lasted many years.

Almost a full decade his senior, a divorcée with three small children, the far more cosmopolitan Alison (née Leviton) read Burnett's work, offered him her wisdom, and shared her network of precious contacts within the New York drama scene. She introduced Burnett to her friend the Broadway producer Delos Chappell, who already had a handful of successful stage credits to his name. Although Chappell was unable to find an immediate home for *An Apple for the Teacher* on Broadway—that came half a decade later—he gave Burnett the necessary encouragement to keep at it. Newly married to his young wife, Frances, living in a rented apartment, and still making car payments, Burnett held on to his day job, continuing to write on the side, often with Alison's aid.

Something had occurred in the summer of 1938 that left a profound impact on Burnett's life, and ultimately on motion-picture history. At the age of twenty-seven, still relatively innocent, unsophisticated, and nominally Jewish, Burnett journeyed with his wife across the Atlantic during his school break. "I had inherited $10,000 from an uncle," he later recalled, "and it was one of my romantic dreams to go to Europe on a big ocean liner. My wife's family lived in Belgium. I had read headlines about Hitler, but they were meaningless until we got to Antwerp and my wife's family asked us to go to Vienna—the Anschluss had just happened—to help other relatives get money out of Austria." By that point, Jews in Nazi-occupied Austria, at least those who were fortunate enough to leave, were prevented from bringing money and other assets with them. "I went to the consulate to get a visa," he recounted further, "and he said, 'Mr. Burnett, I don't know why you're going to Vienna and I don't want to know, but I want to warn you that if you get into any trouble in Vienna this government cannot help you.' He gave me a small American flag to wear in my lapel, and he said, 'You must never go out in the street without wearing this.'" Burnett went to Europe that summer, hoping the journey might serve as a belated honeymoon for him and his wife. He returned with a story he never forgot.

While in Austria, he experienced firsthand the implementation of the Nuremberg Laws and other virulent forms of institutionalized anti-Semitism that had been enthusiastically adopted by the annexed state in May of that year. It was, as he later recounted, "an indescribable horror, a city of marching feet." Milling about the capital city, he stumbled upon a massive sign, bigger than anything he'd ever seen before, "and on the billboard was a caricature of a Jew, and it said in huge letters, MURDERER, THIEF. And we'd sit in the relatives' apartment and hear the marching feet outside." The intensity of the experience, more extreme than he ever possibly could have imagined, stuck with him. While still in Vienna trying to make sense of the situation, asking lots of questions and hearing plenty of tragic stories, Burnett learned of the so-called refugee trail, the treacherous escape route that Jews and others deemed undesirable by the Third Reich were left to travel after the Nazis came to power. "It led from Marseilles to Morocco," explains film historian Charles Francisco, "back across the Mediterranean to Lisbon and—with luck—to eventual safety and freedom in the United States." This is the path outlined on the animated map insert and described in the *March of Time*–like voice-over narration by Lou Marcelle at the start of *Casablanca*.

During the same fateful summer that Burnett visited Austria, high-ranking Nazi official Adolf Eichmann—later made infamous during his 1961 trial in Jerusalem—established Vienna's Zentralstelle für jüdische Auswanderung (Central Agency for Jewish Emigration), which saw to it that Jewish property and other valuables remained in Austrian (read: Aryan) hands. In complete defiance, Burnett and his wife, Frances, boarded a railroad car bound for the border carrying with them a large cache of illegal goods belonging to Frances's Viennese relatives. "When we got on the train, I had diamond rings on every finger and my wife was wearing a fur coat in August," he remembered, describing their scheme to smuggle out the family's prized possessions. A near brush with a border guard—with Murray running a high fever and a camera hidden beneath a pillow in their train compartment—didn't keep the Burnetts from doggedly pursuing their goal, eluding party officials, and making their way through the increasingly impenetrable demarcation lines of Nazi-controlled Europe.

One night, after Murray and his wife arrived in the South of France, having successfully smuggled out the contraband, they visited a smoky nightclub on the outskirts of Nice, on the road to Monte Carlo, perched above the Mediterranean. It catered to a mixed clientele made up of refugees and military officials of all political stripes. The patrons spoke in a babel of foreign tongues, and there was a black pianist, a crooner from Chicago, who was busy working the crowd playing a set of popular jazz standards. Burnett was especially fond of the pianist, whose songs brought him back to his student days at Cornell and whose enchanting voice soothed the audience—"a great contrast to the tragedy and tears," he recalled—and provided them with hours of welcome distraction. Taking in the scene, Burnett purportedly turned to his wife and said on the spot, "What a setting for a play!" Thus was the idea for *Casablanca* born.

Upon returning to New York, with the idea simmering in his mind for the next year or so, Burnett announced to his writing partner, with an uncommon sense of urgency: "No one can remain neutral, God damn it, Joan. No one can remain neutral." They wrote the play, as Burnett later told a reporter from the *Los Angeles Times*, in "the white heat of anger—anger at stupid people who refused to acknowledge that Hitler and Nazism were a threat." Burnett and Alison labored feverishly, for six straight weeks in the summer of 1940, while he was on school break. Putting in long days, they worked out of Alison's well-appointed, spacious apartment on West Fifty-Fourth Street. Their method of collaboration went something like this: he would plant himself at the typewriter, hunting and pecking, while she paced, smoking one cigarette after the next, dictating dialogue aloud. Some of the pages stayed, others got crumpled into a ball and tossed on the floor. It was a continuation of their habit, developed in months leading up to summer, of writing together in the afternoons. "Joan nourished me," Burnett commented many years later. "I went to her apartment after school, and she would give me lunch. She was a marvelous cook. She was a beautiful woman.

I needed Joan. Don't for a moment think I didn't. In a way, I think she was my mother." (Around this same time, Burnett received extensive therapy for his childhood maternal conflicts from renowned Viennese-born analyst Theodor Reik.) Over the years, a number of critics, film historians, and fans have speculated about a possible romantic relationship between the two writers, even suggesting a marriage that never took place, but theirs was strictly a professional affair, all maternal feelings notwithstanding.

As they settled into a rhythm, they invented many of the central characters—including the cynical saloon keeper Rick and the elusive black marketeer Ugarte—as well as the general arc of the plot. The play was originally to be set in wartime Lisbon, which, as historian Neill Lochery has recently suggested, bore many real-life affinities with the fictional atmosphere that Burnett and Alison concocted: "broken romances; desperate refugees trying to obtain correct paperwork and selling the family jewels to finance their onward passage; a thriving black market as supply dictated that the prices of diamonds fell to record low levels; cafés and hotel bars full of refugees and spies scattered across the city center and along Lisbon's coastline resort." Lisbon proved to be the target destination sought by those left stranded in Vichy-controlled North Africa—it was one of the very last European cities from which refugees could gain transatlantic passage or, if they had especially deep pockets, even catch the Pan Am Clipper. Amid a web of subterfuge and desperate flight, Casablanca, a city that neither Burnett or Alison had visited, became the chosen hub for such dramatic tensions from the refugee trail to play out.

With each passing week, the two writers continued to spin their story. They hit a stumbling block when it came time to explain how these refugees might gain access to the free world. Of course, any stateless subjects had to have exit visas of some kind, documents that would enable them to leave a Vichy-ruled zone. But how could they come up with a reasonable plot device? The two writers reached a standstill. "One of Joan Alison's favorite ploys to combat writer's block," explains Francisco, "was an exuberant 'Let's go shopping.'" On this particular day, the two writers strolled a few blocks up Fifth Avenue from Alison's apartment to Bergdorf Goodman, where they did a little indulgent browsing among the luxury goods. Alison tried on a few fancy coats, feigning genuine interest in the purchase, while Burnett looked on bemusedly. By the time they left, reentering the din of the city streets—yes, like many literary and cinematic legends, this may merely be the stuff that dreams are made of—they had purportedly hatched the idea for "letters of transit," those fictional golden tickets that ensure safe departure, almost like Dorothy's ruby slippers in *The Wizard of Oz*, which had been released a year earlier.

The draft Burnett and Alison completed in the summer of 1940 contains much of the raw material, not to mention the well-chiseled characters and inspired plot points, that would be transported to the big screen some two years later. Of course, the love story is there, folded into the tale of stranded refugees, and the righteous cause that must ultimately triumph above all else. Perhaps more remarkable still, Burnett and Alison managed to capture the very mood and atmosphere of a city that neither of them had seen before.

From the opening lines of exposition, the scene is indelible. "The bar of RICK'S CAFÉ, Casablanca, French Morocco, 1941," it begins:

> About eleven o'clock of a summer's evening. This is the bar of an expensive and chic night club which definitely possesses an impalpable air of sophistication and intrigue. There is a hectic excitement about the people and the entertainers that manifests itself in speech and manner. [. . .] Along L. wall Centre is a door leading to the gambling and dance rooms, from which, at intervals, bursts of music and voices can be heard. These increase in volume whenever the door is opened. At L. front, is a table at which a man in tuxedo with white summer jacket is seated. Further front is another table marked "RESERVED." Along R. wall, set into it, are three tables and a number of seats. At extreme R. corner, is a small piano on wheels, salmon colored, ornate, and eye-filling. There is a NEGRO on a stool before it. The walls are decorated with rare tropical birds, flamingoes, etc. and huge palm fronds. The place is full of people, at bar and tables, in evening dress and uniforms. People entering head for the bar, some seek admittance to the gaming rooms, but only after they have been silently approved by the MAN sitting at the table nearest the L. door. He is RICK, an American of indeterminate age. There is a drink before him, untouched. The NEGRO, in bright blue slacks and sport shirt, open at the throat, touches the keys of the

piano softly, playing STARDUST, taking liberties with it. There is a hum of voices, chatter, laughter.

The evocative atmosphere described on the first page of Act I of Burnett and Alison's ninety-seven-page, three-act script is immediately recognizable to anybody who has seen the film that Warner Bros. would later release. There's Rick, his café, even his white dinner jacket; Sam, the "Negro" musician (also called The Rabbit in the play, for his infectious rendition of the popular jazz standard "Run, Rabbit, Run"), with his trusty upright piano on wheels; the lively mixed crowd; and the vaguely exotic décor (Warners would later repurpose sets evocative of the North African streets originally designed for *The Desert Song*, released a year after *Casablanca*).

Soon the action begins, with the arrival of the obsequious Ugarte ("Bowing slightly," as the stage directions read), asking to have a drink with Rick, who responds with words familiar to *Casablanca* initiates: "You know my rule." Of course, Rick never drinks with customers (it will take a jovial, pear-shaped waiter named Carl, absent from the stage play, to remind us). Next arrives a rather pushy fellow named Forrester-Smith, eager to make his way to the roulette table. He's not from the Deutsche Bank, as the film will have it, but a fop from the upper rungs of English society ("a stout, red-faced gentleman, very British, in tweeds"). "Now look here!" he tells Rick. "I've been in every gambling room between Honolulu and Calcutta, and if you think that I'm going to be kept out of a bloody dive like this without going to the authorities, you're very much mistaken, sir." And Rick, in control, snarls his retort: "Your money's good at the bar," adding what will likewise be repurposed as his comeback line, "You're lucky the bar's still open to you."

Throughout these initial pages of the first act, not only are there large swaths of dialogue that will be kept entirely intact in the subsequent screenplay and into the movie, but also quite a few important set pieces and character depictions. For example, there is the exchange between Ugarte and Rick about the thief's most recent haul: "Letters of transit signed by Marshall Weygand. They cannot be rescinded or questioned." Later, when Ugarte expresses a few pangs of guilt, Rick gets in a line that might have made theatergoing audiences of the 1940s squeamish, and surely would have made the Hays Office, responsible for enforcing censorship in the name of the Production Code, shudder. "You remind me of a pimp who's had a windfall," he says. "When he quits, he's so sorry for the girls." Burnett and Alison introduce the chummy friendship between Rick and the morally dubious, skirt-chasing prefect of police Luis Rinaldo (later Louis Renault), who in the play has a fully articulated fetish for innocent young girls: "There is something that attracts me about these unawakened girls, something that challenges. . . ." Rinaldo's rallying cry, "*Pour le sport*, Ricky, *pour le sport*," leads him to trade his own crooked iterations of the law for various services rendered by his underage victims. Finally, Rinaldo and Rick, who learns from his friend of the arrival via the refugee trail of Czech underground leader Victor Laszlo, place their bets on his prospects of flight.

The stage play, as Burnett and Alison first sketched it, holds certain information that will later be deemed either extraneous or detrimental to the plot that is ultimately told. For instance, when Rick dismisses the obedient Rinaldo as a "Gestapo spank" (a term retained in the film), the prefect of police produces a file kept on the mysterious American barman: "Richard Blaine, American. Age (here I shall be discreet) formerly a prominent and successful attorney in Paris. Married to the daughter of Alexander Kirby. Two children. Left Paris in 1937 because. . . . We will pass over that. Your wife obtained her divorce in Reno, in 1939 and has custody of the children." Some of the other trimming and modification concerns the ancillary characters introduced by Burnett and Alison. Although Rick's abandoned plaything Yvonne makes an appearance in their rendition, she's much more forward than on screen ("Rick has no soul," she asserts, "but he's nice to sleep with"). Likewise, Rick's long lost paramour, Lois Meredith, an American with a sordid past, arrives on the arm of Laszlo radiating an attitude more suggestive of Mae West ("It isn't the first time," she boasts to Rinaldo when he commends her for having Rick break his rules and join them for a drink, "you must read my memoirs"), or perhaps a naughty American cousin of Ilsa Lund, than of the restrained European she will become in the film. For his part, Laszlo is presented as a man with access to bank accounts containing millions of dollars raised by the resistance, held in Prague and other cities across Europe, which the Gestapo is intent on seizing; it's money rather than names of other key members of the resistance that the Nazis demand.

Yet despite the many later, largely self-serving assertions to the contrary, much of the wartime political rhetoric attributed to individual characters as well as the essential shades of French Moroccan ambience are drawn from the play. We learn, for instance, of Rick's overriding neutrality. "This is a place of entertainment," he declares after breaking up an argument. "When you come here you leave your political opinions behind." Still later, when introduced to Captain Strasser—who will earn a promotion, to major, for the movie—Rinaldo describes his friend approvingly: "Rick is unlike any American you have ever met, Captain. He is *completely* neutral." The owner of the Blue Parrot nightclub, Rick's down-market competitor, makes an appearance in the first act, bearing the name Señor Martinez (later Signor Ferrari), and as in the film, he puts in an offer on Rick's Café and on Sam, both of which are rebuffed by Rick.

In the hands of Burnett and Alison, Sam the piano player harbors the same boundless loyalty as he does two years later on screen. He covers for Rick, trying to prevent his friend's ensnarement with Lois. His original lines of dialogue remain unchanged in the screenplay: "Boss, we'll take the car and drive all night. We'll get drunk. We'll go fishin' and stay away until she's gone." Likewise, in the stage play Lois hums the opening bars and even sings a few lines of its most famous stanza before Sam agrees to play their forbidden torch song "As Time Goes By." It was an all-time favorite from his college days, and Burnett played the 1931 recording by beloved crooner Rudy Vallee over and over at Cornell, driving his fraternity brothers mad and wearing out the recording in the process. Finally, in Burnett and Alison's rendition, we learn of Rick's pained

Playwright Joan Alison soon after selling Everybody Comes to Rick's *to Warner Bros.*

memory of his Parisian tryst with Lois at La Belle Aurore and of Lois's penchant for wearing blue.

While writing the play, certain characters were molded around composites of people that Burnett and Alison either knew personally or had read about. Burnett often claimed that Rick was a mix of an ideal version of "himself and a college roommate." Here Alison took a different view: "I always scream when he identifies with Rick, because he was a country boy, unsophisticated. Both of my husbands were wide-shouldered and fine athletes, and Rick was my concept of a guy that I would like. Clark Gable." The name Laszlo, Burnett often recounted, derived from Laszlo Bellak, a 1930s Jewish-Hungarian table tennis champion, a gold medalist in Paris and Berlin, and émigré to America. As for the female lead, the inspiration may well have come from across Burnett's desk. "Murray's concept of sophisticated was me," insisted Alison. "Lois was based on me." An extant photo of Alison, taken at a restaurant in New York the day that she and Burnett sold their play to Warner Bros., two days after Christmas 1941, shows her wearing an elegant gown and a floral brooch and boasting the well-coiffed hair—popularly known then as "victory rolls," owing to their V shape—of a Hollywood movie star.

Over the course of the play's remaining two acts, additional core story elements get taken up—many of them retained, in some form or another, in the final film. We witness the rekindling of amorous feelings between Rick and Lois, who returns alone to see her former lover; hear her guilt-ridden pronouncement of Laszlo's heroic virtues ("He's one of the few men willing to lift up his voice and tell the world to fight for what he believes in"); and are exposed to Rinaldo's persuasive skills in convincing Rick that he's merely being played for a sap. Rick and Laszlo square off, lobbing a few acid lines at each other. And perhaps most important, near the close of the second act, when a group of German officers begins to sing an amped-up rendition of the beloved Nazi anthem "Das Horst Wessel Lied" (later changed, when rights couldn't be secured for the film, to "Die Wacht am Rhein") Laszlo exhorts Sam to play the "Marseillaise" ("Rick nods to the Rabbit almost imperceptibly," as the stage directions have it, "and the RABBIT begins to play"). We then encounter the young, naïve Bulgarian newlyweds Jan and Annina—here given the family name Viereck ("square" in German), perhaps an in-joke for Burnett and Alison—and catch wind of their emotional conversation, replayed verbatim in the screenplay, in which Annina seeks Rick's advice as to how she should handle Rinaldo's proposition to exchange visas for sex.

The final act allows Rick to reveal the true allegiances hidden beneath that otherwise impenetrable carapace of his. He helps the Bulgarian couple secure safe passage ("a kind of peace offering to love," as he calls it), using one of the prized letters of transit to secure them a spot on the plane to Lisbon with Victor and Lois. He has them say a prayer for Ugarte, who is thought to have committed suicide in Nazi custody. And after duping Rinaldo, holding him at bay while the others flee, Rick gives his dramatic farewell in a scene that holds more than a mere germ of one of Hollywood's most famous finales:

Rick: (Sharply) You're going, Lois.

Lois: No, no, no! You fool, I'm in love with you again. It's true that I came here for an exit visa, when I saw you my knees went weak. I'm . . .

Rick: You're going, Lois. There nothing here for you. You told me . . . I'm finished . . . all burned out . . . Victor's still fighting, and he needs you, Lois.

Lois: (Frantically) I don't care. I'm . . .

Rick: Get out of here, Victor, for God's sake . . .

Victor: (Pulling her towards the door) Rick, are you sure it's worth it?

Rick: (Forcefully) I'm sure . . . you've got a job to do.

Victor: (Sweeping LOIS with him towards the door) Thank you, Rick, and no matter what you think . . . you're still fighting.

Rick allows himself to be arrested by an irate Strasser, explaining his motives in his last line, the very last in the play, to an inquiring Rinaldo: "For the folding money, Luis, for the folding money. You owe me five thousand francs." The stage directions indicate that Rick walks off with Strasser as the curtain closes.

WHEN THEY FINISHED a draft of the play, Burnett and Alison found a talented New York agent named Anne Watkins who took an immediate interest in the property and soon had it optioned for an undisclosed sum by Broadway producers Martin Gabel and Carly Wharton. Unsure of its potential on Broadway, the producers, operating out of an office on West Forty-Second Street, approached playwrights Ben Hecht and Robert Sherwood, both of whom purportedly voiced their approval after giving it a read. "The play doesn't really need a major rewrite," they reported back to the producers. Things looked up, at least for the moment.

A more serious issue arose when Wharton questioned the putatively immoral—and, for many theatergoers of the 1940s, objectionable—portrayal of Lois. It's clear enough in the play that Lois has sex with Rick when she returns alone to try to get the letters of transit. Wharton demurred, as she later explained it, "as strongly as anyone with an open mind could object" to it. There were, additionally, some lingering concerns about the ending, in which Rick gets whisked away by the Nazis (this was, rather presciently, the kind of thing that would pose a red flag for the Office of War Information a couple of years later). Reluctant to make substantive changes to their precious script—a young playwright named Louis Weitzenkorn is said to have taken a quick pass at it—even if that might give it better chances on Broadway, Burnett and Alison instead urged their agent to give Hollywood a whirl.

While they were still shopping the play out west—it bounced around different studios for well over a year—the two writers worked on a few other original pieces, hoping that they might either land a spot on Broadway or, perhaps, reach the hands of an eager studio professional in Hollywood. One of these was a play that shared a bit of thematic overlap with *Rick's* and took the form of an anti-Nazi spy thriller. Given the working title *One in a Million*, it focused on the threat of Nazi infiltration in the German-American Bund, a topic that Warner Bros. had taken up in its 1939 production of *Confessions of a Nazi Spy*. They showed their play to émigré director and actor Otto Preminger—later brought in to Warners' Burbank studios and tested for the role of Major Heinrich Strasser—who optioned it, but he eventually passed when it became clear that the duo's real focus remained fixed on *Rick's*.

For Burnett and Alison, that particular script was first priority; it was a story that *had* to be told. "It was a cautionary tale," observed David Margolick of the *New York Times* in 1985, "a warning that, as fascism marched forward, good men and women everywhere had to take a stand." Warner Bros. already had a reputation for supporting the cause, having made a few stridently anti-fascist pictures in recent years. Producer Hal B. Wallis, the big man on the lot who was in the process of negotiating with studio head Jack Warner to supervise a number of signature productions of his own, was particularly receptive to such ideas. "Five days after Pearl Harbor, I found a script [*Rick's*] on my desk that was destined to become my toughest assignment, the most famous picture I ever made, and a legend that has lasted until this day," notes Wallis in his breezy memoir *Starmaker*, written with Charles Higham. He goes on to call the property "an obscure play" that was "written by two unknowns" and that, in his somewhat questionable telling, "had been turned down by every studio in town" (at least one producer at M-G-M is said to have put in a lowball bid of $5,000 but couldn't get support from the higher-ups at his studio, and Paramount allegedly made an offer on it as well). Wallis readily admits that the initial story by Burnett and Alison contained many of the key components of the movie, if merely in the rough. "The script needed a great deal of work," he adds, "but I liked it. The story of a laconic American solving the problems of Europeans would have definite appeal in those troubled times."

On December 22, 1941, a studio memorandum from Wallis's office was sent to story editor Irene Lee (née Levine), head of the Warners story department and the studio's first champion of the play: "Mr. Wallis would like you to please get him a price on the story *Everybody Comes to Rick's* and get reactions on it from three or four people." The first reaction came, a day later, from associate producer and contract writer Jerry Wald: "What dialogue I read in the synopsis was very good, and I think we should be able to get a good picture out of it." That same day, veteran screenwriter Robert Lord wrote to Lee, "I suspect that with enough time and effort a picture could be got from this very obvious imitation of *Grand Hotel*." Just a few days later, on behalf of the studio, Wallis acquired the rights to Burnett and Alison's play for $20,000—the most money ever paid, at that time, by a Hollywood studio for an unproduced play and more than twice the purchase price of Warners' acquisition of Dashiell Hammett's *The Maltese Falcon* the previous year—for what would become Warner Bros.' Production No. 410 on its slate of films for 1942. It's hard to know the real reason for the unprecedented sum. Wallis had been impressed with the box-office performance of the Casbah-rocking romance *Algiers* (1938), an American adaptation of *Pépé le Moko* starring European heartthrobs Charles Boyer and Hedy Lamarr. He also liked its vaguely exotic, simple but catchy one-word title. On New Year's Eve 1941, he sent around a memo to all departments at the studio announcing, "The story that we recently purchased entitled *Everybody Comes to Rick's* will hereafter be known as *Casablanca*."

ALTHOUGH HE'D ALREADY made the purchase, Wallis wasn't yet done surveying the different opinions of writers on the lot, carefully weighing his options before assigning it to a single individual or team. An official slogan at Warners, a string of words found printed at the bottom of all studio memoranda, was "Verbal messages cause misunderstanding and delays (please put them in writing)," and the paper trail for its productions was appropriately vast. Screenwriter Aeneas MacKenzie dispatched a memo to Wallis's secretary Paul Nathan on January 3 offering his unvarnished views. "I think we can get a good picture out of this play," wrote MacKenzie. "But it isn't a pushover; because certain characterizations—such as Rinaldo—need very definite strengthening and certain basic situations present problems from the censorship angle. The pre-action relationship between Rick and Lois, for example, is one which does not seem permissible in film." Not everyone shared the optimism that MacKenzie and others articulated in the first round of readings. Fellow writer Wally Kline wrote to Wallis a couple of days later, expressing his concerns about the "highly censorable situations" in the play and about retaining the ending. "It will be a tough job to get a satisfactory picture out of this material," he wrote, "but I believe it can be done." The following day, Robert Buckner, a seasoned producer and screenwriter at Warners, then hard at work on *The Desert Song* (1943), offered an unambiguous dissenting view. "I do not like the play at all, Hal," Bruckner's note began. "I don't believe the story or the characters. Its main situations and the basic relations of the principals are completely censorable and messy, its big moment is sheer hokum melodrama [. . .] and this guy Rick is two-parts Hemingway, one-part Scott Fitzgerald, and a dash of café Christ." True as some of his assertions may seem today, Buckner proved to be in the minority among the preliminary readers.

In fact, by early February, Wallis was in the thick of negotiations with the Epstein twins, Julius and Philip, who had already earned numerous accolades at the studio, with films like *Four Wives* (1939), *No Time for Comedy* (1940), *Strawberry Blonde* (1941), and *The Man Who Came to Dinner* (1942), and who were eager to work on the script. "We thought the play would make a wonderful movie," recalled Julius nearly half a century later. "It had a lot of juice to it." After a stint as an office boy and New York press agent, Julius had begun writing at Warners in 1934, then in his midtwenties. His brother Philip joined him a few years later. Their specialty was "champagne comedy," often buoyed by snappy dialogue with a healthy dose of wit (*Gift of Gab* was, fittingly enough, one of Philip's early stories). They had long since proved their talents when it came to adapting stage plays, and they were also known around the studio for their ability to get otherwise sagging screenplays up onto their feet, adding "a little zip to the script," as director Raoul Walsh once put it.

Born in 1909 on Manhattan's Lower East Side, "the Boys"

*The writers Julius (*left*) and Philip (*right*) Epstein in their office at Warner Bros.*

or "Julie and Phil," as they came to be known in Hollywood, were raised in a small apartment on East Broadway above a doctor's office. Having arrived among the early waves of minimally educated Jewish immigrants from Eastern Europe, their mother worked as a housekeeper and their father maintained a livery stable. Already an avid movie- and theatergoer as a child, Julius served as editor in chief of his school newspaper at Erasmus Hall High School, in the Flatbush section of Brooklyn, where he and Philip were both varsity boxers; Julius initially harbored aspirations of becoming a sportswriter. The twins went on to attend Penn State University, where both boxed in the intercollegiate bantamweight division and where Julius served as team captain during their senior year, in 1929. While at Penn State, Julius, who become a political science major, enrolled in a playwriting course, eventually churning out more than half a dozen original scripts by the early 1930s. ("They were just hack work," he later recalled.)

In 1933, Julius was summoned to the West Coast to ghostwrite a script sold to Warners by a college classmate of his and their mutual friend Jerry Wald (the same Wald who would later read *Everybody Comes to Rick's* soon after its arrival at the studio). His friends were in a pickle, as they had sold the script on spec and couldn't figure out how to finish it themselves. Julius got a crash course in screenwriting by watching a production on the lot at Paramount—*College Humor*, costarring Bing Crosby and Mary Carlisle—just days after arriving in Los Angeles, and he promptly banged out the script to seal the deal for his friends. As a result of these events, and the crooked arrangement with Wald, he is thought to have served as inspiration for the fictional character of Julian Blumberg, the nebbishy playwright whose work gets plagiarized by the ruthless antihero Sammy Glick, modeled in part on Wald, in Budd Schulberg's acclaimed 1941 Hollywood novel *What Makes Sammy Run*? Unlike Blumberg, however, Epstein managed to hit the ground running. Within a year of his arrival, he landed the first of two consecutive seven-year contracts at Warners, and his dear brother Philip—who was known for finishing Julius's sentences and vice versa—followed closely behind.

Inveterate pranksters, the Epsteins enjoyed a well-deserved reputation in Burbank for having something of an antiauthoritarian streak, holding forth for hours on end at the writers' table in the studio commissary. The frequent butt of their jokes was studio boss Jack Warner, a man who, as Jack Benny once quipped, "would rather tell a bad joke than make a good movie." The twins once swiped Warner's stationery and dashed off a note to a handsome, young actor named Don Taylor, an old friend of theirs from Penn State, in which they slyly ridiculed Warner's known tendency to ask Jewish actors (famously John Garfield, né Jacob Julius Garfinkle) to change their names. "All of us at Warner Bros. are looking forward to your great career as an actor," they wrote in the voice of Jack Warner, "and to a long and fruitful relationship with you under your new name of Hyman Rabinowitz."

According to Leslie Epstein's personal account of his father and uncle, in "Duel in the Sun," Philip and Julius were active, loyal members of the Screen Writers Guild. When a number of writers picketed on the lot, sometime in the 1940s, several members of the union were allegedly targeted and roughed up by "goons" hired by Warner. Julius is said to have suggested, never missing a beat, that the studio motto be changed from "Combining Good Picture-Making with Good Citizenship" to "Providing Good Picture Making with Good Marksmanship." Years later, during the anti-Communist witch hunts of the McCarthy era, Warner allegedly handed over the names of the Epstein twins—and several others, all of whom had been in contract disputes with him—to the House Un-American Activities Committee ("Those boys are always on the side of the underdog," he accused). When asked, in a questionnaire they were sent by HUAC, whether they had ever belonged to a subversive organization, they both answered in the affirmative. The name of said organization? Warner Brothers.

Among the things that drove Jack Warner especially crazy was the twins' habit of arriving at the studio in the afternoon. One day, when no longer able to put up with it, he confronted them. "Read your contract," he barked, "It says you have to be on the lot by nine in the morning. What makes you two different from everybody else? Butchers have to be at the butcher shop at nine. Clerks have to be behind their desks then, too. Even presidents of banks have to show up at nine." In response, the twins sent Warner the unfinished pages they were then working on with a note attached to them: "Why don't you tell a bank president to finish the script." That plucky attitude—in particular, the immense joy taken in ridiculing figures of power—found its way, in tone and sensibility, into the screenplay they ultimately hatched from *Everybody Comes to Rick's.*

By the time they were assigned to the project, in February 1942, the Epsteins were relatively experienced working in both a credited and uncredited capacity at the studio. The twins had collaborated with producer Hal Wallis on *Strawberry Blonde* and with director Michael Curtiz, soon to be tapped for *Casablanca*, his sixty-first feature for the studio, on *Four Wives*. Julius and writer Lenore Coffee, who would later be among the many at the commissary writers' table asked to sprinkle pixie dust on the inchoate *Casablanca* script, had been nominated for best screenplay for *Four Daughters* (1938). Still, they understood the inner workings of a system whose supposed genius didn't often reward the writers. "Everybody at the studio was a script doctor—'Who isn't doing anything at the moment? Here, see what you can do with these scripts,'" Julius told film historian Patrick McGilligan in a 1983 interview. For Epstein, during the 1940s, it didn't much matter whether you received credit for a picture, since you were on contract and the studio knew the extent of your contribution; they were the ones who paid your salary, which didn't depend on the final tally of fixes made or adaptations written in a given year. "There were seventy to seventy-five writers at Warners—it wasn't called the motion picture *industry* for nothing," he recalled half a century after the production. "It was like an assembly line."

What the Epsteins were particularly good at was dialogue, often of the cheeky variety, and many of the final *Casablanca* screenplay's finest and most mordant lines can be traced back to them. The fast-paced, testosterone-laden banter between Rick and Renault bears their signature ("How extravagant you are, throwing away women like that," remarks Renault when Rick brushes off the advances made by Yvonne in the first reel.

"Someday they may be scarce."), as do the pair's intermittent bouts of verbal sparring ("I just paid out twenty. I'd like to get it back," Rick tells Renault when making their bet on Laszlo's chances of escape. "Make it ten," responds Renault. "I am only a poor corrupt official"). Carl, the waiter with the tongue of a borscht belt entertainer (or, in the case of character actor S. Z. Sakall, picked to play him, a Hungarian cabaret artist), was born at their shared desk, as was much of the acerbic dialogue written for that other great source of mischief and deception, Signor Ferrari: "As the leader of all illegal activities in Casablanca, I am an influential and respected man."

As for the screenplay's occasional moments of sexual innuendo—more refined and suggestive than in the stage play—they seem to have the Epsteins' fingerprints on them, too: for instance, when Annina tells Rick that both she and husband arrived at his café escorted by Renault, he replies, with an implied wink and a nudge, "Captain Renault is getting broad minded." And then there's the inspired final scene of the screenplay in which an utterance by Renault, after Rick unloads his gun into Strasser's chest (i.e., "Major Strasser has been shot"), may well be "the single best use of the passive voice in movie history," as *New Yorker* critic David Denby remarked. After a pause and barely a heartbeat, Renault follows it with that other most famous line of dialogue, whose murky origins lie in a car carrying the Epstein twins somewhere along that curvy patch of Sunset Boulevard. As Philip's son Leslie tells it, stopped at a red light at the corner of Beverly Glen, still wracking their brains for the perfect formulation, they both turned to each other and, in unison, cried out: "Round up the usual suspects!"

When faced with the near impossible task of doling out the precise share of credit for "that celebrated piece of patchwork picturemaking," as McGilligan aptly calls *Casablanca*, the Epsteins undoubtedly deserve a healthy chunk. They took the first crack at the script—after the initial round of evaluations and treatments had been written up by MacKenzie and Kline—and then worked on it in earnest after returning from a four-week stint in Washington, D.C., where they were collaborating with Frank Capra on the *Why We Fight* series in March. A draft of the script from April 2, 1942, kept in the Warner Bros. archives in Los Angeles only has their two names listed on it.

While they were away, however, Wallis put the script into a number of different hands, including those of Howard Koch, a relatively new contract writer at Warners, who was occupied with several other projects when *Casablanca* arrived on the scene. Born in New York City in 1901, Koch had studied law at Columbia University before becoming a writer. He got his start at Orson Welles's Mercury Theatre, collaborating with John Houseman on a series of radio plays, including the sensational 1938 Halloween episode of *War of the Worlds* announcing an attack by Martians. Koch landed at Warner Bros. sometime in the late 1930s, and worked with Wallis soon after on the Bette Davis vehicle *The Letter* (1940). He also served as one of the screenwriters, together with John Huston, on the highly successful war drama *Sergeant York* (1941), a film that allowed

Koch to become more explicitly invested in what he saw as the noble fight against tyranny. It was a political reflex that he would rely on again in *Casablanca.* A man of the left, yet without party affiliation, Koch would soon write *Mission to Moscow* (1943) for Warners, a sympathetic portrayal of Russia directed by Curtiz. He would later be subpoenaed by the House Un-American Activities Committee and ultimately forced into exile in England, spending many years on the industry's blacklist.

When he received drafts of the Epsteins' script from Wallis, Koch did not often share the twins' approach. "They apparently see the situations more in terms of their comic possibilities," he wrote in a memo to Wallis of May 11, 1942, "while my effort has been to legitimize the characters and develop a serious melodrama of present-day significance, using humor merely as a relief from dramatic tension. I am not presuming to decide which is the better way to attack the picture, but certainly they are different from the ground up." Koch was keen on giving Rick, in particular, more political depth; his gunrunning habit in Ethiopia and his anti-fascist combat in Spain came from Koch (as did, presumably, his presence on the Gestapo's blacklist in Paris). Koch was responsible for Rick's key line of dialogue—providing a vital flicker of humanity—in response to Ferrari's bid on Sam, "I don't buy or sell human beings." In a direct volley, the Epsteins gave Ferrari his rather dark, humorous reply: "It's too bad. That's Casablanca's leading commodity."

In that "powderkeg of political tension," as Warners story analyst Stephen Karnot first described the atmosphere evoked in Burnett and Alison's rendition of *Rick's*, Koch was often intent on emphasizing the ideological underpinnings; he had hoped, for instance, to insert a rather heavy-handed scene in which Laszlo coaxes Renault into toasting with him to *liberté, égalité,* and *fraternité.* "Within the confines of a studio that both Koch and Julie Epstein describe as 'a family,'" observes Aljean Harmetz, "Koch rewrote the Epsteins to give the movie more weight and significance, and the Epsteins then rewrote Koch to erase his most ponderous symbols and to lighten his earnestness."

A bit later in the production, when Wallis sensed trouble with the love scenes, he brought in yet another writer, Casey Robinson, with whom he had just worked on the blustery Bette Davis romance *Now, Voyager.* It's unclear whether Wallis had already been showing Robinson, one of the studio's most valued and best-paid writers, drafts of the script along the way. Whatever may have preceded his official involvement, on May 20, 1942, Robinson submitted his "Notes on Screenplay 'Casablanca'" to Wallis's office. As he wrote at the outset, "my impression about *Casablanca* is that the melodrama is well done, the humor excellent, but the love story deficient. Therefore my comments are almost all concerned with the latter." He offered a number of ideas on how to beef up this particular aspect, and the document makes clear that Robinson had even written test scenes, centering on the romance.

Among the various suggestions that Robinson made was to replace the slightly overexperienced American Lois, from Burnett and Alison's play, with a European woman of greater virtue and nobility. "Something very specific gave me this idea," he told Joel Greenberg in a 1974 interview. "I was falling in love with a Russian ballerina named Tamara Toumanova; writers sometimes have such personal reasons." (True to form, when the Epsteins first caught wind of this change while they were still in Washington working on *Why We Fight*, they dashed off a caustic note to Wallis on hotel stationery: "While we handle the foreign situation here, you try to get a foreign girl for the part. An American girl with big tits will do. [. . .] Love and kisses, Julie and Phil.") Robinson's final contribution may be measured more in terms of what he added to the dramatic mood than to the dialogue. Julius Epstein insisted in his interview with McGilligan that Robinson's only lasting contribution to the script was the line "A franc for your thoughts" in the Parisian flashback, "which I always thought was a terrible line."

Not all of the film's famous snippets of dialogue came from the screenwriters alone. There are indeed those that, over the years, have been attributed to others involved in the production. For instance, a number of Bogart biographers, film historians, and critics have claimed that the actor prevailed upon director Curtiz, adding his two cents to the shooting script in the case of both "Here's looking at you, kid" and "Of all the gin joints in all the towns in the world, she walks into mine!" In retrospect, given the high number of tweaks to the dialogue, this seems entirely plausible. "We were making changes in the script every day during shooting," Julius Epstein told Stephen Bogart in his *Bogart: In Search of My Father* (1995). "We were handing in dialogue hours, even minutes, before it was to be shot." As for the film's last line of dialogue ("Louis, I think this is the beginning of a beautiful friendship")—delivered by Bogart in what was ostensibly the very last round of retakes—it originated, we are given to believe, with the producer himself. Wallis claims in his memoir to have chosen it over an anemic alternate line ("Louis, I might have known you'd mix your patriotism with a little larceny"), and at least Robinson corroborates Wallis's claim. Regardless of its origins, it remains one of the film's most memorable utterances. Or, as David Thomson puts it, "Today, that shameless get-off line speaks to the lasting bonds of affection between golden-age Hollywood and ourselves—the tarnished coinage of movies."

For many years, after the celebrated screenplay earned an Oscar for the Epsteins and Koch and brought considerable fame to all involved, moments of intermittent quibbling about the full extent of each individual contribution took place. In 1973, Koch published a revisionist account in *New York* magazine—reprinted that same year as the preface to the published screenplay—in which he famously took far more than his fair share of credit. He began the piece by discrediting wholesale the work of Burnett and Alison: "The play provided an exotic locale and a character named Rick who ran a café but little in the way of a story adaptable to the screen." Not since James Agee who, in his barbed contemporary review of the film in *The Nation*, lambasted *Everybody Comes to Rick's* (presumably without ever having read it) as "one of the world's worst plays," had anyone taken such a pot shot. Koch went on in the same piece to describe how he started the artistic process from scratch—just him and "a dozen brown pencils, Eagle Number One," at his desk at Warners—from the first "Fade In" to the film's finale. "When I sent down to the set the last scene and wrote *The End* on the screenplay," he writes somewhat imaginatively, "I felt like a weary traveler who had arrived at a destination but with only the foggiest notion where he was or how he got there." Burnett and Alison filed a $6.5 million libel lawsuit against Koch and his publisher for taking sole credit on their story. "Koch has an awfully bad memory," remarked Alison, who insisted further, "there is enough glory in *Casablanca* for both the original authors and screen adaptors."

Five years later Koch published his memoirs, the shamelessly titled *As Times Goes By*, and changed his tune ever so slightly. "When it was all over and the words *Fade Out, The End* had been typed on the much-revised and multi-authored script," he writes there, "I had only the foggiest notion of what

The writer Howard Koch accepting the Academy Award for Best Adapted Screenplay of 1943.

sort of film would emerge from the composite of our efforts." (In that same version, Koch refers to *Rick's* as "an unproduced play by Murray Burnett and Jean [*sic*] Alison.") Even if Julius Epstein would later poke fun at the award-winning screenplay, calling it "slick shit," he wasn't especially thrilled about being written out of the script's creation. As Epstein commented, after the initial piece by Koch was published, "I've always liked Howard. I think his memory is just wrong, and he is thinking the wishful thought." Robinson, for his part, asserts: "I do know that the boys wrote the police stuff and the comedy, and they wrote it very well. And the breaking into and closing down of the club ['I am shocked, *shocked* to find that there is gambling going on in here!']—they wrote that. So what it came to was I wrote the love story." Robinson also claims, rather disingenuously, to have been the first to read the play for Wallis ("It was set in Casablanca, Africa, and there the relationship with the picture almost ends."). A decade and a half after he stoked the fire with his essay in *New York* magazine, Koch took a more philosophical position on the film's creation: "I've got almost a mystical feeling about *Casablanca*. That it made itself somehow. That it needed to be made and that we were all conveyers on the belt, taking it there."

The closest we may get to a definite answer as to who wrote the bulk of the screenplay can only come from reading the hard evidence left behind from the production, and it tells a different story. For instance, on the finished draft, dated June 1, 1942, the Epsteins' names are listed first and in the largest type, and below them in a slightly smaller font is Howard Koch (even Koch himself notes this in his revised comments).

Similarly, on the production budget prepared a day later and reprinted in Rudy Behlmer's *Inside Warner Bros.*, the Epstein brothers receive the highest salaries among writers on the film ($15,200 apiece, for their twelve weeks on the assignment, compared with Koch's $4,200 for approximately seven weeks); the budget also accounts for fees paid to writers Wally Kline ($1,983), Aeneas MacKenzie ($2,150), and Lenore Coffee ($750), with an additional $6,350 listed for "Script Changes," possibly used to supplement the additional payment to Robinson, who is said to have earned a total of $9,000 for three weeks on the film.

THIS SAME BATTLE against anonymity and lack of proper acclaim followed playwright Murray Burnett for the rest of his life. After the success of the film, he and Alison found their way to Hollywood and were both hired as writers at Paramount at a salary of $1,000 per week. Despite the lucrative paycheck, neither of them found a proper fit at the studio, where among other things they were assigned a Bob Hope comedy. "Remember we were not screenwriters," Alison recounted in 1990. "They wanted us to go through all their old scripts that they wanted redone. I'm not a plagiarizer. I couldn't work on anybody else's idea." That, however, is how much of Hollywood works, as Burnett found out more than once. In June 1962, in the case of *Burnett v. Lambino*, he charged Metro-Goldwyn-Mayer with plagiarizing *Hickory Stick* (what was originally *An Apple for the Teacher*) in the 1955 film *The Blackboard Jungle*. He lost in court.

A decade and a half later, when Burnett and Allison filed a libel suit against Bogart biographer Nathaniel Benchley (they argued that his claim that their play "died before it ever reached Broadway" was libelous), *Variety* ran its piece on the trial under the snide title "Lose it Again, Sam." And lose they did. Burnett later sued Warners to have the rights of his characters returned to him and lost that as well. "These characters are part of me, and I have great regard for them—even Ugarte," Burnett told journalist David Margolick in 1985. "I want them back." The contract that he and Alison had signed, perhaps naïvely, over forty-three years earlier, however, stipulated that they "give, grant, bargain, sell, assign, transfer and set over" to Warner Bros. the complete rights "to every kind and character whatsoever, whether or not now known, recognized or contemplated, for all purposes." In other words, they didn't stand a chance. "Plaintiffs may play it again," wrote Justice John A. K. Bradley of New York State Supreme Court in his ruling on the $60 million suit filed in 1983, "but they must do it in United States District Court."

"We called it 'the curse of *Casablanca*,'" Burnett's widow Adrienne, a Hungarian-born actress who met Murray when she played in the Broadway production of *Hickory Stick*, told me from her home in Honolulu. "When a movie is a great success, everybody wants to take credit for it." It was also part of the "curse," as she continued, that Murray Burnett, for much of his adult life, was left "trying to get credit for something that everyone else was taking credit for." Even late in life, when Burnett was finally given his proper due, the curse followed him. "You know the story about the man who was tried for stealing a chicken and acquitted," he is quoted as having said in his obituary of September 1997. "For the rest of his life, people say, 'That's the guy who stole the chicken.'"

Throughout his long career, Burnett continued to work on other projects, yet many of them led him back to Rick. In the early 1950s, he wrote a radio series called *Café Istanbul* (later renamed *Time for Love*), starring Marlene Dietrich as Mademoiselle Madou, in which, either consciously or subconsciously, he crafted a number of spin-off scenarios from the play that he and Alison had written. In November 1952, *The New Yorker* ran a story about Dietrich and her radio performance: "Miss Dietrich read on until she came to 'All that evening the smoke had swirled and eddied about the Café Istanbul in nervous circles, as if looking for escape.' 'This *eddied* is English?' she inquired. 'Sure it's English,' said [director] Burnett. 'Take it out,' said Miss Dietrich. 'If I don't know it, they won't know it in Idaho.'" As Adrienne Burnett says of Dietrich's part in *Istanbul*, "I think to a great extent, she was a female version of Rick." Up until his death in 1997, Burnett held on to blueprints for a sequel to *Everybody Comes to Rick's*, a fifteen-page typescript he kept in his desk drawer, in which Rick runs a bar in Estoril, Portugal, on the outskirts of Lisbon, with Renault still in tow.

In April 1991, the original version of *Everybody Comes to Rick's*, under the more commercially viable name *Rick's Bar Casablanca*, was finally staged at London's Whitehall Theatre; it starred British actor Leslie Grantham, best known for playing a villain in the popular BBC television series *East Enders*, as Rick. Its run lasted less than a month. "I'm very proud of the play," said Burnett defiantly from London, after winning back the rights in his final $100,000 settlement with Warners. "Listen, there would have been no movie *Casablanca* if this play had never been written." After reading a piece in the *Los Angeles Times* discussing the London premiere of Burnett and Alison's play, which featured a few barbed comments from Burnett regarding the lack of proper credit, Howard Koch finally came around to see things in a different light. In a letter to the editor, he wrote the following:

> In "You Must Remember This" (May 14), Murray Burnett, co-author with Joan Alison of the play *Everybody Comes to Rick's*, complains that he did not receive sufficient credit for its contribution to the film *Casablanca*, and he may be right. When Warners assigned me the story, I had not read the play. We were facing a deadline, the camera was on our heels, so the material I was working on was limited to what I inherited from Julius and Philip Epstein, which I assumed contained what was useful from the original play. Having read the play more recently, I believe the complaint was, at least to some extent, justified. After 50 years, memories can be faulty and mine was in this case. If I have undervalued *Everybody Comes to Rick's*, I am sorry and hope that the play will have a big success in London and its audience will realize that its contribution to *Casablanca* was substantial.

Reviews of *Rick's Bar Casablanca*, however, were not quite as generous in their evaluation of the play. Writing in the *Evening*

Standard, Milton Shulman called it "an exercise in cinema cultdom relying on collector mania rather than anything else." The review in the *Sunday Times* found cause to praise Grantham's West End debut but criticized the improbability of some of the choices made in the production: "Would a Bulgarian Jew on the run wear his yarmulke in a city swarming with SS soldiers?" Many critics found the marquee tagline "You must remember this" prompted unflattering comparisons to the film. An unnamed reviewer sent to London by *Variety* voiced similar concerns about the disadvantage of the play due to the film's unforgettable dialogue and performances, but found some virtue in the original political thrust of the work by Burnett and Alison: "What does come across a bit more in the play is its clarion commitment to freedom and human dignity. The authors clearly were out to rally public sentiment against the then-spreading Nazi scourge." Still, the overwhelming tenor of criticism was unmistakably negative. Charles Osborne from the *Daily Telegraph* was perhaps the least charitable of the lot: "*Rick's Bar Casablanca* should have been left to rest on its laurels in Mr. Burnett's bottom drawer, and I advise anyone feeling nostalgic about *Casablanca* simply to rent the movie from their nearest video library."

IN THE YEARS since the film's release, the highly acclaimed screenplay—ranked number 1, in 2001, by the Writers Guild of America in its 101 Greatest Screenplays—has attained a mythical, if not a mystical status in the eyes of many. Regardless of any lingering authorship questions, it remains one of the most frequently taught scripts to aspiring writers and actors, first championed by the American screenwriter guru Syd Field, who died in 2013 and whose 1979 best-selling handbook *Screenplay: The Foundations of Screenwriting* was long considered the screenwriters' bible. Mapping out his three-act structure, and the "plot points" that make them cohere, Field devotes significant attention to *Casablanca* at several junctures in his book, even beginning a chapter on "The Scene" with a paean to that storied screenplay:

> *Casablanca* is an extraordinary film experience, one of those rare and magical moments that reside deep within our collective film consciousness. What makes it such a great film? What makes it stand out so vividly in the fabric of our film experience? Many things, of course, but in my own personal opinion, Rick is a character who, through his words and actions, sacrifices his life for the higher good. In *The Hero with a Thousand Faces*, Joseph Campbell says the hero has to "die in order to be reborn." [. . .] In their screenplay, Julius and Philip Epstein and Howard Koch have fashioned a character who is tough and fearless and possessed of a strong moral center and a proverbial heart of gold.

Years later, the competing screenwriting guru Robert McKee famously included a multihour annotated reading of the *Casablanca* screenplay in his weekend seminars, which he has given in cities across the globe since the 1980s. "We know characters better than we know our friends," he wrote in his 1997 guide *Story: Substance, Structure, Style and the Principles of Screenwriting*, "because a character is eternal and unchanging, while people shift—just when we think we understand them we don't. In fact, I know Rick Blaine in *Casablanca* better than I know myself. Rick is always Rick. I'm a bit iffy."

Over the years, countless actors, writers, and directors have been inspired by the work of Field (James Cameron, Judd Apatow, Tina Fey) and of McKee (Ed Burns, John Cleese, Brooke Shields, Joel Schumacher). The latter continues to offer his workshops with staggering frequency and even earned a small tribute, played by actor Brian Cox, in Spike Jonze's 2002 film *Adaptation*. In his 2003 *New Yorker* profile "The Real McKee," Ian Parker observes, "He screened *Casablanca* over six hours, and afterward (his shoes kicked aside) he reached an extraordinary crescendo of metaphysical, motivational talk (being and becoming, Schopenhauer and Derrida) that discovered in 'As Time Goes By' the richness of a *Hamlet* monologue."

Despite the seemingly sacred place that the *Casablanca* screenplay has reached in Hollywood lore, a wicked hoax ("The Great Script Tease") was nonetheless perpetrated in 1982, when the journalist and aspiring screenwriter Chuck Ross sent around a freshly typed copy of the complete text under the less identifiable title *Everybody Comes to Rick's*. With minimal changes (Sam became "Dooley") and authorial attribution given to the phantom scribe "Erik Demos," Ross submitted it to 217 entertainment agencies. The results are as revealing as they are surprising: 90 refused to read an unsolicited manuscript; 7 never responded (18 additional copies ostensibly were presumed lost by the U.S. Postal Service); 8 noticed a certain similarity to *Casablanca*; 33 recognized it outright (the rest, apart from a handful who expressed tentative interest, are unaccounted for). Among the various comments given as feedback: "I strongly recommend you leaf through a book called *Screenplay* by Syd Field, especially the section pertaining to dialogue"; "Too much dialogue, not enough exposition, the story line is weak, and in general didn't hold my interest"; "I think the dialogue could have been sharper and I think the plot had a tendency to ramble." For Ross, the exercise demonstrated not just the inability of contemporary talent agents to recognize talent—let alone a world-famous screenplay—but also the insurmountable odds stacked against unknown writers.

When Howard Koch learned of the hoax, several years later, he published an opinion piece in the *New York Times* in which he expressed a profound sadness: "One of the most popular films of all time was either rejected or not recognized." The movie industry of the mid-1980s, in Koch's estimation, was no longer what it had once been. "The common denominator is money," he remarked ruefully, "and the product is no longer leavened with love." Among the letters sent to the *Times* in response to Koch's piece was one written by a former story editor at Kings Road Productions, Renee Cho, who had read and rejected the phony screenplay. "The reason I rejected it was not because I didn't like it or recognize it," she wrote, "it was because the story has been done to perfection, and there's no need to do it again."

Chapter 2

USUAL SUSPECTS

Like so many of the decisions that went into this tangled Hollywood production, the casting of *Casablanca* has long been a source of intense speculation, rumor, and misinformation. It started on January 5, 1942, barely a week after Warner Bros. acquired the property, when the studio issued a red herring of a publicity announcement in *The Hollywood Reporter*, one of the industry's leading trade publications: "Ann Sheridan and Ronald Reagan co-star for the third time in Warners' *Casablanca*, with Dennis Morgan also coming in for top billing. Yarn of war refugees in French Morocco is based on an unproduced play by Murray Burnett and Joan Alison." Reagan was never a serious contender to star, and in retrospect such doctored publicity items, quite common at the time, seem to have been aimed more at making boldfaced names out of lesser-known contract players at the studio than at disseminating reliable information to the public (in the case of Sheridan and Reagan, they costarred in *Kings Row*, which was released by Warners soon after the press notice appeared). A few weeks later, Warners casting director Steve Trilling sent a memo to producer Hal Wallis, urging him to "please figure on Humphrey Bogart and Ann Sheridan for *Casablanca*."

As we know, Sheridan, the studio's "Oomph Girl," who had played opposite Bogart in the noir-themed road movie *They Drive By Night* (1940), didn't land the career-making role of Ilsa Lund (she might have been a better choice for Lois Meredith, Ilsa's more libertine American counterpart in the original stage play). Bogart first had to overcome fleeting opposition from studio head Jack Warner. "What do you think of using [George] Raft in *Casablanca*?" Warner wrote Wallis in a memo on April 2. "He knows we are going to make this and is starting to campaign for it." Asserting his authority on what would later be billed, like *Now, Voyager* before it, "A Hal B. Wallis Production," Wallis countered Warner with an unambiguously worded memo on April 13: "I have thought over very carefully the matter of George Raft in *Casablanca*, and I have discussed this with Mike [Curtiz], and we both feel that he should not be in the picture. Bogart is ideal for it, and it is being written for him, and I think we should forget Raft for this property." As it turns out, *Casablanca* wasn't really "being written" for anyone. Sure, lines were tailored to specific actors after casting was over and done with. But nearly every one of these decisions came with its share of back-and-forth negotiation and compromise.

The three lead actors in the film, not to mention the ensemble of supporting players, are now so inextricably identified with it that it's difficult to think of their later screen roles without immediately remembering their performances in *Casablanca.* It's even hard to watch their earlier work without anticipating the roles they'd play on the soundstages and back lot at Warners in the summer of 1942. The studio executives may have considered various alternative casting options, and the lead actors may have initially expressed some reluctance to embrace the inchoate story, but today they all seem born to play the roles assigned to them. There is no Rick Blaine without Humphrey Bogart, no Ilsa Lund without Ingrid Bergman. True, Paul Henreid wasn't Wallis's first choice for Laszlo. Weeks after the misleading publicity announcement of Dennis Morgan, Wallis first tried in vain to get Dutch-born actor Philip Dorn, who played an anti-Nazi resistance leader for Warners in *Underground*; then the French actor Jean-Pierre Aumont, a true war hero, tested for the part in April; and finally, there was the idea, soon abandoned, of casting Joseph Cotten. And yet Henreid came to embody the earnest, principled commitments of the Czech freedom fighter.

Each of the three leads came to *Casablanca* from a very different place in their respective careers. Bogart, then forty-two years old, had already acted in close to fifty features, and had reached a point in his life and career where he needed a break from playing gangsters and street thugs (as he did at Warners in the late 1930s in films like *Angels with Dirty Faces*, *King of the Underworld*, and *You Can't Get Away with Murder*) to avoid being forever stereotyped. Having arrived in America from her native Sweden just three years before, the twenty-

Claude Rains, Paul Henreid, Humphrey Bogart, and Ingrid Bergman in a publicity still.

seven-year-old Bergman had appeared in just a handful of Hollywood pictures, none of which allowed her the chance to express her true talents. Likewise, Henreid, then thirty-four, another recent European transplant, was still trying to carve out his proper niche in Hollywood as a leading man.

Although Bogart had already established his rugged screen persona in such earlier Warner Bros. films as *The Maltese Falcon* and *High Sierra* (both 1941), his portrayal of Rick Blaine gave him the chance to play a romantic lead, a character of greater emotional complexity and human vulnerability, that defined him forever. Donning his trench coat and snap-brim hat, the same signature props showcased in the movie's poster art—Bergman later claimed, in conversation with English television host Michael Parkinson, that the actor seemed to wear this outfit in all his movies—Bogie attained international stardom with *Casablanca*. When it came time to renew his contract at Warners, soon after the production wrapped, he also became the highest paid male actor in the world; already in *Casablanca*, he earned over $10,000 more than any other player on the set.

Born in New York City on Christmas Day 1899, the son of a wealthy physician and a successful book illustrator, Bogart grew up in a stately brownstone on the Upper West Side. He attended the Trinity School and was sent off to Phillips Andover Academy for a year, in the hope that it might help him gain admission to Yale. The patrician boarding school didn't sit well with Bogart, however, and he left midyear to join the navy. There he could indulge his love of sailing, first kindled at the family summer house on Canandaigua Lake in upstate New York, and serve his country in the final months of the Great War. "The war was great stuff," he later recalled. "Paris! French girls! Hot damn!"

Back in Manhattan after the war, Bogart landed a job as a stage manager through family contacts and soon began acting in various theater productions—not always with the best results. In 1922, in *Swifty*, one of the early plays in which he earned a role, a critic called his performance a "rather trenchant example of bad acting." By the 1930s, he started to appear in movies, first at Fox and later at Warner Bros., where thanks to actor Leslie Howard, who lobbied in his behalf, he beat out Edward G. Robinson to play Duke Mantee—as he'd done before on Broadway—in the acclaimed adaptation of Robert Sherwood's *The Petrified Forest* (1936). Within a four-year period, from 1937 through 1940, he performed in more than two dozen features. "Most of them were standard products of the Warners assembly line and looked it," writes his biographer Stefan Kanfer. It wasn't long, however, before critics grasped his talent. As a young moviegoer, Pauline Kael often speculated with her friends about when the studio executives would finally recognize the full potential of Bogart. "I don't think he could have been as good as he was in *Casablanca*," she later recounted, "if he hadn't done the *Falcon* first, because he really discovered his powers in the *Falcon*." *Time* hailed his acting in that film as "practically perfect," calling it "the performance of his career."

Bogart hadn't really hit his stride until the early 1940s, when he fulfilled what appears to have been a new need—that is, for an unconventional romantic lead—on screen. His gait, his gestures, mannerisms and speech were entirely his own. Bogie even smoked in his own way. As writer Richard Kluger once observed, "every considered drag and expelled puff of smoke seemed to represent a mocking laugh of bitter defiance." That attitude made him not only attractive to the students and intellectuals who rediscovered him in the 1960s, but also to wartime viewers. "Bogart became the thinking man's patriot," writes critic Andrew Sarris, "liberal, skeptical, sardonic, suspicious at first, but eventually heroic in the service of one unfashionable underdog or another, black, Russian, refugee, colonial." Bogart harbored, and indeed radiated, seemingly organic affinities to these noble, oppressed causes.

What was perhaps less natural for Bogart was the transition to playing a romantic lead. He needed coaching—he was told by his friend Mel Baker to stand still, and allow Bergman to come to him—and often suffered from self-doubt, playing long rounds of chess to ward off the feeling. "I remember, years ago, when I signed him," recalled Sam Jaffe, his agent. "I said to members of my family, 'This man will do romantic roles. There's an interesting look about him, an appearance.' Oh they laughed at me." When a journalist visited the set during the production of *Casablanca*, Bogart admitted, rather sheepishly, that he wasn't really up to "this love stuff" and, to make

Bogart and Henreid play chess on the set as producer Hal Wallis (center) and director Michael Curtiz (right), together with an unidentified studio employee, look on.

matters worse, wasn't sure whether he could do it at all. Ever the doubter, Jack Warner purportedly once asked, "Who would want to kiss Humphrey Bogart?"

Bogart's son Stephen recounted, in his biography of his father, a litany of woes that had to be overcome during the production.

> It was a difficult movie for my father. He spent most of his time in his trailer. He was not happy with the part at first. He wanted to get the girl, but so did Paul Henreid, because that, to some extent, was the definition of stardom: the guy who got the girl was the star. But Bogie also worried that the public would not believe that a woman as beautiful as Ingrid Bergman could fall for a guy who looked like him. He was, after all, a five-foot-ten, 155-pound [. . .] balding man who had spent most of his life playing snarling triggermen.

After the film was released, and Bogart became more widely regarded as a sex symbol, he used to say that he didn't really do anything much differently in *Casablanca*; Bergman looked at him with an amorous gaze and, presto, he had sex appeal.

Bogart sparred continually with Wallis and Curtiz throughout the production, arguing about his lines, about Rick's excessively self-pitying nature, and about other impediments facing the production. When cinematographer Arthur Edeson struggled with the lighting on the first day, Bogie didn't do anything to mask his contempt. In the end, however, he found his rhythm and made what would be one of his most indelible marks on a film. "No one would ever refer to *Casablanca* as an Ingrid Bergman picture or a Paul Henreid picture, or for that matter a Michael Curtiz picture," writes Bogart biographer Kanfer. "It was, and would remain, a Humphrey Bogart movie because he was the one who furnished the work with a moral center. There was no other player who could have so credibly inhabited the role of Rick Blaine, expatriate, misanthrope, habitual drinker, and, ultimately, the most self-sacrificing, most romantic Hollywood hero of the war years."

FILLING THE ROLE of Ilsa was no easy task. When Hal Wallis and casting director Steve Trilling first floated the idea of getting hold of Austrian beauty Hedy Lamarr from M-G-M, the studio's notoriously proprietary Louis B. Mayer gave them an unambiguous no. By the second week of April, months after the misleading publicity notice had announced Ann Sheridan as the lead, Michèle Morgan, who had made a recent splash at RKO with *Joan of Paris*, came into the Burbank studio to test for the part of Ilsa. There had also been studio chatter of considering Morgan's compatriot Edwige Feuillère, but it doesn't seem to have gotten very far. Initially, Wallis was quite taken with Morgan's performance, even announcing publicly that she'd landed the role. Privately, however, he knew exactly whom he had in mind, or so he later claimed. "I wanted Ingrid Bergman for the part of Ilsa," Wallis recalled in his autobiography. "She had just made a tremendous success in *Intermezzo*, and I felt that she was the only actress with the luminous quality, the warmth and tenderness necessary for the role."

Born in Stockholm in 1915, an only child raised in part by her aunt and uncle after her parents' early deaths, Bergman began her acting career as a teenager at the city's prestigious Royal Dramatic Theater School, where Greta Garbo had trained before her. She didn't last long at the school; with just one year under her belt, she took a screen test with filmmaker Gustaf Molander. Bergman served as an extra in several pictures, eventually landing a part as a hotel maid in *Munkbrogreven* (*The Count of the Old Monk's Bridge*, 1935). She appeared in a handful of additional well-received Swedish features, making what was by far her strongest impression internationally with *Intermezzo* (1936), directed by Molander and starring opposite Swedish leading man Gösta Ekman. When the film enjoyed a short run in New York over the winter holidays in 1937–1938, producer David O. Selznick's colleague Kay Brown had a fateful conversation with the Swedish elevator boy at Selznick International Pictures on Park Avenue. You have to see this picture, he purportedly told her; you *have* to see the girl that starred in it. Selznick saw it—the elevator boy was right—and recognized the vast opportunities for Bergman in Hollywood. He promptly arranged to have Brown bring Bergman to America in 1939, the same charmed year in which he produced the Academy Award winner *Gone With the Wind*, to star in the American remake of *Intermezzo: A Love Story* for Selznick's company.

The twenty-four-year-old Swede mesmerized audiences with her performance as Anita Hofmann, a piano teacher who falls in love with the married violin virtuoso Holger Brandt (Leslie Howard). Through the refined lens of Gregg Toland's camera, we can see Bergman conjure many of the same emotions she later displays in *Casablanca*—the understated affection, the brilliant range of enchanting glances, and the seemingly preternatural ability to subordinate personal desire to do what's right. About halfway into the picture, she utters, with profound self-awareness of the fragile nature of their love, "Hold me close, Holger," a sentence laden with the same urgent, throat-constricting cadence she uses to tell Rick, "Kiss me. Kiss me as if it were the last time."

When the film was released, in September 1939, the young Bergman elicited ample praise from American critics and moviegoers. "I had already seen the Swedish version," recalled film journalist Herman Weinberg, "and I was deeply impressed by the freshness and vitality of the young Ingrid Bergman. But seeing it with an American audience and sensing their realization that a star had been born was overwhelming. It was the same feeling I'd had ten years earlier when I first saw [Marlene] Dietrich in *The Blue Angel*." Like Dietrich, Bergman became famous for her unwillingness to conform to the norms of Hollywood. She eschewed the conventional star makeover, refusing to pluck her eyebrows, wear thick makeup, or change her name, and she maintained a level of assertiveness quite uncommon to female actors of her generation. "She was natural and blooming and unaffected," writes critic James Harvey in *Watching Them Be: Star Presence on the Screen from Garbo to Balthazar*, "guileless and seemingly transparent. She offered her onscreen radiance, her purity even (a word she often evoked from reviewers), to the world without reserve or disguise."

Selznick continued to hold Bergman under firm contract, his top talent and most "marvelous property," when in 1941 he negotiated her first American studio films, for Columbia (*Adam Had Four Sons*, a generally forgettable picture in which she played a European governess) and M-G-M (*Rage in Heaven* and *Dr. Jekyll and Mr. Hyde*), mere stepping-stones toward stardom. To acquire her for *Casablanca*, Wallis had to persuade Selznick that the film was worthy of her. When he initially refused to return Wallis's calls, Wallis simply showed up at the Carlyle Hotel in New York, where Selznick was staying, and got hold of him on the house phone. At Wallis's insistence, Selznick finally agreed to meet with Julius and Philip Epstein, the screenwriters known for their gift of gab, to hear more about the project.

The meeting took place one afternoon in early April, while Selznick ate lunch at his desk and the Epsteins spun their yarn ("Tell him anything," Wallis instructed them in advance, "but get Bergman!"). What they delivered was likely "a feat of verbal hocus-pocus," as fellow screenwriter Howard Koch called it, since they themselves were not yet sure of the final shape the script would take. They began their pitch by talking about the languishing refugees, the desperate search for transit visas, and all manner of intrigue, with no mention of Ilsa. Things started to look dire, and they rambled on for quite a while as the producer ate a bowl of soup without ever looking up. But then the Epstein twins decided to use an old Hollywood trick: likening a project to a recent box-office hit. "I said *Casablanca* is going to have a lot of that *Algiers* schmaltz," recalled Julius Epstein years later, "lots of atmosphere, cigarette smoke, guitar music. Selznick looked up and nodded. I knew then we had Bergman." As Bergman recounts in her memoir, "David O. Selznick liked it because at last I was going to wear lovely gowns and clothes and look pretty. Oh, it was so difficult in Hollywood to play against what Hollywood made you."

Selznick profited considerably from the deal he cut with Wallis in late April, earning a handsome fee of $125,000 from Warners—in addition to receiving Olivia de Havilland on loan from the studio—of which he paid only $35,000 to Bergman. Although Bergman expressed doubts about the film ("The picture is called *Casablanca*," she wrote to her friend Ruth Roberts, "and I really don't know what it's all about"), Selznick convinced her that this was an opportune moment, amid rising wartime fears, for the non-naturalized émigré actress to establish herself in Hollywood. She left her husband, Petter Lindström, and their young daughter, Pia, in Rochester, New York, where Petter was completing his medical degree, and took up residence in a small rental apartment in Beverly Hills. Bergman would later become famous, and rather notorious, for the ease with which she set aside her family matters in favor of her career.

With the script having gone through multiple drafts, and the characters still partially in development, Bergman was unsure of her role. In late May, just days before filming began, she held meetings with Wallis, Curtiz, Jack Warner, and Selznick, trying to sort out the lingering questions. "From the very start," Bergman explains in her memoir, "Hal Wallis, the producer, was arguing with the scriptwriters, the Epstein brothers, and every lunchtime Mike Curtiz argued with Hal Wallis.

There had to be all sorts of changes in the script. So every day we were shooting off the cuff: every day they were handing out the dialogue and we were trying to make some sense of it. No one knew where the picture was going and no one knew how it was going to end, which didn't help any of us with our characterizations." From a different vantage point, however, that uncertainty—wittingly or not—helped Bergman to deliver an unusually affecting performance, conveying to the audience that she could well end up boarding that plane to Lisbon with either of her two lovers. When she pressed Curtiz about where her love ought to be directed, he responded evasively, "We don't know yet—just play it well . . . in-between."

As it happened, Bergman may have arrived on set with a personal attachment to the story of the film. In January 1940, when she and her daughter, Pia, traveled on the S.S. *Rex* from Genoa to New York, they made an unplanned stop in Lisbon to pick up additional passengers, some of them making the journey, like the lucky few in the movie she'd shoot two years later, from Casablanca to New York. Although Bergman was not a refugee, unlike the many other actors in the film, she always thought of herself as a *flyttfågel,* a migratory bird or a "bird of passage," as her character is fittingly referred to in the original play. "I don't want any roots," she told the talk show host Merv Griffin in a 1980 interview. In the wake of her scandalous affair with Italian director Roberto Rossellini in 1949, when Bergman was branded "a horrible example of womanhood and a powerful influence for evil" on the floor of the U.S. Senate, she was banished from Hollywood. She would spend the rest of her life and career moving from country to country.

Many years later, after the film attained bona fide cult status, *Casablanca* was *the* picture for which Bergman was best remembered. "Probably the most iconic performances in American film," observed filmmaker William Friedkin in a 2012 documentary about the production, "are Bogart and Bergman in *Casablanca*." The irony, of course, is that despite any suspicions of Bogart's jealous wife, Mayo Methot, there was no offscreen chemistry between the two actors. Bogart spent most of the production alone in his trailer, while Bergman tried to navigate the unsteady course of the script. "In *Casablanca*, I kissed Bogart," she famously remarked, "but I never really knew him." She added, "He came out of his dressing room, did his scene, then fled away again. It was all very strange and distant." To prepare for the movie, Bergman watched *The*

Bogart and Bergman on the set.

Maltese Falcon, still playing in theaters at the time of production, over and over again.

Bergman's Ilsa introduced the world to a stylish yet restrained femininity—sex appeal without sex—as well as European sophistication deployed in a manner so relatable as to be irresistible. "She was a healthy, intelligent, and charming continental heroine," wrote Rudy Behlmer, "a welcome contrast to the usual glamour and exotica." Nowhere did those attributes come to greater articulation than in *Casablanca*. "I made so many films which were more important," Bergman later recalled, "but the only one that people want to talk about is that one with Bogart." Indeed, it was there that her extraordinary beauty and refined acting style won over millions across the globe and even inspired American folksinger Woody Guthrie to write a song about her (never recorded during his lifetime, but played with great relish by British pop troubadour Billy Bragg: "Ingrid Bergman, you're so perty, / You'd make any mountain quiver").

THE SCREEN SENSATION that Bergman caused was hard to match for any actor, American or European, but Paul Henreid did what he could to reach such heights. Born in the port city of Trieste, then still part of the Austro-Hungarian Empire, he trained with Max Reinhardt's theater company in Vienna before making his way into film. After the Nazis came to power, he fled to England, where among other film roles he played an elusive Gestapo agent in Carol Reed's *Night Train to Munich* (1940), and from there to Hollywood via New York.

In a letter of June 23, 1941, written soon after Henreid and his wife, Lisl, landed in California and were living in a rented room at the Beverly Hills Hotel, Lisl wrote to her Berlin-born friend Eleonora von Mendelssohn in New York: "It is a fantastically beautiful climate here, as lovely as in Cannes. We had a magnificent journey; it's such a lovely country, which we won't forget anytime soon. Paul likes it here very much." She added in the same letter, written on hotel stationery, that Paul was busy, involved in many studio meetings, and remained hopeful that his first American film (*Joan of Paris*) would be well received among U.S. critics.

Henreid always maintained that his first love was the theater and, as he wrote in his autobiography *Ladies Man*, for Europeans of his ilk film work was largely "considered a number of degrees below the stage." As he puts it further, "I suppose we considered it slumming. It was a means of making money, the extra car, the new house, but the stage had a certain purity. That was where you displayed your craft and received your inner satisfaction." By the time he reached Hollywood in the spring of 1941, a contract from RKO in hand, his views if not his values would require something of a makeover. "Perhaps I saw filmmaking in a new light," he remarked, "or it may be, if I am completely honest with myself, that I sold out."

At RKO, as part of a lavish dinner meeting at Romanoff's hosted by the studio's publicity team, he quickly became Americanized—or, really, de-Germanized—from "von Hernried," the name to which most of his British films were credited, to Henreid. There they also rolled out the star image that had been manufactured for him ("the suave ladies' man"), with slight alterations made by his wife Lisl, who wouldn't stand for their initial insistence that he be presented to the public as unattached. Still, in 1942, when he went on a nationwide tour for *Joan of Paris*—in which he played the intrepid undercover Free French pilot Paul Lavallier opposite the French sexpot Michèle Morgan—he had to rebuff a round of call girls in Chicago arranged by a publicity man at the studio. In Dallas, things escalated. He was purportedly lured into a women's restroom where a drunken admirer, stark naked, propositioned him: "How about a roll in the hay? You're supposed to be good at that." Outside the stall, cheering fans egged him on, "Go on, give her a good time, Paul. Be a sport."

His stock as one of Hollywood's most desirable leading men continued to rise, much of it owing to a famous scene from *Now, Voyager* (1942), made just before *Casablanca*. The fairy-tale-like story of an ugly duckling turned glamorous princess by a knight in shining armor, it was largely a vehicle for star Bette Davis. But the picture gave Henreid the chance to exude an air of high-pedigree European charm and sophistication. As he tells it, the scene in question, when Henreid lights two cigarettes and places one in Davis's mouth, derives from a habit that he and his wife used to indulge while driving on the continent. "It was an intimate and sensual gesture," he later recalled, "or it could be played that way." Producer Hal Wallis recognized its power: "It's something that's going to make an impression with the audience." And that it did. When the film appeared, the critic for the *New York Herald Tribune* declared, "Paul Henreid achieves his full stature as romantic star."

By the time he received a copy of the script for *Casablanca*, Henreid had signed a seven-year contract at Warners, something he'd done rather hesitantly, but with strong encouragement from his agent, Lew Wasserman, who argued that the film might help protect him from any restrictions placed on "enemy aliens" working in Hollywood. To Wasserman's surprise, Henreid's initial inclination was to pass on the assignment and go on temporary suspension. "What's wrong?" he snapped at his agent, when Wasserman failed to see his point. "Not only is it a terrible script, really rotten, but I don't want to be the second lover in a film, second to Humphrey Bogart!"

It was, of course, playing second fiddle that bothered Henreid most. Eventually, despite his reservations, he accepted the role of Victor Laszlo. In his recollection, it was Albert Maltz (who cowrote the 1942 noir *This Gun for Hire*, but whose name has never been attached to *Casablanca*) and Howard Koch who were assigned to build up the part for him. "I thought Maltz and Koch were a well-matched team, and if anyone could, they would spice up the original Epstein brothers' dreadful script." By this point in his career, Henreid's self-perception as a leading man didn't quite match the role he was ultimately assigned. He fought with Curtiz over specific scenes, especially when it looked like Bogart had the upper hand. In the playing of the "Marseillaise," for example, which requires a nod from Bogie, he objected: "I'm supposed to be a leader of the masses, and here I have a stinking little band, and I can't get them to do what I want!" Later in life, Henreid liked to claim, rather imaginatively, that he'd prevailed upon the studio to write into his contract a special clause stipulating that he would get the girl.

LESS CONCERNED WITH star treatment was Claude Rains, Warners' standby for the mild-mannered, English type who looks good in a well-tailored tweed suit, with a pipe in his mouth, then in high demand. The British-born actor had been a contract player at Warners in the 1930s. He'd already earned an Academy Award nomination for best supporting actor in Frank Capra's *Mr. Smith Goes to Washington* (1939) and had played opposite Henreid in *Now, Voyager*; he'd go on to earn three more nominations, including one for *Casablanca*, but never win. Indeed, Rains's Captain Renault retains much of the chummy, dry wit of Dr. Jaquith, the benevolent psychiatrist in the earlier picture with Henreid. No casting was necessary; he was the only actor ever considered for the part of Captain Louis Renault.

When *Now, Voyager* was released, the *New York Times* singled out Rains for his "polished and even-tempered performance." Originally a theater actor, he made a career in Hollywood playing supporting roles, many of them rather affable and droll. He was a consummate professional—*Casablanca* was his thirty-second film—known to study his lines obsessively, and generally kept to himself during the production. "Rains avoided the fray," writes his biographer David Skal, "to the point of brown-bagging his lunches and avoiding the studio commissary and its personalities and politics." Although he had many of the wittiest lines in the film, he was not as much of a joker as were some of the other cast members (especially Peter Lorre). One exception concerns an oft-told story about a disagreement over the speed of his entrance during a particular scene. After being exhorted by taskmaster director Curtiz more than once to make his entrance with "more energy," he allegedly shot through the door riding on a bicycle.

Although he often played upper-class sophisticated characters, and although his voice came to embody that very world, Rains was not born into wealth. Seven of the ten children his mother had brought into the world before him—he was delivered, the first son in the family, on a brass bed in the cramped quarters of his parents' London flat on November 10, 1889—had died soon after birth. His father had been a silent-film actor, but not one to nurture his son. Young Claude didn't make it past the first years of primary school; he spoke with a thick Cockney accent, the patois he learned in the streets of Brixton, and struggled throughout his youth with speech difficulties. Before he hit his teens, Rains sold newspapers for W.H. Smith, worked as a page boy, sang in a church choir, and, following his military service in London Scottish regiment during the Great War, found his way to the theater and ultimately to film.

By the mid-1930s, Rains had laid permanent roots in America. His mother passed away just weeks before the principal photography of *Casablanca* commenced, when *Now, Voyager* was still in its final weeks, and the hyperconscientious actor took no time off to mourn, nor did he make the transatlantic journey to attend the funeral. Whatever solace he sought was generally found in the tranquility of the 380-acre farm that he bought in Chester County, Pennsylvania in 1941. He drove there the moment that filming of *Casablanca* was over, and by the time talk of possible retakes for the final scene came up—an idea, quickly jettisoned, of having Rick and Renault in Free French uniform, shot at night in thick fog aboard a freighter on Warners Stage 7—he was long gone.

During the production, Rains struck up a friendship with Bogart. They were known on occasion to go for drinks together after a hard day on the set. Rains also grew quite fond of Bergman, who held a certain affection for the actor. Yet, he had little patience for Henreid (whom he allegedly called "Paul Hemorrhoid" when the actor wasn't around). Similarly, Henreid found Rains to be "a big baby" and "an unbelievable prima donna." None of these tensions, however, compromised Rains's performance on screen, where he delivered acid-laced lines with exceptional wit and flair. "Mr. Rains is properly slippery and crafty as a minion of Vichy perfidy," wrote Bosley Crowther in the *New York Times*. As important, however, are the glimpses of humanity that he offers the audience, the overriding sense that his commitments to Vichy—if we can dignify them with such a term—are about as deeply rooted as are his scruples. He may leap at the sound of Major Strasser's command, but he is just as quick to cover for Rick and to toss that tainted bottle of Vichy water into the wastebasket in the film's final moments.

In the film's opening credits, Claude Rains's name comes first in the list of names that fill out the second frame—after the trio of headliners Bogart, Bergman, and Henreid—followed by Conrad Veidt, Peter Lorre, and Sidney Greenstreet. Perhaps because of Veidt's status as one of Weimar Germany's most celebrated film actors and the star of internationally acclaimed movies like Robert Wiene's *Das Kabinett des Dr. Caligari* (*The Cabinet of Dr. Caligari*; 1920) and *Orlacs Hände* (*The Hands of Orlac*; 1924), he was paid $1,000 more per week than Rains and considerably more than either Lorre or Greenstreet. "I have the feeling I am stealing money from Warner Brothers," he once told actor Leonid Kinskey, who plays the bit part of Sascha the barman at Rick's. "I arrive in the morning, put on my uniform of Nazi Major, stick a monocle in my eye [*sic*], and now and then deliver short speeches with a slight German accent."

Like most of his German actor colleagues, Veidt studied under Max Reinhardt and had a lengthy career on the stage before going into film. In the late 1920s, he appeared in a couple of silent films made for Universal, including Paul Leni's *The Man Who Laughs* (1928). He then returned to Europe, but Veidt was among the earliest of the Weimar-era stars to leave Germany after Hitler's ascent to power—he was married to a Jewish woman—relocating to England in 1933; he took British citizenship in 1939, and for years he gave vast amounts of his earnings to support the British war effort. He landed in Hollywood in 1940, after starring in Michael Powell's highly successful Technicolor fantasy *The Thief of Bagdad* (1940), produced by Alexander Korda, and soon found himself playing a series of menacing Nazi types.

"Now the European actors driven out by the Nazis have more work," observed one émigré critic while *Casablanca* was in the final phase of postproduction. "They find employment in the many war films which are currently being produced.

Marvelous irony of fate: to become known—indeed, to get star treatment—for playing the part of the bestial Nazis who destroyed us." Veidt seemed somehow aware of this fate and took it as his special task to present the threat of Nazism to an American audience. "I know this man well," he told a studio publicist of his role as Heinrich Strasser. "He is the reason I gave up Germany many years ago. He is a man who turned fanatic and betrayed his friends, his homeland, and himself in his lust to be somebody and to get something for nothing."

Veidt's Major Strasser has none of the sinewy, languid movements that he brought to the character of Cesare the somnambulist in *Caligari*, but his screen presence is no less ominous. He rattles off the list of offenses committed against his beloved Third Reich by Victor Laszlo, pieces of caviar still dancing on his tongue; conducts his crew of Nazi goons singing "Die Wacht am Rhein"; and careens down the road—or, rather, against Warners' rear projection—toward the Casablanca airport with a look of maniacal determination on his face. Throughout his illustrious career, Veidt brought boundless passion and conviction to everything he did. Alas, in April 1943, just months after *Casablanca* was in wide release, he died at the age of fifty from a heart attack sustained on the golf course at the Riviera Golf Club in Pacific Palisades.

Peter Lorre was another member of the unusually large crop of German-speaking émigrés on the set. The great character actor was born Ladislav Löwenstein, on June 26, 1904, in the outer provinces—in what is today Slovakia—of the Austro-Hungarian Empire. As a young boy, he moved with his family to Vienna, where he attended primary and secondary school and, eventually, after a false start as a business student at the Wiener Handels-Akademie, fell in with the city's young theater and coffeehouse crowd. One of his earliest acting teachers, the psychoanalytically inspired dramatist Jacob Levi Moreno at Vienna's Stegreiftheater (Improv Theater), saw in his young pupil an extraordinary gift for "swapping skins with another's feelings and being." Moreno also suggested to his pupil a swapping of names: he purportedly took the first name Peter after his friend the Viennese poet Peter Altenberg, and adopted the last name Lorre—said to mimic the speech of a parrot—as a means of retaining the same initial as his two birth names. Lorre performed onstage in Vienna, Munich, Breslau, and Berlin before making his Austrian screen debut as a dental patient in the late silent *Die verschwundene Frau* (*The Missing Wife*, 1929).

While playing Galy Gay, the lead in Brecht's *Mann ist Mann*, at the Berliner Staatstheater in 1931, Lorre caught the attention of director Fritz Lang, who promptly cast him as the Grieg-whistling child murderer in *M*, released later that year. Lorre made an enormous splash with his performance in Lang's film, impressing viewers and critics across the globe. In the United States, critic William Troy wrote of Lorre's "flawless acting" in *The Nation*, likening his delivery to that of the greatest actors of Greek and Elizabethan drama. "The modern psychopath, through Peter Lorre's acting," he wrote, "attains the dignity of the tragic hero." No less than Charlie Chaplin would soon hail Lorre as "Europe's greatest actor."

While many of the European émigrés had trouble adjusting to Hollywood, Lorre, who arrived in 1935 via England and a short stopover in Paris, was relatively quick to assimilate, despite giving off the initial impression of a "rococo cherub gone slightly astray." This didn't ensure good roles, however, as Lorre continued to find himself playing a long list of oddballs, villains, and characters of ambiguous sexuality and dubious origin. After appearing in a motley assortment of horror films and thrillers, and as the title character in some half dozen pictures from the Mr. Moto series, he found his way to Warners for *The Maltese Falcon.* Playing opposite Bogart as the well-coiffed dandy Joel Cairo—a man with multiple passports and precious few scruples—he set off alarm bells at the Hays Office. "We cannot approve the characterization of Cairo as a pansy as indicated by the lavender perfume, high pitched voice, and other accoutrements," wrote censorship czar Joseph Breen. In his unmistakably queer characterization of Cairo, he somehow slipped by the censor, however, with the same spectacular ease that he slides by the doorman of Rick's Café in his first appearance as Ugarte in *Casablanca.*

Even though he has comparatively little screen time, Lorre commands the audience's attention from that first moment onward. "Like a blanched weasel, he whisks into view," writes his biographer Stephen Youngkin, "fawning and fulsome, oozing greasy charm and puffing on a cigarette, turning even the simple act of smoking into a menacing art." When the film was released, most reviews focused their attention on Bogart and Bergman, leaving little room for discussion of the film's other players. There were, however, some critics who recognized the magnetism of Ugarte. "Lorre is in and out of the picture in the first reel," wrote the unsigned reviewer from *The Hollywood Reporter*, "yet the impression he makes is remembered."

When Lorre wasn't in front of the camera, he was often cooking up pranks on the set. Among his favorites was taking an eyedropper dipped in water and using it to put out Curtiz's cigarette whenever he'd leave one in an ashtray unattended—anything to fluster the director. He once got the obsessive Claude Rains to believe that he hadn't studied properly for a nonexistent scene that Lorre made up. And Paul Henreid tells how Lorre managed to persuade the studio's sound guys to wire the room in which Curtiz was known to have his afternoon trysts with young actresses, as if taking a page from Captain Renault's lecherous playbook, thus projecting the amorous sound track, as it were, over the set speakers (his booming voice, heard throughout the corridors: "Oh yes, yes—oh, God, yes"). Although they do not appear in any scenes together, one of Lorre's favorite partners in crime, Sidney Greenstreet, with whom he was paired in more than half a dozen films at Warners, was generally at the ready to assist in these schemes. In *Hollywood Unseen*, a recently published photo album, there's a magnificent shot, snapped a year or so before *Casablanca*, of Greenstreet dressed as Santa Claus and Lorre behind him wielding a baseball bat, bulging eyes trained on his would-be target's head, looking determined to decapitate Father Christmas.

It seems somehow fitting that Greenstreet, *The Maltese Falcon*'s "Fat Man," was born in a town called Sandwich, in southeast England, in 1879. A former touring member of Ben

Peter Lorre and Sydney Greenstreet clowning around.

Greet's Shakespearean Repertory Company, he enjoyed intermittent success on the English and American stage before, at the age of sixty-two, he crossed the Atlantic and shimmied his way into the studio interiors at Warner Bros. Starting with *The Maltese Falcon*, he acted in a staggering twenty-four films in eight years. "It has always been a convention of the film industry," writes David Thomson, "to 'introduce' potent new players. But few introductions have been as dramatic as that of Greenstreet: monstrous, over sixty, hostile, and so clearly familiar with every wrinkle in the world's corruption. Where could his bulk have been hiding?" As Thomson adds, "It was a happy chance that his first film put him in the company of Peter Lorre, for they were inspired, tormenting company held together by some unspoken perversity."

Greenstreet's fly-swatting Signor Ferrari delivers some of the great lines in *Casablanca*. His comeback to Rick, after the American saloon keeper takes the moral high ground on the question of selling Sam to him, is delivered with just the right amount of unction and sleaze, declaring human beings, refugees in particular, the North African outpost's most valuable commodity. Like Rains's self-conscious performance of the crooked official, Greenstreet's Ferrari is fully aware of his deceitful behavior. "Carrying charges, my boy, carrying charges," he says to Rick when Rick questions the booze that's siphoned off each shipment due to him. In his later screen appearances, before passing away from diabetes in 1954 at the age of seventy-four, Greenstreet often played equally duplicitous, conniving, hard-nosed characters.

While Greenstreet had haggled with Wallis over the proper fee for his performance, his role proved to be far less difficult to fill than that of Sam the piano player. Lest we forget, Sam had been central to the unproduced play that Burnett and Alison wrote in the summer of 1940, and even more central to Burnett's formative experience that night at the magical French nightclub overlooking the Mediterranean Sea two summers before. The jazz standards that the black pianist played then—and the character that would play them in the film—helped convey that aching, nostalgic feeling and intense longing, evoked in the story Burnett re-created with Alison upon his return from Europe.

Some of the earliest communiqués sent to Warners casting director Steve Trilling concerned this critical part: "In one of our proposed pictures, *Casablanca*, there is a part now written for a colored man who plays the piano in the night club," wrote Wallis in a memo of February 5, 1942. "I am thinking of making this a colored girl, and when I was in New York I saw Hazel Scott at the Uptown Café Society. She would be marvelous for the part. I understand that there is a colored girl out here now appearing in a Felix Young night club and I wish you would see her and tell me what you think. The one out here is Elena [Lena] Horn[e]." Acclaimed singers, both Scott and Horne were fixtures in the New York City jazz scene at the time. Although Trilling would inquire about the possibility of casting the two female singers—he is said to have considered Ella Fitzgerald as well—by April, Wallis reversed course and had Curtiz do screen tests with the stage and screen performers Dooley Wilson and Clarence Muse. Wallis's initial inclination was to give the part to Muse, a former vaudeville entertainer then under contract at M-G-M, but without any stated reason, possibly cost or possibly looks, Warners general counsel R. J. Obringer gave the final announcement in early May that Wilson would be given the part.

Arthur "Dooley" Wilson had grown up in show business. Born in Tyler, Texas, in 1886 (some sources give the year of his birth as 1894), as a young boy he learned to sing and dance in vaudeville, minstrel shows, and traveling theater companies.

He joined an all-black repertory group, the Pekin Stock Company, in Chicago and mastered the drums while continuing to act. He earned his reputation through a popular number, done in whiteface, in which he appeared on stage dressed as a leprechaun and sang "Mr. Dooley" in a thick Irish brogue. "It wasn't hard to play an Irishman," he told journalist Dorothy Kilgallen, whose profile of Wilson, "Here Comes Mr. Dooley," appeared in *Collier's* in 1944. "I made up as white as you."

By the 1920s, having relocated to Harlem, he was appearing regularly at the local clubs. When he played at the Sontag on Lenox Avenue, a young Irving Berlin is said to have been among his regular fans; Berlin purportedly liked to give Wilson a five-spot to play his own version of the composer's "Alexander's Ragtime Band." Around that same time, Wilson joined a band called the Red Devils, which soon made its way across the Atlantic to perform in Europe, playing clubs like Le Grand Duc in Paris. While in Europe, the Red Devils even made an appearance in North Africa, to play at a party in honor of distinguished British military officer T. E. Lawrence, better known as Lawrence of Arabia. "He didn't pay much attention to the place," notes Kilgallen, "it was just another job to him. Nothing tapped him on the shoulder, no prescient voice whispered in his ear, 'Remember this name—Casablanca. It will mean something to you twenty years from now.'"

Wilson soon enjoyed considerable success on the stage. In the late 1930s, he landed a part in *Of Mice and Men*, touring the country; next, he played opposite Ethel Waters as Little Joe Jackson, the lead in *Cabin in the Sky*, during its enormously successful run, from October 1940 through March 1941, at the

Martin Beck Theatre on Broadway. This brought Wilson to the attention of Hollywood scouts, and he signed a short-term contract with Paramount in 1941, acting in four features during his first year alone.

Most of his film roles were limited to what African-American actors of his generation were expected to play in Hollywood—ancillary characters such as personal valets, shoeshine boys, chauffeurs, cooks, and other domestics. In one of several films he finished for Paramount before working on *Casablanca*, the Bob Hope vehicle *My Favorite Blonde* (1942), he played a Pullman porter. With Sam, however, Wilson had a part that allowed him greater emotional depth and complexity, and far more substantial dialogue. Sam helps to propel the film forward, his deep voice conveying an abundance of grace and humanity, his gimlet eyes leading the viewer to understand the full significance of Ilsa's return. He's a genuine friend to Rick, his sole traveling companion, and the one character who tries to shield him from pain, offering to get drunk and go fishing with him to avoid the torturous revisiting of his love affair. He's also the friend who, in the Paris flashback, breaks the news of Ilsa's rejection.

One technical problem had to be surmounted, however, for Wilson to accept the part: he didn't know how to play the piano. And so staff musician Elliot Carpenter—who had played piano and bass in the Red Devils with Wilson in the 1920s and composed music for poet Langston Hughes—served as a ghost pianist, tapping away at the keys off screen while Wilson mimicked Carpenter's hand movements. (In 1997, actor Johnny Depp wrote a piece for *The Hollywood Reporter*

Production still of Dooley Wilson and Bogart.

in which he expressed his colossal disappointment upon learning that Wilson had to fake it: "As much as I hate being the dog that pees on your beautiful lilacs," he wrote, "it is someone's duty to tell you that Dooley Wilson apparently could not play the piano.") Wilson did all the singing himself, not only the iconic "As Time Goes By," but popular jazz standards like "It Had to Be You" and "Parlez moi d'amour," as well as the film's sole original composition, written by Jack Scholl and M. K. Jerome, "Knock on Wood." Wallis wasn't totally sold on Wilson's voice—he issued a memo to the head of the studio's music department, Leo Forbstein, near the end of the production, to "begin looking immediately for a Negro with a good crooning voice to double all of Dooley Wilson's songs"—but eventually decided to scrap his plans for dubbing. After the film was released, Carpenter and Wilson took their show on the road, playing at a USO party for servicemen in Washington in July 1943, among other venues.

A review of the film published in the *New York Amsterdam News*, one of the few black-owned newspapers, took due note. Under the banner title "Wilson's Role in *Casablanca* Tops for Hollywood" (and the subhead "Stars in Pic with Bogart: Warner Brothers Show That It Can Be Done"), the opening lines announced: "*Casablanca* the much-talked-about film that has had such a long and successful run at the Hollywood Theatre on Broadway is one every colored person should make it his business to see since no picture has given as much sympathetic treatment and prominence to a Negro character as occurs in this story of war intrigues in North Africa." The author of the review, Dan Burley, a nightlife columnist and managing editor at the paper, went on to observe: "There's not the slightest semblance to the objectionable Uncle Tomming that characterizes most of the Hollywood output. Instead, there is an effort to blend Wilson's admitted talents into the picture with the resultant effect *Casablanca* has on the minds of those who saw it." He ends with a discussion of the remarkable scene in which a glass of champagne is poured for Sam to join in Rick and Ilsa's celebration of their brief moment of shared euphoria during the flashback in Paris.

In his autobiography, Hal Wallis contends that he chose not to have Clarence Muse as Sam because "he seemed too much a caricature of a black type in the test." After putting a tentative hold on Muse, he ultimately decided to go with Wilson, having first seen him on the stage in *Cabin in the Sky* and been impressed by his performance as Little Joe. The part of Sam ("The Rabbit"), as adapted from *Everybody Comes to Rick's*, was already relatively well developed, and the screenwriters and the studio were generally supportive of its underlying theme of racial integration and interracial friendship. The bitter truth, however, is that Wilson's rate of $3,500 was less than some of the other white supporting players (Greenstreet earned $7,500). This is especially glaring, considering that the mountains of fan mail he received at Warner Bros. matched, or even surpassed, that of Hollywood's major stars. In his review of the film in the *New York Times*, Bosley Crowther called Wilson a major discovery ("a Negro 'find'"): "Mr. Wilson's performance as Rick's devoted friend, though rather brief, is filled with sweetness and compassion which lend a hopeful mood to the whole film."

To be sure, what was portrayed onscreen was not a realistic depiction of contemporary America but rather an imaginary North African utopia. "In the jungle, the desert, and the smoky interiors of Rick's Café," writes film historian Thomas Doherty, "Hollywood projected racial pluralism onto a landscape beyond American borders." After *Casablanca*, Wilson acted in the all-black musical *Stormy Weather* (1943), as part of a distinguished ensemble that included Lena Horne, as well as Cab Calloway, Fats Waller, and Bill "Bojangles" Robinson. Soon frustrated with the lack of possibilities for career advancement, he returned to the New York stage, playing—

with tragic irony—an escaped slave in *Bloomer Girl*, at the Shubert on Broadway and in off-Broadway revivals, up until his death in 1953.

IN THE DECADES after *Casablanca*, the principal actors continued their lives and careers, while remaining forever linked to the film. Bogart's fame continued to grow, owing to the critical success of pictures like *To Have and Have Not* (1945) and *The Big Sleep* (1946), both directed by Howard Hawks, and *Key Largo* (1948), directed by his friend John Huston. For many years, he remained one of America's most iconic and best paid actors, even if he wasn't always the easiest for producers and directors to get along with.

Although Bogart generally preferred to avoid the glare of the spotlight, and especially preferred sailing the high seas on his fifty-four-foot yawl the *Santana*, he occasionally had trouble avoiding it. In an event that came to be known as the "Panda Fracas," reported in all the New York City tabloids, sometime in the wee hours of September 26, 1949, Bogie and his drinking pal Bill Seaman landed at New York's El Morocco nightclub with two giant stuffed panda bears in tow. While they occupied a table for four, downing a few rounds of drinks, they were approached by a twenty-two-year-old self-proclaimed "model" named Robin Roberts, who allegedly tried to abscond with one of the pandas. Bogart tried to stop Roberts and in the process, she slipped to the floor; soon her girlfriend stepped in, then their dates got into the tussle, and eventually a lawsuit was born. A few days later, in Mid-Manhattan

Court, Bogart admitted to being drunk ("who isn't at three o'clock in the morning?"), but denied that he'd ever strike a woman ("I'm too sweet and chivalrous. Besides it's too dangerous"). He prevailed in the end, but the damaging headlines remained. "Bogart's a hell of a nice guy until around 11:30 pm," former comedian and Hollywood restaurant owner Dave Chasen famously remarked. "After that, he thinks he's Bogart." The actor would even reenact these volatile, explosive tendencies, flickers of which we see in Rick Blaine, in later films like Nicholas Ray's *In a Lonely Place* (1950), in which he plays the unhinged war veteran turned screenwriter Dixon Steele.

Soon after his death in 1957, after such acclaimed late films as *The African Queen* (1951) and *The Caine Mutiny* (1954), the cult of Bogie took firm root on American and European soil. Among students, he became widely viewed as a countercultural hero, a champion of the weak and oppressed while among hippies he became the source of a popular figure of speech: "Don't Bogart that joint," a direct reference to his iconic smoking style, became the title of a popular late-1960s rock ballad (also known as "Don't Bogart Me") by Fraternity of Man, famously used on the soundtrack of *Easy Rider* (1969). The Bogart revival only grew with time. "One does not go to see Humphrey Bogart, *as Sam Spade*," wrote James Baldwin in the mid-1970s, "one goes to see Sam Spade, *as Humphrey Bogart*." Not everyone, however, was quite so taken with the actor. "I hated Humphrey Bogart," insisted *Everybody Comes to Rick's* cowriter Joan Alison. "I thought he was a common drunk." Bogie frequently butted heads with the studio executives in the front office and was also known to wrestle with directors. When working with Billy Wilder on *Sabrina* (1954), the two argued incessantly. "I examine your ugly face, Bogie," Wilder once taunted him. "I look at the valley, the crevices, and the pits of your ugly face, and I know that somewhere under the sickening face of a shit—is a real shit." A more revealing statement, however, in light of the nascent Bogie cult was delivered in the form of a question by Marta Toren, playing Violette in *Sirocco* (1951): "How can a man so ugly be so handsome?"

When Ingrid Bergman's biographer Charlotte Chandler first made her acquaintance, late in life, the actress offered up a line that she presumably had delivered before: "I feel sometimes people are disappointed when they meet me because they are expecting Ilsa from Casablanca, and instead they get Ingrid from Stockholm." *Casablanca* was a halo that she wore—even if it occasionally must have felt more like an albatross—for the rest of her life. "I was never so talented in selecting for myself the best and the most successful films," she explained, "although I dreamed of being independent and successful enough to do so. A film I definitely would *not* have selected was *Casablanca*, and it is my best-loved, best-remembered film. Everywhere I go, people ask me or *tell* me about *Casablanca*." In the 1960s, she spoke to students at Harvard University and was simply amazed to hear them quote lines from the film that they had committed to memory. Soon after, at the British Film Institute, she had the opportunity to view the film on the big screen. "I really thought it was a very good movie," she admitted in 1973, almost incredulously, in a televised interview with Michael Parkinson. Although she certainly made superior, critically acclaimed films—from George Cukor's *Gas-*

light (1944) and Alfred Hitchcock's *Notorious* (1946), her Italian pictures with Roberto Rossellini, all the way up to Ingmar Bergman's *Höstsonaten* (*Autumn Sonata;* 1978)—*Casablanca* remained her international calling card.

In the epilogue to her memoir, Bergman writes about being invited back to Hollywood in November 1979 as the guest of honor at the Variety Club of America. The event, billed as a children's benefit in her name, took place on Warners Stage 8, where the set for Rick's Café Américain was rolled out one last time. The rather clichéd stage directions for the event had the seventy-one-year-old Paul Henreid opening the doors for her and saying, "Ingrid, come in. Welcome back to Rick's and let's have a glass of champagne." They then raised a glass "to Bogie," who had passed away twenty-two years earlier, "And to Mike Curtiz and all the others." By that time, Curtiz had been dead more than a decade and a half; Peter Lorre died soon after him, and Claude Rains followed Lorre. Both Sidney Greenstreet and Dooley Wilson had long since checked out, even before Bogie. In Dooley's place, seated at the upright, was Café Society pianist Teddie Wilson, who asked Bergman to hum "As Time Goes By." The moment she begins to hum, Frank Sinatra, standing behind her, chimed in with one of the more famous covers of Herman Hupfeld's song.

"I feel about *Casablanca* that it has a life of its own," she admitted near the end of her life. "There is something mystical about it. It seems to have filled a need, a need that was there before the film, a need that the film filled." When asked in 1974 about the appeal that the film retains, she told Richard Anobile, "I think because of the sentimental things, and the glorification with the 'Marseillaise' being sung and all that. I think that's what people like. I think they miss that in modern films. You have everything in that movie from love to heroism and murder and whatnot."

Much as Paul Henreid's complaints about not getting the proper star attention in the film may appear today like the behavior of a Hollywood screen diva, his concerns about being overshadowed by Bogart were not entirely misplaced. He shared top billing with Bogie and Bergman and tried as best as he could to share the spotlight—even if he is now occasionally thought of mockingly as "that other guy," as Harry, played by Billy Crystal, calls him in *When Harry Met Sally* (1989), where he's branded as the epitome of sexless boredom. Unlike Bogie and Bergman, both of whom have enjoyed cult followings and countless revivals, Henreid has been largely forgotten. "People think he is French," insists his daughter Monika, a former actress. "No one can pronounce his name. He is known as Victor Laszlo, but spent much of his life in L.A., working and directing. He gave Richard Dreyfuss his first film job; he discovered Burt Reynolds." Henreid directed such films as *Live Fast, Die Young* (1958) and *Dead Ringer* (1964), the latter made with Bette Davis for Warner Bros. Yet, much like the other two principals, more than anything else, Henreid would be identified for his performance in *Casablanca*. As *Christian Science Monitor* reporter Robert Marquand mordantly noted at the close of an article weighing the skewed legacy of the actor, "if Henreid hadn't done the movie, he probably would have regretted it. Maybe not today, maybe not tomorrow, but soon, and for the rest of his life."

As for that misleading announcement about the casting of Ronald Reagan, it leaves something to think about. "More than one film critic has speculated," writes film scholar Dana Polan, "that if this casting had actually happened and Reagan had garnered success, he would not have remained consigned to the lesser ranks of Warner Bros. actors and may have had a more successful acting career, thereby removing the temptation to leave acting for politics. World history might have been very different, the speculation goes!" The truth of the matter, however, is that Reagan, a second lieutenant in the U.S. Cavalry Reserve, was called into active duty just months after Pearl Harbor, well before the film's production had begun. His commitments, in other words, were not limited to those of Colonel Jack Warner. In the 1970s, while still governor of California, he responded to a letter from one of his supporters in which he addressed the question of casting in *Casablanca*. "It was one of those magic blessings every actor dreams of," he wrote admiringly of Bogart, whom Reagan had gotten to know working on such pictures as *Dark Victory* (1939) at Warner Bros. "He became a top star and deservedly so but he remained the same unassuming, nice guy he'd always been."

Chapter 3

I STICK MY NECK OUT FOR NOBODY

During the 1930s, and into the early '40s, as the Great Depression continued to cast its long shadow and distressing memories of the Great War were still fresh in the minds of most Americans, politicians and the public at large were disinclined to meddle with the political affairs of Europe. Even after Hitler's stunning ascent in Germany in January 1933, and the gradual rise of fascism in Italy, Americans showed little interest in waging an opposition. Hollywood, for its part, was no exception. Most studios, still reliant on significant revenue streams from the European export market, which into the mid-1930s constituted 30 to 40 percent of its box-office profits, fiercely avoided subjects that could be construed as offensive or insensitive. A typical attitude, voiced by M-G-M producer Irving Thalberg after returning from a trip to Germany in 1934, was "Hitler and Hitlerism will pass." The imposition of the anti-Jewish Nuremberg Laws in 1935 didn't stop most studios from continuing to retain cordial business ties with Nazi Germany, nor did the ruthless expansion of the Third Reich. "Fascism tipped the European applecart," wrote journalist Helen Zigmond in a sobering report from December 1938, several months after the Anschluss and just weeks after the violent pogroms of Kristallnacht, "and Hollywood, instead of crying out against the bunglers, still scrambles for the fruit."

Although not without fault, Warner Bros. was among the earliest studios to address the threat of fascism and to halt its operations in Nazi Germany. There may have been personal reasons for this—the Warner (né Wonskolaser) family, Jews from the Polish provinces, had experienced pogroms firsthand—or it may also have had something to do with the unflinching, streetwise reputation that the studio earned in the early 1930s. In his 1965 autobiography, Jack Warner told a story, more of a legend than fact, of a studio employee in Germany who was beaten to death by Nazi thugs in 1933. "I immediately closed our offices and exchanges in Germany," he recounted, "for I knew that terror was creeping across the country." As far back as Harry, Sam, Albert, and Jack Warner's first jointly produced film, *My Four Years in Germany* (1918), a silent feature based on the autobiography of former United States ambassador to wartime Germany James Gerard, there was a notable desire on the part of the brothers to reflect political currents on screen (in that film, as in Warners productions of the 1930s, it was the threat of German wartime aggression). Unlike most of their counterparts at the major Hollywood studios, the Warners didn't shy away from public debate. "He had the toughness of a brothel madam, and the buzzing persistence of a mosquito on a hot night," the North American–born Jack, head of production throughout the war years, once said of his Polish-born brother Harry (né Hirsch Moses), president of the studio.

"While no one would ever have accused Warner Brothers of being the classiest studio in Hollywood," writes Neil Gabler in *An Empire of Their Own: How the Jews Invented Hollywood*, "most would have conceded that it was the most aggressive, cantankerous, and iconoclastic." Having earned a name for itself by introducing a long line of scrappy, often working-class and vaguely ethnic stars (James Cagney, John Garfield, Edward G. Robinson, Paul Muni, Joan Blondell, Bette Davis, Myrna Loy, among others), the studio was unafraid of taking on projects that might stir up controversy, such as the mob-themed features of the early 1930s—movies like *Little Caesar* or *The Public Enemy*—or films that focused on the sociopolitical issues of the day. As Jack Warner told a reporter from the *Brooklyn Eagle* in 1938: "Every worthwhile contribution to the advancement of motion pictures has been over the howl of protest from the standpatters, whose favorite refrain has been, 'You can't do that.' And when we hear that chorus now, we know we must be on the right track."

Harry Warner expressed his determination, as early as the spring of 1933, "to expose Hitler and Nazism for what they truly were." He would soon sign off on anti-Nazi cartoons made by the studio's animation unit later that year, and he would work on various ideas for a string of anti-Nazi features. Harry and Jack Warner were perhaps the only studio heads in town to support the Hollywood Anti-Nazi League (HANL); they also helped provide the space for the radio program *America Marches On*, jointly produced by HANL and the American Legion. In March 1938, Jack Warner hosted a dinner honoring the Nobel Prize–winning German novelist Thomas Mann, one of the most vociferous critics of the Third Reich, an event that was covered in the pages of *Variety* ("the first time a studio head organized and participated in an anti-Nazi activity"). "In their zeal to caution the world about growing Nazi aggression," writes historian Michael Birdwell in *Celluloid Soldiers: Warner Bros.'s Campaign Against Nazism*, "Warner Bros. ran afoul of nascent fascist organizations in America, isolationists in and outside of government, and the industry's own in-house censorship organ, the Production Code Administration." For them, the fight against fascism was not something that could be easily brushed aside.

The specter of war, and the big moral decisions that came with it, permeated everything from the source material of *Casablanca* to the very climate into which it emerged. The moment that a copy of Burnett and Alison's play first landed at the Burbank offices of Warner Bros., on December 8, 1941, the day after the Japanese attack on Pearl Harbor, its potential as a successful war drama was duly recognized. In the notes attached to the synopsis he prepared on December 11, junior script reader Stephen Karnot, who would soon leave his post at Warners to work at a defense plant, observed: "Excellent melodrama. Colorful, timely background, tense mood, suspense, psychological and physical conflict, tight plotting, sophisticated hokum." Owing to its irresistible dramatic content, and its potential appeal to mass audiences, Karnot recommended it as a "box-office natural" for Bogart.

Along similar lines, in Aeneas MacKenzie's report, the screenwriter gave Wallis assurances that the story's commercial viability were outweighed only by what he highlighted as the play's greatest strength. "Behind the action and its background," he wrote, "is the possibility of an excellent theme—the idea that when people lose faith in their ideals, they are beaten before they begin to fight. That was what happened to France and to Rick Blaine." This early evaluation of Burnett and Alison's work proved rather prescient, as the central motif that MacKenzie underscored was preserved, and indeed amplified, in the final picture, rushed into release soon after Allied troops arrived in North Africa in November 1942.

Warner Bros. performed, in addition to its primary function of delivering class-A popular entertainment, a few politically minded offscreen roles: Harry Warner organized a committed group of ex-servicemen at the studio known as the "Warvets" to oversee security on the lot, keeping a lookout for air raids, while Jack Warner donned the uniform of a U.S. Army Air Force lieutenant colonel, even signing his name "Col. Jack Warner." Before they had begun formal work on the script, in February 1942, the Epstein twins heeded their own patriotic call to duty. "Frank Capra went to Washington to do a series called *Why We Fight*," Julius Epstein recounted in an interview from the 1980s, "and he asked my brother and me to go along to work on it. We said we would; the studio said, 'No, you've got to do this picture.' We said, 'We're going anyhow.' We never did a line before we went to Washington."

Their main assignment for Capra, helping to develop the screenplay for the first installment of the series, *Prelude to War* (1942), offered a kind of documentary counterpart to what they would soon fictionalize in *Casablanca*. It made the most powerful case, initially aimed at American recruits and later released to the broader public, for America's entry to the war. "One of Hitler's chief secret weapons has been [his] films," remarked Capra in 1942. "We will now turn that weapon against him." The fundamental idea, then, was rather didactic: to teach and inspire the recruits and to offer them a morale-building basis for battle. As the insert by Secretary of War Henry Stimson announces at the start: "The purpose of these films is to give factual information as to the causes, the events leading up to our entry into war and the principles for which we are fighting." As for the Epsteins, they contributed some of the same pluck and proficient storytelling—without their signature wisecracking, snappy wit—that had become the hallmarks of their work at Warners and that helped the film earn the award for best documentary at the 1943 Oscars ceremony.

When the twins returned to Hollywood four weeks later, they brought with them an intensified spirit of engagement with which they endowed their characters and the underlying tension of the inchoate *Casablanca* screenplay. Similarly, Howard Koch, who helped revise the drafts prepared by the Epsteins, never lost sight of the drama unfolding in the global arena. "Mike [Curtiz] leaned strongly on the romantic elements of the story," recalled Koch years later, "while I was more interested in the characterizations and the political intrigues with their relevance to the world struggle against fascism." Much like the fictional Rick Blaine, Koch himself had experienced a similar kind of political transformation, from a figure of quiet pacifism into a rather strident anti-fascist and vocal proponent for military intervention, sometime in the late 1930s. He helped to inject these core tenets into his characterization of conscientious objector turned unlikely World War I hero Alvin York, played by Gary Cooper, in *Sergeant York*, the highly successful biopic that Warners released a little over a year before *Casablanca.* He revisited them again, most famously, in the cynical saloon keeper *cum* resistance fighter named Rick Blaine.

Relatively early on in the film, Rick announces his neutrality and his refusal to take sides in an ugly world, as he's seen walking almost in lockstep with Captain Renault, the French prefect of police and unabashed political opportunist. The two men make their way through the lively main hall of Rick's Café Américain, where Sam is seated at the piano entertaining a raucous mixed crowd, when Renault shares the news that he's preparing to make an important arrest that night, "a murderer, no less." He advises Rick, who shows a brief flash of concern in his eyes, to avoid interfering. "I stick my neck out for nobody," retorts Rick unequivocally, with a good dose of swagger, taking a deep drag on his cigarette, a slight poker-face grin barely visible on his face. It's a line he'll soon repeat, when the mercy-seeking Ugarte (Peter Lorre) is whisked away by the Vichy police right before his eyes, and will gloss once more before the film's denouement. Renault applauds him, suggesting that

Ugarte (Peter Lorre) being whisked away at Rick's.

such a response is "wise foreign policy," a policy that numerous American public officials and their far-flung constituencies outside of Burbank had widely supported up until 1941, the year portrayed in the film. A Gallup poll conducted during the early war years suggested that more than 90 percent of the American public favored neutrality.

Such slogans as "No Foreign Entanglements," emblazoned upon placards carried by protesters in Washington, and captured in the Capra documentary that the Epstein brothers helped write, garnered considerable approval among Americans. In September 1941, a set of hearings was convened by a U.S. Senate Subcommittee on War Propaganda, chaired by Idaho Democrat Senator D. Worth Clark. The hearings were designed to address a resolution sponsored by two hard-nosed isolationist senators, Republican Gerald P. Nye of North Dakota and Democrat Bennett Champ Clark of Missouri, calling for "an investigation of any propaganda disseminated by motion pictures and radio or any other activity of the motion picture industry to influence public opinion in the direction of participation of the United States in the present European war." Both senators displayed unmasked contempt for the film industry, which they considered a bastion of Jews, Communists, foreigners and other subversive, immoral forces threatening to undermine America. "Go to Hollywood," exclaimed Nye in his opening salvo. "It is a raging volcano of war fever. The place swarms with refugees." In the eyes of the isolationist faction and its political bedfellows (America First, Father Charles Coughlin, the Silver Shirt Legion), the foreign-born moguls, those "Merchants of Death on Sunset Boulevard," had sought to advance a dangerous interventionist agenda. Fueled by a potent mix of nativism, xenophobia, and anti-Semitism, Nye's probe was aimed at determining how many of these suspicious, ostensibly warmongering productions "were the work in part or in full of refugees or alien authors."

Among those summoned to testify was the Polish-born Harry Warner, some of whose recent films—specifically, *Confessions of a Nazi Spy* (1939), *Underground* (1941), and *Sergeant York* (1941)—were singled out for negative scrutiny. In public, Harry was far more reserved than the famously brash, toothy, and flamboyant Jack, who was known for his off-color sense of humor. As president of the studio, Harry was deeply attentive to financial matters, but also a man with a strict moral compass and the tremendous zeal to fight a good fight.

"He has two major interests," declared a 1937 profile of Harry Warner and his studio in *Fortune* magazine, "business and morals." In Warner's congressional testimony, delivered on September 25, he defended the studio—whose patriotic motto, "Combining Good Picture-Making with Good Citizenship," would almost seem designed to inoculate the company against any such charges—and denied all complicity in the promotion of war hysteria. "We're not newcomers," he insisted, deflecting fears of alien infiltration. "We helped pioneer the motion-picture industry. We are not interlopers who seized control of a large company by some trick." Harry Warner remained unrepentant about *Sergeant York*: it was "a factual portrait of the life of one of the great heroes of the last war," he asserted. "If that is propaganda, we plead guilty." Likewise, of his other war-themed productions, he claimed that the accusing parties had never even bothered to watch them. As he summarily stated, "In truth the only sin Warner Bros. is guilty of is that of accurately recording on the screen the world as it is or as it has been."

Three years before the hearings in Washington, in his self-appointed role as the moral voice of the studio, Harry Warner had made public his "intention of making important social pictures to combat Fascism." He saw it as his duty, as he wrote in the pages of the *Christian Science Monitor*, "to educate, to stimulate, and to demonstrate the fundamentals of free government, free speech, religious tolerance, freedom of press, freedom of assembly and the greatest possible happiness to the greatest possible number." Several of the studio's highly regarded features from the period blended, almost seamlessly, these cornerstone beliefs into timely stories that were, at least on their historical or geographic surface, far enough removed from the current sociopolitical situation to elude the ire of Joseph Breen and the Production Code Administration (the official Hollywood censorship body informally known as the Hays Office) and the isolationist faction in Congress. *The Life of Emile Zola* (1937) reworked the Dreyfus affair, giving contract star Paul Muni the chance to make a dramatic plea for religious tolerance and social justice. Two years later, in *Juarez* (1939), Muni again played the title character, this time Mexican national hero Benito Juárez, who immortalized the democratic spirit of independence. "The struggle of the remarkable Mexican to save his nation for its own people," wrote Warner in the same piece in the *Christian Science Monitor*, "is so surprisingly paralleled by the world events today that the timeliness of the subject matter is obvious."

A short feature that Warners released the same year, *Sons of Liberty*, directed by Michael Curtiz, earned the studio an Oscar for best short subject. It also provided the rare opportunity to portray a Jewish historical figure more explicitly—after great pains had been taken to downplay the ethnicity of Alfred Dreyfus in *The Life of Emile Zola*—in the character of Haym Salomon (Claude Rains), a Polish-Jewish immigrant in colonial America who saw it as his patriotic calling to help finance the Revolution and who, as Birdwell suggests, stood in as a "filmic embodiment of Harry Warner." Like the studio boss, Salomon is widely identifiable as a model citizen and a loyal patriot.

Undoubtedly the studio's most controversial picture, which

New York's German-Jewish newspaper *Aufbau* would hail as "America's first anti-Nazi film," was *Confessions of a Nazi Spy* (1939); it marked the first time a major studio invoked the otherwise taboo term "Nazi" in a title (its chief advertising slogan, "The first picture that calls a swastika a swastika," made this plain). Directed by the Ukrainian refugee filmmaker Anatole Litvak, and based on a newspaper story of foreign espionage on the home front, written by former FBI agent Leon G. Turrou and later expanded as the best seller *Nazi Spies in America* (1938), *Confessions* emerged largely from the efforts of the Hollywood Anti-Nazi League. Composed of refugee actors, writers, directors, and producers, alongside a sizable segment of prominent left-leaning American studio professionals, HANL was founded in 1936 by Czech-born radical Otto Katz. Later known as a highly elusive Soviet spy, Katz was famous among members of the film colony for his persuasive recruitment efforts and was thought by some to have served as partial inspiration for *Casablanca*'s underground resistance fighter Victor Laszlo. He was also a model for the anti-fascist hero, played by Paul Lukas, in Warners' 1943 adaptation of Lillian Hellman's play *Watch on the Rhine*.

Together with actor Edward G. Robinson, who himself was born in Romania as Emanuel Goldenberg, HANL leaders urged Hal Wallis and Warners to address the subject of a Nazi spy ring that had taken root within the New York branch of the German-American Bund. "The world is faced with the menace of gangsters who are much more dangerous than we have ever known," remarked Robinson, who became a star in Warners' acclaimed gangster picture *Little Caesar* less than a decade before. "And there's no reason why the motion pictures shouldn't be used to combat them." Similarly, *Los Angeles Times* gossip columnist Hedda Hopper noted at the time of production, in a statement that would seem to apply equally well to *Casablanca*: "scores of actors, the great majority of them natives of Germany, clamored to have a role in the film."

The finished film opened in New York City on April 28, 1939, the same day that Hitler announced, in a speech delivered before the Reichstag, his plans to march into Poland. Although it earned mixed reviews, it demonstrated Warners' stubborn determination to make films that openly addressed the Nazi threat despite—or, perhaps, because of—the vocal opposition aimed at the studio. During the film's production schedule and after its release, the company was the subject of violent threats, bullying, and intimidation at home and abroad, including from the German consul in Los Angeles, Georg Gyssling; the German-American Bund; and Father Coughlin. According to Birdwell's detailed account in *Celluloid Soldiers*, the film was banned across Scandinavia, as well as in several countries in continental Europe and South America, its screening prompted public hangings of theater owners in Poland and even the burning of a Warner Bros. theater in Milwaukee, Wisconsin. Groucho Marx, who would later butt heads with the studio, had nothing but praise for the film. "I want to propose a toast to Warners," he announced in a moment of uncommon seriousness, after seeing *Confessions*, "the only studio with any guts."

By his own telling, after a private viewing of the film by top Nazi officials at Hitler's alpine retreat in Berchtesgaden, Jack

Warner earned a spot on the Nazi extermination list. Never one to back down from a fight, Warner told a reporter from the *New York Times*:

> Our fathers came to America to avoid just the sort of persecution that is taking place in Germany today. If we wish to keep the United States as the land of the free and the home of the brave, we must do everything we can to destroy the deadly Nazi germs of bigotry and persecution. I consider this picture our greatest contribution and we shall produce it regardless of the consequences, regardless of the threats that have been pouring in on us, regardless of the pressure that has been brought against our organization by certain forces, even within the industry, which have an interest in seeing the picture abandoned.

Blending documentary with fictional drama, and offering a powerful broadside against isolationism by showing the threat of fifth columnists as imminent, *Confessions* was praised by some critics for offering a new form of "movie journalism." In it, we follow FBI agent Renard (Robinson) as he uncovers the vast network of planned Nazi infiltration—repeatedly underscored in a montage of newspaper headlines, maps, newsreel and documentary clips (even a few from Leni Riefenstahl's 1935 Nazi propaganda film *Triumph of the Will*), and an ominous procession of goose-stepping shadow figures. By the film's end, the gathering threat of Nazism gets drowned out by "America the Beautiful," which reverberates triumphantly.

"We're not Europe," says a patron at a New York diner in the final scene, alluding to the string of capitulations and to recent news of the Nazi spy convictions. "The sooner we show 'em that, the better."

Scenes from *Confessions* would later find their way into Capra's *Why We Fight* series and even earn a small comedic homage from Warners animation unit in the Looney Tunes short *Confusions of a Nutzy Spy* a few years later. In that version, Porky Pig hunts down a German-accented lynx that infiltrates America with the intent to bomb it to smithereens. Fleetingly, the "Missing Lynx," as he's called in the cartoon, dons a Hitler disguise, little mustache and all, and gives the Nazi salute, barking "Sieg Heil." If it wasn't already the case in 1939, by the time of the animated *Confusions*, in January 1943, the Nazi threat was a topic of popular concern, subjected both to serious and satirical scrutiny, and ready for mass consumption.

Although he was berated for *Confessions*, Harry Warner, who quickly found himself on the right side of history, held a trump card in his hand during the congressional hearings: a telegram he'd received a few months before from Senator Nye responding to the film. It was written in surprisingly effusive terms, the kind of language normally reserved for the Warners publicity team. In his testimony, the studio head happily produced the document from his breast pocket and read it aloud: "THE PICTURE IS EXCEEDINGLY GOOD. THE CAST IS EXCEPTIONALLY FINE. THE PLOT MAY OR MAY NOT BE EXAGGERATED BUT ONE THAT OUGHT TO BE WITH EVERY PATRIOTIC AMERICAN. [. . .] ANYONE WHO TRULY APPRECIATES THE ONE GREAT DEMOCRACY UPON THIS EARTH

WILL APPRECIATE THIS PICTURE AND FEEL A NEW ALLEGIANCE TO THE DEMOCRATIC CAUSE." Around the time of the hearings, *New Yorker* author, screenwriter, and humorist Leo Rosten published his investigative work *Hollywood: The Movie Colony, the Movie Makers*. There he cast a critical eye on the "Hollywood Legend," the candy-coated mythology surrounding Tinseltown, while also noting a few of the film industry's bona fide achievements. "It will be to Hollywood's credit," he wrote, holding up the recent work at Warner Bros. for special praise, "that its anti-Fascist activities predate the swing in American public opinion and diplomacy. It will be to Hollywood's credit that it fought the Silver Shirts, the German-American Bund, and the revived Ku Klux Klan at a time when few realized their ultimate menace."

On December 2, 1941, less than a year before *Casablanca* had its New York premiere, and just days before the United States entered the war, Warners released yet another anti-Nazi film, *All Through the Night*. This modestly budgeted picture starred both Humphrey Bogart and Conrad Veidt, featured a large cast of foreign-born bit players, and was overseen by Hal Wallis; it was also drawn from a story by none other than *Hollywood* author Rosten, under the assumed name Leonard Q. Ross. Like its more celebrated successor, it charts the gradual move from isolationism to active engagement in sports promoter and gambler-with-a-heart-of-gold "Gloves" Donahue, the debonair protagonist in a pressed double-breasted suit and snap-brim hat played by Bogart. The film wastes no time getting its point across, opening with a scene of Donahue's cronies lining up formations of toy soldiers and tanks on the table of a

New York City lunch counter, plotting the best course of attack for the British to beat the Nazis ("catch 'em with their panzers down"). When asked for his opinion on the matter, Gloves responds, in uncanny anticipation of Rick Blaine: "I can't be bothered. That's Washington's racket. Let them handle it." But as the plot unfurls, Donahue becomes the wise-minded citizen who cracks the Nazi conspiracy led by Herr Ebbing (Veidt) and his followers (including the devious Pepi, played by Peter Lorre with extra relish).

Despite its incongruous, slapdash mix of screwball comedy and wartime melodrama, the film's most redeeming achievement was to break the widely held taboo against any reference to concentration camps—Dachau is mentioned several times—and to work in a few populist slogans. "We gotta wake up!" says one character after trouncing a band of Nazis at a New York underground meeting, using baseball bats in lieu of artillery. And as Leda Hamilton (Kaaren Verne), a German woman exploited by Ebbing but finally saved by the chivalrous Donahue, says in the film's final minutes, "It's about time someone knocked the Axis back on its heels." To which Donahue replies, with plenty of swagger, "It's about time someone knocked those heels back on their axis!"

A KEY STRAND of the history in the making that the Hollywood studio self-consciously sought to record, as Harry Warner insisted in his testimony before Congress, was to recognize the Nazi threat across the globe. This is precisely how *Casablanca* opens—with a stream of credits beamed over a map of

Africa, a few resonant bars of the "Marseillaise," and a fade-out to a spinning globe. The very first words uttered in the film, delivered by narrator Lou Marcelle ("a fifty-dollar job," he later recalled) in a folksy newsreel-style voice-over, are: "With the coming of the Second World War, many eyes in imprisoned Europe turned hopefully, or desperately, toward the freedom of the Americas." Among the throngs of exiles languishing in North Africa, Rick, who for untold reasons is banished from his home, claims to be interested neither in world affairs ("Your business is politics," he announces to the visiting Nazi delegation, "mine is running a saloon") nor in the fate of others ("I'm the only cause I'm interested in"). Yet, with remarkable flair and efficiency, the larger political drama manifests itself in the contradictions of his character, in the bitter clash between self-imposed isolation and principled commitment to a far greater cause. Thanks not only to the fortuitous timing of its release, but also to the sly intermingling of history, politics, and fiction, *Casablanca* gave viewers the chance to reflect on the current state of the world (Manny Farber's contemporary review of the film in *The New Republic* ran under the apt title "The Warner Boys in Africa"), while also feeding their appetite for entertainment at the movies—larger-than-life characters, exotic backdrops, heart-wrenching romance, and plenty of glimpses of a universally identifiable, basic humanity.

At its root, we might consider *Casablanca*, as screenwriter Philip Epstein's son Leslie suggested to me, the "transcendent example" of classical Hollywood cinema. "It's got a lot to do with the timing, the war, and all that," he continued. "But also it's *the* signature archetype of how Americans would like to think of themselves, as tough ('I stick my neck out for nobody'), but underneath there's a heart and they do the right thing somehow. It's a tough morality, but it is morality, and Bogart got that across." Among the multitude of archetypes in which the film luxuriates, Bogart's portrayal of Rick offers a hard-boiled, world-weary toughness that moviegoers knew well from such previous Bogie performances as Sam Spade in *The Maltese Falcon.* ("Go ahead and shoot," he tells Ilsa, exuding the same cold cynicism as that gumshoe, when she points a revolver at him in the dark of night. "You'll be doing me a favor.") With *Casablanca*, remarks Pauline Kael, Bogart "established the figure of the rebellious hero—the lone wolf who hates and defies officialdom (and in the movies he fulfilled a universal fantasy: he got away with it)." As early as *The Petrified Forest* (1936)—in which costar Leslie Howard brands Bogie's character, Duke Mantee, "the last great apostle of rugged individualism"—the figure of Rick Blaine almost seems to be waiting, not yet fully born, to assert his true self.

Rick's implied status as an outlaw, a frontier renegade, further links him to a long line of heroes of the American western, men who similarly know when to do the right thing, even if it means taking the law into their own hands. (Think of Gary Cooper in Fred Zinnemann's *High Noon*, made a decade after *Casablanca*, and the vigilante justice inflicted upon the band of criminals, stand-ins for Nazi thugs, on the American frontier.) The rich nuances expressed in Bogart's face, those deep caverns of conflicted humanity, have inspired movie love in countless viewers, including filmmaker, critic, and program director of the New York Film Festival Kent Jones, who recently confided to a group of students that the origins of his own cinephilia lie in that most famous of Hollywood visages. Bogart recalls, as Jones put it, the magic of classical Hollywood cinema but just as forcefully evokes the offscreen battles that soldiers were fighting overseas at the time of his meteoric rise.

Jones later spoke with me about his initial viewing of the film in the early 1970s, while on vacation in London with his parents, and how for him—as for millions of other spirited young moviegoers—Bogart quickly became "a counterculture hero." Not only did Jones adorn his childhood bedroom walls with posters of Bogie, an affinity he shared with Allan Felix, the fictionalized hero of Woody Allen's Broadway hit *Play It Again, Sam* (1969), but using an old tape recorder he captured the audio track of a televised broadcast of the film—the most televised movie of the 1970s—to listen to later in bed. It wasn't so much a teenage obsession, he explained to me, as "it was a connection politically in the sense that I too had reached the point: 'I'm sick of all this crap.'" Bogart's hardened attitude, not to mention his rebellious streak, spoke to a new generation at odds with the ruling power and still looking somehow to act, to do the right thing.

Along similar lines, Barbara Deming, in her examination of American movies of the 1940s, speaks of Rick as an "unlikely warrior." Having spent the early part of that decade working as a film analyst for the Library of Congress, writing what became *Running Away from Myself: A Dream Portrait of America Drawn from the Films of the Forties* (1969), Deming looked at the protagonists of such films as "the products of a deep crisis of faith." Rick is no exception. "At the film's beginning," she writes, "the hint is dropped that the hero may be speaking words he does not mean. He is presented as a cipher, a man with a mask, and the film poses the question: if it should come to a trial, might he not possess a fighting faith more real than all the rest?" As viewers, we are invited to believe in Rick's hidden ability to rise above his professions of neutrality, his intermittent wallowing in self-pity, and to fight the good fight. "This is the film's real magic," Deming continues, "not only does it bring to the question the right answer; it brings the right answer without letting the audience become fully aware of what the question is; it drowns out the bitter cries without letting the audience become fully aware of what the cries have been all about."

One of the clever ways in which the film sneaks in the political dimension—and, indeed, drops more hints about Rick's true convictions—is by couching it within the tense romance between Rick and Ilsa. *Casablanca* "recasts propaganda as a romantic act," as critic Karina Longworth, who hosts a classic Hollywood podcast called *You Must Remember This*, puts it. The political lines can thus be traced along the string of romantic plot points. Of course, Ilsa serves as the unwanted reminder of Rick's past, the figure who, in tandem with their long repressed song, recalls the torrid and ultimately ill-fated affair they enjoyed during the spring of 1940, when the Nazis marched into Paris. She causes him not only to break one of his cardinal rules—to drink with customers at his café in Casablanca—but also to become unhinged in the process. As Rick sits alone after hours, throwing back one shot after the next and doing all that he can to overcome the shock of

Ilsa's sudden appearance, he asks Sam, seated across from him improvising on the piano, "If it's December 1941 in Casablanca, what time is it in New York?" On this long night, in the pre-dawn hours vaguely evocative of the actual conditions surrounding the Pearl Harbor bombings, Sam claims that his watch has stopped running. Rick replies, with yet another glimmer of vulnerability, "I bet they're asleep in New York. I'll bet they're asleep all over America."

When Rick stubbornly, bitterly insists that Sam play "As Time Goes By," the flashback to his spring romance with Ilsa begins. While much of that particular interlude is aimed at offering up fleeting images of their happy past together, it also offers a window onto the war and the Nazi aggression across Europe. Locked in a tender embrace, midway through the flashback, Ilsa and Rick hear the sound of artillery fire. "Ah, that's the new German 77," says Rick matter-of-factly, betraying his knowledge of military artillery (as one of many examples of Hollywood bending historical accuracy, there was no German 77—apart perhaps from the 77th division of the Luftwaffe—used in World War II). "And judging by the sound, only about thirty-five miles away." Much later, during a face-off in Rick's apartment, when an emboldened Ilsa is intent on getting her hands on the precious letters of transit, she counters Rick's flippant dismissal of the cause that Laszlo supports. "It was your cause, too," she insists. "In your own way, you were fighting for the same thing." And, perhaps unsurprisingly, ultimately, it is Ilsa who finally brings Rick back into the fold, helping him to resolve his crisis of faith.

On the airport tarmac, Rick tells her, in one of the film's

most famous, oft-quoted scenes, "Ilsa, I'm no good at being noble, but it doesn't take much to see that the problems of three little people don't amount to a hill of beans in this crazy world." Of course, the screenwriters, director Michael Curtiz, and producer Hal Wallis needed Rick to bid farewell or face the wrath of the Production Code Administration; he couldn't run off with a married woman—even their Parisian romance had to take place under the presumption of Laszlo's death—and thus violate one of the Code's foremost moral prohibitions. As film historian Thomas Doherty puts it, "The film needs Rick to stick his neck out and commit to the Allied cause at the same time it needs to respect the sanctity of the bonds of matrimony. [. . .] One reason *Casablanca* endures in the popular movie memory is the aberrational decisiveness of its climax, which tackled and resolved the question of dual loyalties head on."

In order to heighten the suspense of the film, the Nazis portrayed on screen had to reflect the same menacing threat that Harry Warner underscored in his 1941 Senate testimony and depicted in such earlier films as *Confessions of a Nazi Spy* and *All Through the Night*. Without relying on mere parody or caricature, Major Strasser conveys an unmistakably diabolical air, his venomous lines delivered with the fervor of a madman. Similarly, the other Nazi officials in his entourage do all that they can to intimidate and threaten those in their midst. In a cruel ironic twist of history, these same Nazis were played by refugees, perhaps most famous among them Veidt, who had fled the very regime whose officials they were now embodying on screen.

Near the start of the film, when we hear snatches of conversation from refugees seeking a way out, a pair of Germans in uniform march by leaving a trail of untranslated words in their wake. "*Ich verstehe es gar nicht. Wir sollten eine viel stärkere Hand haben in Casablanca*" ("I don't understand it at all. We should have a much stronger hand in Casablanca"), one of the officers asserts, referring both to the halfhearted devotion to Vichy rule of law and the go-for-broke card games being played at Rick's. Later on, at Signor Ferrari's Blue Parrot, we're told by its proprietor that the Germans have "outlawed miracles" when it comes to dreaming up escape routes. And yet despite the overriding tragic predicament, there are brief moments of comic relief in which the Germans, no longer merely diabolical, become the butt of the joke. When Renault tells headwaiter Carl that he should be sure to give Major Strasser a good table, he responds, with the well-timed wit of a vaudeville player: "I have already given him the best, knowing he is German and would take it anyway."

Despite all professions of neutrality and political indifference, Rick offers perceptive viewers a few glimpses of his true allegiances vis-à-vis the Nazis from the very moment he's introduced. As he sits alone at his table, playing a solitary chess game, puffing away on his ever present cigarette, and giving the okay to sundry financial transactions and to the traffic that his doorman Abdul (Dan Seymour) monitors, the head of the Deutsche Bank (Gregory Gaye) attempts in vain to gain entry to the café. Rick shakes his head, prompting Abdul to give his canned "private room" excuse. Undeterred, the German insults and threatens Abdul, at which point Rick coolly approaches the door. As he tries to sort things out—at the very same instant that Ugarte suddenly shows up, slicked-back hair and unctuous grin in place, slithering his way through the half-closed door—the German becomes increasingly haughty and indignant, handing Rick his visiting card. The fact that he's frequented gambling parlors from Honolulu to Berlin doesn't impress Rick, who promptly, unrepentantly, tears up his card. "Your cash is good at the bar," he tells him. The German storms out, announcing that he'll report Rick to the *Angriff*, the actual Nazi propaganda newspaper founded by Joseph Goebbels. In this otherwise rapid and minor exchange, Rick is fleetingly branded a political subversive, or simply an anti-Nazi.

Later on, after Ugarte has been captured and Rick is invited to join Strasser and his men at their table, he once more wraps himself in the mantle of political neutrality. Rather than admitting his nationality to Strasser, Rick declares himself a "drunkard" ("Which makes him a citizen of the world," as Renault sees it). But he strikes a slightly defensive, if not patriotic position when asked if he can imagine the Nazis in New York. "Well, there are certain sections of New York, Major, that I wouldn't advise you try to invade." Ultimately, after Strasser tries to show that Rick has not always been so uncompromisingly neutral, he leaves politics behind at the table and returns to his work as a saloon keeper. (Off screen, when accused of being a Communist by the turncoat John L. Leech in early 1940, Bogart issued a formal statement declaring a similar kind of political neutrality to that which he maintains in the film: "I have never contributed money to a political organization of any form. That includes Republican, Democratic, Hollywood Anti-Nazi League or Communist Party.")

Of course, the film's most rousing political scene—one that appealed even to those critics, like Manny Farber and Pauline Kael, who were generally less susceptible to Hollywood hokum—comes when Rick and Laszlo meet man-to-man in Rick's office soon after the former has started to show a few cracks in his steely shell by allowing the young Bulgarian Jan to win at the roulette table ("a gesture to love") so that he and his wife can afford exit visas. The scene begins with the bold reassertion of Rick's worldview. "I'm not interested in politics," he declares to Laszlo, in a litany of disingenuous excuses after hearing that the movement needs his support. "The problems of the world are not in my department," he continues. "I'm a saloon keeper." Laszlo is quick to remind Rick of his earlier involvement in anti-fascist causes, in Ethiopia and Spain, but cannot persuade him to relinquish the letters of transit at any price—a matter he's told, rather bluntly, to take up with his wife.

Then in a swift transition, shot at a low tilt from outside Rick's office, the two men, now standing atop the stairs, hear a boisterous rendition of "Die Wacht am Rhein" sung by a group of Nazi officers seated around Strasser's table. Laszlo rushes down the stairs approaching the band members. "Play the 'Marseillaise'!" he commands them, with a sudden torrent of urgency, echoing Rick's earlier demand that Sam play "As Time Goes By." "Play it!" he insists. Rick gives the band members his nod of approval, another silent gesture of his shifting allegiances—a gesture that we've already seen at work earlier in the film—and they, together with the masses of refugees crowded into the main hall at Rick's Café, burst into song, drowning out the German chorus in a spectacular show of solidarity. Indeed, it is "one of the most stirring sequences in history," as director Steven Spielberg calls it. "If you know the movie, you remember the guy's face," remarks Kent Jones, referring to the trumpet player who looks across the room to Rick for approval before playing the French national anthem. "And Bogart gives them the go-ahead. Then you take the shot of the Germans giving up and sitting down, and then you have the moment, the thing that really makes it, when it really starts to build up with the Spanish guitarist; then, more obviously, when Yvonne starts singing. But it's really the way that it is, that it moves from bit by bit, that is almost emblematic of the whole movie."

Laszlo (Paul Henreid) conducting "La Marseillaise."

The incremental rise of the "Marseillaise"—an anthem that bespeaks a patriotic love of France and of freedom, more generally, echoed in the seemingly spontaneous cries of *"Vive la France!"* and *"Vive la démocratie"* by Yvonne and others in the crowd—exemplifies the common will to unite and overthrow tyranny, an impulse that Rick's own evolution likewise encapsulates. "Everybody in Casablanca came to Rick's," explained playwright Murray Burnett four decades after the film's release, "but everybody must come to a decision. Now that's pretty abstruse, but that's why I titled it *Everybody Comes to Rick's*. It was a double meaning."

Film critic J. Hoberman recounts that during the war, when his mother was a student at Brooklyn College, she attended a screening of *Casablanca* at one of New York's grand picture palaces in the Flatbush section of that borough. During the "Marseillaise" scene, many people in the theater—politically minded students, perhaps, possibly fellow travelers—stood up and sang along. "This made a huge impression on me," he remarked. "And I mention this whenever I've taught the film."

During postproduction, in early September 1942, Hal Wallis dashed off his "Music Notes" concerning the film. The first of these reads: "On the 'Marseillaise,' when it is played in the cafe, don't do it as though it was played by this small orchestra. Do it with full scoring orchestra to get some body to it." Like other important scenes in the film, among them the famous finale on the fog-drenched tarmac, the principal actors were not fully aware of how things would finally be composed and edited. Paul Henreid wrote in his memoir, "I am described by the Germans as a great leader of the masses, a man who can command obedience," and yet during this particular scene he notices the "musicians look away, then back to me before they start playing, and I conduct them, singing myself." He promptly approached the director, demanding answers: "What the hell is going on? Why do they look away and then back at me?" The quick-talking Curtiz smoothed things over, assuring Henreid that all would be fine: "It will establish that Bogie is on your side." Bogart, however, was just as much in the dark as Henreid. When he arrived to shoot the scene, he was reportedly told by Curtiz: "You've got an easy day today. Go on to the balcony, look down and to the right, and nod. Then you can go home." After many protestations, insisting on knowing the finer details, Bogart followed the orders given to him by Curtiz. "It's a scene that even after thirty years," observed writer Nathaniel Benchley in his 1975 book on Bogart, "prickles the scalp and closes the throat, and for all Bogart knew he was nodding at a passing dog."

Owing to the emotional intensity of such scenes, David Thomson has called *Casablanca* "the first women's picture made for men." While not quite a blustery 1950s Douglas Sirk three-handkerchief weepie, it elicits a thoroughly empathic response in the viewer. The witty subtitle of a piece of criticism on the film from the 1970s speaks to this: "If It's So Schmaltzy, Why Am I Weeping?" Even today, many decades removed from the war and from the original context in which the film appeared, it's hard to watch the singing of the "Marseillaise" without getting a bit misty-eyed. "*Casablanca* reassured its male audience (the source of the national anxiety regarding World War II intervention)," writes film scholar Robert B.

Ray, "that one could accept responsibilities without forfeiting autonomy." That very debate plays itself out in the ensuing confrontation between Rick and Laszlo. "Don't you sometimes wonder if it's worth all this?" asks Rick. "I mean what you're fighting for?" As if citing Harry Warner's testimony before the U.S. Senate, Laszlo replies: "We might as well question why we breathe. If we stop breathing, we'll die. If we stop fighting our enemies, the world will die." Like Ilsa, Laszlo detects Rick's true commitments buried underneath his steely shell. "I wonder if you know that you're trying to escape from yourself," he tells Rick, "and that you'll never succeed." Of course, Rick finally comes around to Laszlo's side, rekindling the beliefs that perhaps had never left him. As Laszlo remarks to Rick in his parting words: "Welcome back to the fight. This time I know our side will win."

"Perhaps the essential reason why *Casablanca* is now a classic, a cult, and a legend" wrote Ingrid Bergman in her memoir, "is that it was concerned with *our* war! Rarely, if ever, have an actor and actress had the opportunity to work so dramatically, if unknowingly, on our emotions, when defeat seemed a possibility and victory far away. *Casablanca* had a major impact on the Allied war effort." Or, as Aljean Harmetz puts it in her account, echoing to a large degree the sentiment expressed both by Bergman and by Leslie Epstein, "There are better movies than *Casablanca*, but no other movie better demonstrates America's mythological vision of itself—tough on the outside and moral within, capable of sacrifice and romance without sacrificing the individualism that conquered a continent, sticking its neck out for everybody when circumstances demand heroism. No other movie has so reflected both the moment when it was made—the early days of World War II—and the psychological needs of audiences decades later."

IN LIGHT OF the congressional hearings that he was forced to endure in September 1941, Harry Warner could no longer contain his glee that *Casablanca* had been so seemingly prescient, or at least magically timed. "Remember that it was completed and ready," he told *Variety* (whose review called the picture "splendid anti-Axis propaganda"), "weeks before our forces invaded North Africa and that, almost on the heels of the first invasion barge to touch African soil with our soldiers, it was on the screen, helping in its definite way to interpret the action for you, to explain Vichy France to you." Warner was fundamentally correct, if also trumpeting historical events to his company's advantage. Operation Torch, which culminated in the landing of Allied forces in North Africa on November 8, 1942, occurred just as the studio was rushing to get its release print into canisters and ready for special delivery to New York's Hollywood Theatre in time for the premiere on Thanksgiving Day.

In the run-up to the premiere, the studio couldn't have asked for better PR from the wire services. United Press dispatched a report from London on November 11 under the auspicious headline "Tanks Batter Casablanca," indicating that the Free French resistance forces were engaged in a pitched battle against Vichy troops and that General George S. Patton's American forces were making inroads. A day later, and exactly two weeks before the film's first public screening, the *New York Times* reported that the city of Casablanca had indeed surrendered to the Americans. Sensing an opportunity on their hands, the Warners sales department immediately issued advertisements of the film with such slogans as "Nothing could be more timely!" and "As exciting as the landing at Casablanca!" The slogans paid off at the box office—the premiere was accompanied by a military parade, no less—where 31,000 tickets were sold in the first week alone. The Hollywood Theatre's 1500-seat auditorium, including the standing-room section, sold out for every performance. Despite nasty blizzard conditions and icy temperatures, the film grossed $255,000 (a little over $3.5 million in today's dollars) during its ten-week run in New York, a bountiful take and the kind of first-run figures that presage a major hit.

As the film was making its way into wider release, the Casablanca Conference, held in the North African city from January 14 to January 26, 1943, with Franklin Delano Roosevelt, Winston Churchill, and Charles de Gaulle in attendance, gave it yet another historical boost. "Now, Rick Blaine was not just the fulcrum of a melodramatic movie," observes Stefan Kanfer in *Tough Without a Gun: The Life and Extraordinary Afterlife of Humphrey Bogart*. "He was a symbol of the nation itself, at first wary and isolationist, then changing incrementally until it headed in the opposite direction." By February 1943, *Casablanca* was screening at two hundred theaters across Roosevelt's America, earning $3.7 million that year alone—roughly $52 million in today's dollars—a sum that, while not quite the obscene box-office take of our current summer blockbusters, represents a notable success by any measure.

Like Rick, President Roosevelt had not always been an advocate for America's entry to the war, nor an outspoken foe of Vichy. In fact, U.S. foreign policy traversed many of the same fault lines as did Rick, Renault, and the extended cast of *Casablanca*. Trying to steer clear of major confrontations with the isolationist faction, in 1940 and much of 1941—that is, before the American entry to the war—Roosevelt maintained friendly relations with Vichy-controlled France and showed little inclination to meddle in foreign affairs. At some point during the same Senate hearings attended by Harry Warner, Roosevelt received a satirical telegram lampooning the events and the basic policy of isolationism: "HAVE JUST BEEN READING BOOK CALLED HOLY BIBLE. HAS LARGE CIRCULATION IN THIS COUNTRY. WRITTEN ENTIRELY BY FOREIGN-BORN, MOSTLY JEWS. FIRST PART FULL OF WAR-MONGERING PROPAGANDA. SECOND PART CONDEMNS ISOLATIONISTS."

By September 1941, the U.S. president conveyed to Vichy leader Marshal Philippe Pétain his firm wish to avoid German incursions into French North Africa. While continuing to press Pétain from afar, America retained its ties to Vichy up until the Allied landings in early November 1942—or, in filmic terms, until Renault makes his final about-face, joining Rick in the cause of anti-fascist resistance and tossing the bottle of Vichy water once and for all into the trash bin. Roosevelt prepared a recorded message for the French people to be broadcast after North Africa was under Allied control. "I know your farms, your villages, your cities," he declared, "I salute again, and reiterate my faith in Liberty, Equality, Fraternity." And, as if channeling the patriotic fervor of Yvonne and the crowds of supporters in Rick's Café, he signed off, *"Vive la France éternelle!"*

On New Year's Eve 1942, after a small party at the White House, President Roosevelt retired to his study for a private screening of *Casablanca.* "The film's message was clear," writes Warren F. Kimball in *The Juggler: Franklin Roosevelt as Wartime Statesman*, "war threatened romance." The film may, in its own way, have helped steer American foreign policy in a new more interventionist direction. At the very least, it was, as Richard Raskin suggests, "in part a private joke, savored by those few guests at the New Year's Eve Party who knew that the president was secretly arranging to depart for Casablanca." When John Lardner had reviewed the film in *The New Yorker*, just a few weeks earlier, he commented of the studio: "They may feel that General Eisenhower has merely served them well as an advance agent." There almost seems to have been a tacit pact made between politics and entertainment. Indeed, the Warners publicity department quickly issued a press release titled "De Gaulle Asks Warner Bros. for Special Screening of *Casablanca* in London." According to the release, de Gaulle hoped to show the film to his senior staff and other anti-Vichy leaders. "*Casablanca* had a special premiere, in which the Fighting French Forces participated, at the Hollywood Theatre three weeks ago," announced the publicity item, "The picture, which is breaking all attendance records in its New York run, ordinarily would not be seen in London for some time."

Humphrey Bogart would soon tour North Africa himself, as part of a Hollywood delegation on a multistop United Service Organizations (USO) junket. Schmoozing with the GIs, Bogart quoted lines from his film roles, foremost among them Rick Blaine, while the soldiers sang "As Time Goes By" accompanied by accordionist Ralph Hark. Bogart remained an unabashed supporter of Roosevelt, even making a series of public endorsements in the 1944 election. He took considerable heat for this, from both Republicans and conservative moviegoers, even from *The Hollywood Reporter*, which urged actors to avoid addressing political subjects in public. Angered by what he perceived as censure, Bogie published a feisty response, aptly titled "I Stuck My Neck Out," in the *Saturday Evening Post*. "When the 'treat 'em nice so long as they stay in their sound stage cages and perform entertaining tricks but rap their noses when they come out of them' school of thought finds a champion in Hollywood motion picture trade paper, I think it is time for one of the 'menagerie' to speak up." Bogart went so far as to compare the threat of boycott, then directed at outspoken actors, with tactics employed by the Nazi regime. With his signature swagger, first perfected in his muscular portrayal of Rick Blaine, he insisted, "I'm going to keep right on sticking my neck out, without worrying about its possible effect upon my career."

More than seven decades later, the message of Rick's struggle has not lost its immediacy. The Second World War is long over, the battle against Nazi tyranny a past victory, but in its place, other wars and other conflicts continue to challenge humanity. In an opinion piece titled "There's a Little Rick in All of Us," published in *Newsweek* in October 2002, political commentator Chris Matthews offered a series of reflections just months in advance of the Iraq War. "It may not always seem this way," he opens his essay, "but Americans don't like to fight." This explains, in his eyes, the unease felt by many when President George W. Bush and his advisors began to beat the drums of war (a very different war, morally and otherwise, than the battle that Rick joined). There remains, as Matthews put it, "a stubborn strain in the American character that resists intervening in foreign places unless we're attacked." For Matthews, this same character maps onto Rick, who gradually feels the threat of evil. "When his ideals, his love and his country are on the line," writes Matthews, "Rick will commit himself to the war against evil he now sees in his face." He rightly notes the risk—one that failed to be heeded properly in the Iraq War—of "moving from reluctant warriors to bullies spoiling for a fight," tracing the tradition embodied in Rick Blaine all the way back to the political rhetoric of Benjamin Franklin and Thomas Jefferson, continuing into the twentieth and twenty-first century.

When Kathy Kriger, a former commercial counselor at the U.S. embassy in Morocco and current owner of Rick's Café in the actual city that was merely re-created on the Warner soundstages in the summer of 1942, weighed the predicament she faced living in North Africa in the days after the 9/11 bombings, she observed the rising tide of xenophobia and anti-Islamic sentiment across Europe and the United States.

"Continuing to serve as a commercial attaché wouldn't do much to change that," she writes in the opening pages of *Rick's Café: Bringing the Film Legend to Life in Casablanca*, "I realized as the credits rolled [while rewatching *Casablanca*], but opening Rick's Café might remind Americans of the values we exhibited during World War II: sacrifice for the greater good, sympathy for the underdog, the willingness to take a stand. Americans would clearly see something unique about Morocco if an American woman on her own could create the iconic gin joint in today's Casablanca." While that region is still far from settled, at least some of the cultural restrictions may slowly have been lifted: in February 2015, for the first time ever, the Doha Film Institute gave the people of Qatar the chance to see *Casablanca* on the big screen in what may have been a Gulf nation premiere.

Around the same time, in the immediate wake of the January 2015 *Charlie Hebdo* shooting—in which eleven people were killed by Islamic terrorists who stormed the Parisian offices of the satirical newspaper—French politicians delivered an impromptu rendition of the "Marseillaise" on the floor of the French National Assembly. When Paris experienced another round of terrorist attacks in November of that same year, leaving more than a hundred civilians dead, the "Marseillaise" was sung by fans as they evacuated a soccer stadium in Paris on the night of the attacks and again when French students at New York's Union Square gathered to mourn and, in the days that followed, at sporting events and concerts held in London, Philadelphia, Chicago, and Los Angeles. This melodious outpouring was, as one journalist noted, "an expression of solidarity with the people of France, and of outrage at the carnage caused by the terrorists." The original song, once the favored anthem of French revolutionaries, reflects this tension. "On the one hand it is a revolutionary tune that extols not just liberty but the values of the new world," explained French historian Michel Vovelle, "while on the other hand it is a war song that expresses, with zeal sometimes deemed 'sanguinary,' the patriotic sentiments of an embattled nation." Thanks to *Casablanca*, the "Marseillaise" may be one of the few national anthems sung by noncitizens, who may not know all its words but know its emotional weight.

Three-quarters of a century after *Casablanca*'s initial release, we continue to wrestle with our own variations of the moral dilemmas faced by Rick, that archetypal reluctant hero, seeking resolve not only in its music, but in its message. "It's just a movie," screenwriter Howard Koch admitted already in 1989, "but it's more than that. It's become something that people can't find in values today. And they go back to *Casablanca* as they go back to church, political church, to find something that is gone from our values today."

Chapter 4

SUCH MUCH?

At a small table tucked away beneath the cavernous arches of Rick's Café Américain sit an elderly European couple dressed in what appear to be their best clothes. A portly man with silver hair and round spectacles, outfitted in the typical costume of a Viennese waiter, rushes up to the table. The endearing Carl announces his presence in a string of untranslated, Austrian-accented words: "*Ich bin schon hier, Herr Leuchtag. Ich habe ihnen den feinsten Cognac gebracht. Trinken nur die Angestellten*" ("Here I am, Herr Leuchtag. I brought you the finest cognac. Only the employees drink it."). After pouring a glass of cognac for Frau Leuchtag (Viennese stage and film actress Ilka Grüning) and one for Herr Leuchtag (Austrian-born actor Ludwig Stössel), Carl (the Budapest-born S. Z. Sakall, né Jenö Jacob Gerö, better known to the world as "Cuddles") joins the conversation, which quickly switches to English.

Herr Leuchtag: Carl, sit down. Have a brandy mit [*sic*] us.

Frau Leuchtag: To celebrate our leaving for America tomorrow.

Carl: Thank you very much. I thought you would ask me. So I brought the good brandy and a third glass.

Frau Leuchtag: At last the day has come.

Herr Leuchtag: Frau Leuchtag and I are speaking nothing but English now.

Frau Leuchtag: So we should feel at home when we get to America.

Carl: A very nice idea.

Carl (S. Z. Sakall), Herr Leuchtag (Ludwig Stössel), and Frau Leuchtag (Ilka Grüning) discussing their plans for America.

Herr Leuchtag: (*Raising his glass.*) To America.

(*Frau Leuchtag and Carl repeat, "To America." They clink glasses and drink*)

Herr Leuchtag: Liebchen, uh, sweetness heart, what watch?

Frau Leuchtag: Ten watch.

Herr Leuchtag: Such much?

Carl: Er, you will get along beautifully in America, huh.

This short scene is "unforgettable in its simplicity and beauty," as the late German filmmaker Rainer Werner Fassbinder once remarked, pronouncing it, with just a smidgen of exaggeration, "one of the most beautiful pieces of dialogue in the history of film." It's also an unexpected moment of deep self-awareness, a parody of wooden translation—fumbling for the equivalent English idiom for telling time in German—and greenhorn confusion, which might be taken for the actual experience of newly arrived refugee actors in Hollywood now playing refugees on screen. "The accent," observed a critic for the *New York Mirror* in 1942, "is on accents in *Casablanca*."

The film was made at a moment in history when Los Angeles and its studio fortresses were increasingly flooded with newly arrived German-speaking émigrés. The European Film Fund, established by director Ernst Lubitsch, agent Paul Kohner, and writer Salka Viertel, assisted in bringing refugees to America, providing stipends and securing affidavits for authors and actors, several of them cast and crew members of *Casablanca* (the chief donors to the fund included director Michael Curtiz and actors Paul Henreid, Peter Lorre, and S. Z. Sakall). By the 1940s, more than fifteen hundred film professionals from Germany and Austria alone had landed on the West Coast, where they began to change the flavor of their adopted city. Just a year before *Casablanca*'s release, Janet Flanner published a *New Yorker* profile of Thomas Mann—who went on writing in German long after he relocated to Pacific Palisades—under the provocative title "Goethe in Hollywood," intimating that the exalted German culture of the pre-Nazi era had now been relocated to Southern California. Around this same time, Austrian-born director and actor Otto Preminger, who was initially considered to play the part of Major Heinrich Strasser, is said to have interrupted an unruly crowd of Hungarian film professionals blathering away in their native tongue with a caustic jab: "Don't you guys know you're in Hollywood? Speak German!"

On the set of *Casablanca*, German was frequently spoken between takes among various actors and crew members. If not the official lingua franca, it was the mother tongue of many of the refugees who congregated that summer in Burbank. Even those who hadn't grown up speaking the language—like the St. Petersburg–born actor Leonid Kinskey, who played Sascha the bartender—found ample opportunity to trot out some of the phrases they had learned back in Europe. As Kinskey fondly recalled of his regular conversations with fellow actors Henreid, Lorre, and Sakall, "[my] German at the time was still fluent enough to nod at the right moment and throw in an occasional 'Ach so' and 'Ach du lieber' in a typical Kaffeeklatsch manner."

In his widely read "Hollywood Calling" column, published in

the German-language émigré newspaper *Aufbau*, Hans Kafka (no relation to Franz) reported in January 1942, "Efficiency is still the only thing that counts. Thus far, there have been no signs of discrimination against immigrant collaborators in the picture business. Continuing their directorial duties are Fritz Lang, Robert Siodmak, Anatole Litvak at Fox, Charles Vidor at RKO, Michael Curtiz at Warners." The state of affairs regarding the actors, even if they were often limited to secondary parts, quite a few of which required donning a Nazi uniform, was not terribly different. As Kafka put it in a subsequent column, "it's a grotesque, almost freakish situation; Hitler's gangsters, trying to annihilate all those [European-born émigré] actors finally succeeded to weld them to an almost perfect ensemble and give them the chance of their lives, artistically as well as financially."

Nearly all of the some seventy-five actors and actresses cast in *Casablanca* were immigrants. Among the fourteen who earned a screen credit, only three were born in the United States: Humphrey Bogart, Dooley Wilson, and Joy Page, Jack Warner's stepdaughter, who plays the Bulgarian refugee Annina Brandel. At the studio, Stage 8, where Rick's Café was assembled, was known as International House—the Warner Bros. press kit sent out to exhibitors included a slightly exaggerated gloss on this aspect: "The cast and crew of the production represent so many different nationalities that the set is the most cosmopolitan spot in Southern California." As the headline of a contemporary review in the *Philadelphia Record* announced, "Foreign Stars Enjoy a Boom in

Hollywood." Hailing from more than thirty different nations, the majority of refugee actors in the film served merely as day players, performing small parts—generally either as Nazis or as refugees fleeing the Nazis—most without significant dialogue. Among them, however, were many distinguished European artists with illustrious pasts on stage and screen.

Peter Lorre had arrived in Hollywood only a few years before—initially sharing a single room with a similarly destitute refugee named Billy Wilder—and Conrad Veidt was still relatively fresh off the boat. Lotte Palfi, a former star of the German stage who played one of the many refugees on screen and lived the life of one off of it, has just a single line of dialogue, whereas Trude Berliner, a onetime cabaret performer in Berlin, plays the lonely woman who asks Rick to join her for a drink. Curt Bois, the shifty pickpocket (or the "Dark European," as he's called in the script), had been a child star in Berlin who became a renowned theater and cabaret actor and a devoted disciple of theater impresario Max Reinhardt. His unusually poignant line, "This place is full of vultures, vultures everywhere," is perhaps not merely a thumbnail description of the dicey North African outpost but also a sly inside joke aimed at the recently arrived émigrés in Hollywood.

Film critic Pauline Kael, who otherwise held back praise for the picture—skewering its "special appealingly schlocky romanticism"—showed genuine affection for its large émigré cast. "If you think of *Casablanca* and think of those small roles being played by Hollywood actors faking the accents," she later remarked, "the picture wouldn't have had anything like the color and tone it had." Nor would it have had the same emotional force. The American-born bit actor Dan Seymour, who played the doorman Abdul at Rick's, noticed streams of tears flowing from the eyes of his fellow actors—most prominently, Madeleine Lebeau, who plays Rick's on-again-off-again paramour Yvonne—during the singing of the "Marseillaise." "I suddenly realized," he recalled many years later, "that they were all real refugees."

Lebeau and her then-husband, Marcel Dalio (né Israel Moshe Blauschild), who plays Emil the croupier, had in fact fled Vichy France via Lisbon, the same destination that scores of languishing refugees in the film dream of reaching. Using forged Chilean visas, they managed to gain a spot on a Portuguese cargo ship transporting European refugees to the New World; they made it to Mexico, and crossed the border into California using Canadian visas. Likewise, the film's technical advisor, Robert Aisner, a former lieutenant in the French army, managed to escape from a Nazi concentration camp and follow the refugee trail to Casablanca en route to America. As Anthony Heilbut, author of *Exiled in Paradise*, the most authoritative guide to the German-speaking migration to America during the 1930s and '40s, once remarked, "It would be exciting to think of *Casablanca* as helping to translate the émigré sensibility to an American audience." If we pay closer attention to the many accents, gestures, and intimations captured on screen, it's even more so.

Already present in the film's prologue, the refugee theme—even if ultimately eclipsed by the love story between Rick and Ilsa and the final enactment of Rick's conversion from self-avowed isolationist to a committed partisan—stands at the

Production still of Paris train station from Casablanca. *(For CASABLANCA [1942] ™ & © Turner Entertainment [s16])*

center of the plot, as its very point of departure and the backdrop against which everything else plays out. Immediately after the opening credits fade from the screen, and after a few recognizable bars from the "Marseillaise" that Viennese-born film composer Max Steiner managed to work into the score—he even wrote a short composition that he called "Refuge" to be played, *molto moderato*, in the prologue—the historical narration begins:

> With the coming of the Second World War, many eyes in imprisoned Europe turned hopefully, or desperately, toward the freedom of the Americas. Lisbon became the great embarkation point. But not everybody could get to

> Lisbon directly, and so, a tortuous, roundabout refugee trail sprang up. Paris to Marseilles, across the Mediterranean to Oran, then by train, or auto, or foot, across the rim of Africa to Casablanca in French Morocco. Here, the fortunate ones, through money, or influence, or luck, might obtain exit visas and scurry to Lisbon, and from Lisbon to the New World. But the others wait in Casablanca—and wait—and wait—and wait.

The miniature globe, spinning like a roulette wheel, quickly dissolves to a map insert tracing the routes of passage, the same routes that Murray Burnett had learned about in Europe four summers earlier. This is followed by a montage of stock shots, a kind of visual shorthand, with throngs of refugees on foot, in horse-drawn carriages, on steamships, on bicycles, and in automobiles. The camera finally guides us to a rather stifling, crowded North African street—filmed on the Warner back lot in Burbank—and to the palpable chaos of that world.

The entire prologue was designed by budding filmmaker Don Siegel, then head of the montage department at Warners, who would go on to direct *Invasion of the Body Snatchers* in the mid-1950s. On August 1, 1942, Wallis wrote a memo to Siegel, copying director Curtiz, in which the producer explained the significance of Siegel's assignment, and in particular, the focus on the globe. "For the opening of the picture, immediately preceding the montage of the refugees," Wallis wrote, "we would like to have a spinning globe—an unusual, interesting shot, sketchily lighted. As the globe's spinning slackens and stops,

Abraham Pisarek's photomontage "Wohin?" ("Where To?") from 1935 (left). *The globe insert designed for the prologue of* Casablanca *by Don Siegel* (right).

the camera zooms up to the general vicinity of our locale, and at that point you can dissolve to your montage."

As it turns out, the evocative image of a globe, used as a symbol of desperate flight, was not unique to high-gloss fantasies hatched in Hollywood. In a series of lectures delivered at the University of Graz, in Austria, scholar Joachim Schlör cited an earlier, lesser-known example taken from the visual arts. In 1935, the Polish-born photographer Abraham Pisarek completed a photomontage entitled "Wohin?" ("Where To?"), in which the actors Cläre Anstein and Heinz Heilborn—both of whom perished in concentration camps—stare longingly at a globe enshrouded in storm clouds. It's almost uncanny how much Pisarek's photomontage anticipates the globe that Siegel was asked to design seven years later, both instances underscoring the peril refugees faced in Nazi-engulfed Europe. In comparing the two images, and placing *Casablanca* within the wider context of anti-Nazi films, Schlör draws a critical distinction: "It's important to note that the film [*Casablanca*] does not broach the issue of Jewish persecution in

Europe directly—opposite the Nazis are, on the one hand, the oppressed people ('We come from Bulgaria. Things are very bad there, Monsieur. The devil's got the people by the throat.'); and on the other, the individuals, the *refugees*, whom we get to know as stand-ins for the thousands."

Informing all facets of this larger backdrop is the profound and stirring encounter with the refugee trail as experienced by Murray Burnett during his fateful trip to Europe in the summer of 1938. "I felt at the time and I still feel that no one can remain neutral in a world like that," Burnett remarked in a 1983 interview. "You had to take sides, no matter how cynical you might have been, no matter how much you wanted to be uninvolved. You had to side with the refugees. You had to." But to tell the story on the Hollywood screen in 1942, these refugees would have to be stripped of any obvious ethnic or religious affiliations. They would simply have to be "refugees" congregating at Rick's Café, all of them in the shared predicament—not specific to any one group, as the film has it—of waiting to secure a prized exit visa. "There is a structural absence of the Jewish question," André Aciman, author of *Out of Egypt* and editor of *Letters of Transit: Reflections of Exile, Identity, Language and Loss*, observes. "All these Jews are on screen and yet they cannot address it explicitly. It's all over the screen, but not in the movie."

We first enter the interior of Rick's Café after a quick show of military pageantry surrounding the arrival of Major Strasser and his entourage, and the promise of an arrest of the murderer responsible for killing two German couriers. To heighten the audience's anticipation, Captain Renault, who assures

Major Strasser that he's rounded up "twice the usual number of suspects," insists matter-of-factly, "Everybody comes to Rick's"—which prompts a transition, by way of dissolve, to the café's façade and its glimmering neon sign. Once inside, the camera pans gently across the tables overflowing with patrons to Sam, tapping away at the keys of his piano and singing a medley of jazz standards, and then rests on a few tables, where we catch a few snatches of conversation. "Waiting, waiting, waiting. I'll never get out of here," says one man with a look of total resignation. "I'll die in Casablanca." Next comes a woman trying to offload her diamonds, branded a "drug on the market" by the local merchant dressed in a caftan and wearing a fez ("Everybody sells diamonds. There are diamonds everywhere"), presumably to finance the purchase of exit visas; then a conversation between two men plotting resistance of some kind that is interrupted by a pair of boisterous German officers walking past the table, a trail of ominous words following them: and another table rehearsing an elaborate escape plan ("It's the fishing smack *Santiago*. It leaves at one tomorrow night from the end of the medina, third boat. And bring fifteen thousand francs in cash. Remember: *in cash*.")

We also hear a table conversing in Chinese, juxtaposed with Sascha's toast "*nostrovje*" and the British response ("cheerio"), a cheeky German address of respect ("Yes, Herr Professor"), an Italian thank you ("*mille grazie, signore*"), and finally the French spoken by the croupier at the roulette table ("*Mesdames et monsieurs*"). At the time of the production, there was no shortage of foreign-born extras available through central casting. "The [Warner Bros.'] commissary at lunch, with its mix of nationalities and accents," writes David Denby in a reappraisal of the film in *The New Yorker*, "may not have been all that different from Rick's Café. The people there are all desperate for work, desperate to find a home, yet happy to be alive and stuck in an absurdly sunshiny place and a naïvely optimistic country. The combination of European bitterness and American joy made *Casablanca* possible."

In that same first scene inside Rick's, at the baccarat table, seated next to an elegant Asian woman dressed in a traditional-looking silk-and-sequin costume, a woman with a German accent (Trude Berliner), wearing only one glove, to better grip the cards in her bare left hand, and an elaborate head scarf, asks Carl the waiter if Rick will join them for a drink. Carl's response, asserting one of Rick's cardinal rules—he never drinks with customers—serves as a setup for a variation on a well-worn émigré joke. A man at the same baccarat table proposes that Rick might drink with them if he knew that he ran the second largest bank in Amsterdam, at which point Carl quips, "The second largest? That wouldn't impress Rick. The leading banker in Amsterdam is now the pastry chef in our kitchen. [. . .] And his father is the bellboy." The punch line, of course, is that despite whatever venerated job one may—or may not—have had in the Old Country, and whatever respect may have come with it, the rules no longer apply.

A little less than three months before the world premiere of *Casablanca*, the Austrian-born writer and critic Alfred Polgar, who had been brought to Hollywood with the aid of the European Film Fund in 1938, was asked to contribute an essay to the *Aufbau* newspaper. What he wrote in "Life on the Pacific" contains much of the same irony and wit, not to mention the unabashed sarcasm, as the writings of the Viennese coffeehouse crowd to which he had once belonged:

> I can assure you that life here—if one is in good health, if one's heart isn't troubled by worry about the fate of one's family, friends, and distant acquaintances, if the general and particular reasons to be worried, disappointed, or disheartened aren't overwhelming, if one has enough work, if hope has half-paralyzed the despair about what is happening and about what is not happening, if there's enough money at home and most probably will be there tomorrow—under these conditions life on the Pacific is altogether tolerable, even pleasant.

Throughout the essay, he draws attention to the warm climate and lush vegetation enjoyed by the "Pacifists," as he calls his fellow inhabitants of the West Coast—"roses bloom several times a year"—before talking about daily life in this company town in which hyperbole is so rampant in work-related conversation. "If for instance someone has done something that is common practice on the Pacific, such as writing the story for a film, everyone—family, friends, agents, and people at all levels of the film studio—are sure to find it 'fantastic.' The only one who doesn't think it's fantastic is the author, whose fantastic stories no one knows what to do with."

As the exiled playwright and ill-fated Hollywood screenwriter Bertolt Brecht wrote in his 1942 poem “Der Sumpf” (“The Swamp”), one of the “Hollywood Elegies” cycle he completed while living in Santa Monica that was later discovered among Peter Lorre’s private papers: “I saw many friends, and among them the friend I loved most / Helplessly sink into the swamp / I pass daily.” Within that same cycle, Brecht composed a short poem titled simply “Hollywood.” Its single stanza further amplifies a bitter sentiment about what he must have thought of as the capitalist “means of production” in the dream factories: “Every day, to earn my daily bread / I go to the market where lies are bought / Hopefully / I take my place among the sellers.” Brecht’s past glories as one of Weimar Germany’s greatest dramatists were often summarily forgotten or ignored in Southern California (“Wherever I go,” he wrote in “Sonnet in Emigration,” another exile poem of his, “they ask me, ‘Spell your name!’”), something he shared with the bit actors and the characters they played in *Casablanca*.

Even Carl (not to mention S. Z. Sakall, the actor who plays him) appears to have had a distinguished past, intimated when Abdul calls him “Herr Professor,” as if to suggest that perhaps the jovial waiter had once been a famous scientist or maybe a philosopher before he landed in Casablanca. One of the favorite in-jokes told among German-speaking refugees in the United States concerned two émigré dachshunds that meet in the street: one asks the other, “Were you also once a St. Bernard?” Sakall picked up on this theme in his memoir, *The Story of Cuddles*: “The poor refugees had a hard time settling down. They roamed the streets like masterless dogs. The only joy in their tragic situation was the same innocent little lie.

Lotte Palfi as a refugee desperate to sell her diamonds.

They told the Americans and each other that in the old country they had been prosperous and had held jobs of authority and importance. It was about them that the very, very sad song had been written: *'Ich war einmal ein grosser Bernhardiner'* ['I was once a Big St. Bernard']."

Finding work, it turns out, wasn't quite as easy as some had imagined. "I told myself, America is a 'melting pot,'" writes Lotte Palfi in her *Memoirs of an Unknown Actress: Or, I Never Was a Genuine St. Bernard*. "With all the nationalities that came together there, speaking different variants of English, I was certain my accent would not stand in my way. Never, never had I been more wrong. True, I did get tiny parts now and then, but only when they needed someone to play a German. Months and often years went by between jobs." She adds later in her account, describing her bit parts mostly in anti-Nazi pictures: "I would work a day or two, rarely three, and then sit around for months taking an undeserved vacation." The one and only line she has in *Casablanca*, uttered while trying to sell her diamonds ("But can't you make it just a little more, *please*?"), seems to underscore her offscreen predicament as well, searching in vain for more fully developed film roles and a steadier source of income. (Alfred Polgar, in his "Life on the Pacific," pointed to the dark irony that the great biblical saga of human suffering was known to the English-speaking world as the Book of Job.)

The jowl-wiggling Sakall, who went by the name of Yani before he became Cuddles, began his life in Budapest, in 1883, under the reign of Habsburg emperor Franz Joseph—the subtitle of his memoir, fittingly enough, is *My Life Under the Emperor Francis Joseph, Adolf Hitler, and the Warner Brothers*—where he very quickly became part of the city's theater and cabaret scene. Like many other ambitious Hungarian Jews of his generation, including director Michael Curtiz (three years Sakall's junior), he moved to Vienna in the 1920s, becoming a regular member of the Leopoldi-Wiesenthal cabaret troupe as well as a beloved comedy actor in Austria's nascent film industry. Later, while in Germany, or what he more playfully called the "Hungarian colony in Berlin," Sakall trained with such theater giants as Max Reinhardt and Erwin Piscator. He also tried his hand as a screenwriter and producer, acting in several silent features and in one of the earliest German sound films, *Zwei Herzen im Dreiviertel Takt* (*Two Hearts in Waltz Time*; 1930), before returning to Hungary in 1933. He continued to

Everybody comes to Rick's: the émigré actors S. Z. Sakall (as headwaiter Carl), Marcel De La Brosse (as a German officer), and Leonid Kinskey (as bartender Sascha).

act in dozens of Hungarian films until 1939, when he narrowly escaped to New York on a ship sailing from Rotterdam.

Upon arriving, the linguistically challenged actor went with his wife, Anna (or "Boszi") for breakfast, in uncanny anticipation of Herr und Frau Leuchtag. Wanting to order scrambled eggs, a favorite of his, he implored the waiter at the hotel restaurant, "Eier!" Not quite sure what to make of this Teutonic utterance, the waiter looked askance. "Somehow he realized I was speaking Goethe's language," Sakall recounts sardonically, "and he replied politely: 'Nix German!'" After an ensuing series of comic miscommunications with the manager—including an effort to draw the shape of an egg and being accused of mocking the manager's bald head—Sakall's wife recommended in vain that her husband might want to attend English classes at night school. While still at the New York hotel, Sakall received a telegram from émigré producer Joe Pasternak in Hollywood: "MR. YANI SAKALL, FILM STAR, NEW YORK. STAY THERE THREE MORE WEEKS AND PICK UP ENGLISH LANGUAGE." Sakall promptly replied: "MR. JOE PASTERNAK, OPTIMIST, BEVERLY HILLS." The need to master English quickly subsided for the Hungarian actor. "Once I arrived in Hollywood," he writes, "my language troubles were over. There I found Laszlo Kardos, Laszlo Fodor, Laszlo Vadnay, Aladar Laszlo and about another ten or fifteen Laszlos—all Hungarians and all potential and helpful interpreters."

Director Michael Curtiz's struggles with the English language were legendary. "So many times I have a speech ready, but no dice," he famously quipped in 1944 upon receiving the Oscar for best director for *Casablanca*. "Always a bridesmaid, never a mother. Now I win, I have no speech." During the shoot, Curtiz had frequently reassured producer Hal Wallis, who was worried about various unfinished patches in the script, "Don't worry vat is rough—I make it go so fast no one vill notice." He once referred to a group of extras as "separate together in a bunch," and Leonid Kinskey tells of a moment on the set when Curtiz became increasingly impatient after an assistant took too long to fetch new pages. "The next time I have to send a silly fool," he purportedly said, "I'll go myself!" A childhood friend of Curtiz, Sakall had worked with the director while still in Vienna, and spent long stretches of time with him at Warners. "Those who tell tales here in America about Mike's exotic English," Sakall notes in his memoir, "should have heard him speak German."

Not everything in Hollywood was easy for actors like Sakall. While he had been quite a star on the other side of the Atlantic, here he was essentially unknown, a dachshund. "On the whole, my Yani is very depressed," wrote his wife, Boszi, in a letter of June 6, 1939, to their family in Hungary. "In Europe he was always used to being fêted, applauded, celebrated, and he misses it here. We roamed the streets for days and no one paid the slightest attention to us. [. . .] Thank God, the doctor whom we called found nothing wrong with him. 'This is a psychological symptom,' he said with a smile: 'He is a 'ham'—that's all." Less than a year later, people began to recognize Sakall, even to ask for an occasional autograph, and all was better—well, apart from being mistaken by a Hollywood police officer for Sidney Greenstreet. Some of Boszi's letters home almost read like vaudeville comedy sketches: "Yesterday we went to a cinema where you could drive in with your car. Yani likes it very much. In Europe he drove *only once* into a cinema with his car, and they took away his license."

Lotte Palfi and Sakall surely were not alone in their experiences. Marcel Dalio had been something of a national celebrity in his native France before fleeing the Nazi occupation for America. Like his countryman Jean Renoir, who also left for Hollywood—or what he called "a club for disenchanted Europeans"—after the fall of France, he had to reinvent himself. While previously Dalio had starred opposite Jean Gabin and Erich von Stroheim as the Jewish soldier Rosenthal in Renoir's *La Grande Illusion* (*Grand Illusion*; 1937) and played the charming marquis in *La Règle du jeu* (*The Rules of the Game*; 1939), in Hollywood he was resigned mainly to minor roles. When images taken from Dalio's earlier screen roles were used to depict the stereotypical Jew on Vichy propaganda placards, Dalio recalled in his memoirs, "at least I had star billing on the poster." "There he is with this bit part in *Casablanca*," screenwriter Philip Epstein's son, the novelist Leslie Epstein, told me, "it's amazing. In fact, *Casablanca* has a roll call of so many of these refugees that—maybe that's, subliminally, part of its appeal, that Europeans see themselves." The many instances in which refugees almost seem to be enacting their true-life destinies on screen also brought a few instances in which these same actors reenacted their fictional roles off the set. As Aljean Harmetz explains it, on June 22, 1942, while Madeleine Lebeau filmed the scene in which she returns to Rick's Café arm in arm with a Nazi officer (played by fellow refugee Hans Heinrich von Twardowski), Dalio had his day in court to file for divorce alleging Lebeau's infidelity.

As for Twardowski, who began his film career playing a supporting role in *The Cabinet of Dr. Caligari* and who fled the Nazis to avoid persecution as a homosexual, he was forever limited to playing Nazis in Hollywood. After being cast as S.S. chief Reinhard Heydrich in Fritz Lang's *Hangmen Also Die!*, less than a year after *Casablanca*, he sent an urgent telegram to his dear friend the theater actress Eleonora von Mendelssohn in New York. "I'M VERY MISERABLE AND UNHAPPY AND I WANT TO RETURN TO NEW YORK. I PLAYED IN FRITZ LANG'S PICTURE THE ROLE OF HEINRICH [*sic*] HEYDRICH," he began. "PLEASE ASK BRECHT HOW I DID IT AND TRY TO RECOMMEND ME TO BERGNER," he continued, referring to the famous Viennese actress Elisabeth Bergner, then preparing to star in *The Two Mrs. Carrolls* on Broadway, "FOR THE ROLE THEY OFFERED TO STROHEIM WHO CANNOT DO IT ON ACCOUNT OF A MOVIE ENGAGEMENT. TALK TO BERGNER ABOUT ME, PLEASE." Like many other of the émigré actors confined to brutal typecasting in a cycle of war pictures at Warners and elsewhere, Twardowski, who became a naturalized American citizen in July 1943, dreamed of a return to the stage. "I am ready to come to New York at a moment's notice," he wrote Mendelssohn.

Some of the bit parts that émigré actors played in *Casablanca* were so minor that they soon drifted from memory. "Paul Panzer, born in Würzburg, serves coffee and cocktails," remark the Austrian film scholars Brigitte Mayr and Michael Omasta. "Lutz Altschul, from Baden near Vienna, now calling himself Louis Victo Arco, has a walk-on part as a refugee, as he had done in the anti-Nazi films *Underground, Berlin Correspondent*, and *All Through the Night*." Trying to recall the supporting role he had played in *Casablanca*, in a phone interview from Berlin nearly half a century after the production, Curt Bois commented modestly: "I have such a small part. If one of the audience coughed while I was stealing from a man his money and then he stopped coughing, he didn't see me anymore. It was such a small part. It was no part at all." In truth, the pickpocket is not terribly essential to the main story of the film, and yet the part contains its own share of psychological complexity and its deeper bearing on the subplot concerning the nameless refugees.

Moments before Bois appears on screen as the "Dark European" with his crafty hands, the "usual suspects" are rounded up and loaded into a wagon by the Vichy police. We witness clear expressions of anxiety, panic, crushed dreams, and a failed escape attempt—captured in a string of reaction shots amid the chaos—that Bois, playing the pickpocket, is soon asked to translate for the naïve English couple. "Two German couriers were found murdered in the desert," he recounts, "the *unoccupied* desert. This is the customary roundup of refugees, liberals, and uh, of course, a beautiful young girl for Monsieur Renault, the prefect of police." For this short moment, Bois serves as a storyteller of sorts—talents that would be put to use years later when coaxed out of retirement to play Homer in Wim Wenders's *Der Himmel über Berlin* (*Wings of Desire*; 1987)—explaining to the English couple, and to the audience, the subplot of the film. Before proceeding to swipe the Englishman's wallet, he notes, once more underscoring the plight of the dispossessed: "Unfortunately, along with these unhappy refugees the scum of Europe has gravitated to Casablanca. Some of them have been waiting years for a visa." Bois himself became a naturalized U.S. citizen before returning, thoroughly disenchanted with Hollywood, to East Berlin after the war.

The many fleeting glimpses of individuals left stranded in *Casablanca* highlight what novelist Erich Maria Remarque, in *Die Nacht von Lissabon* (*The Night in Lisbon*; 1962), calls "the refugee glance—an imperceptible lifting of the eyelids, followed by a look of blank indifference, as if we couldn't care less." As Remarque further observes, "The refugee glance is different from the German glance under Hitler—that cautious peering around in all directions, followed by a hurried exchange of whispers—but both, like the forced migration of innumerable Schwarzes [Jewish families] from Germany and the displacement of whole populations in Russia, are part of twentieth-century civilization."

Although history was fictionalized in the film, the real-life events often had a tangible connection to members of the production. "Curtiz's recent problems with getting some of his family out of Hungary had brought home to him the refugee situation," remarked film programmer Ronald Haver in an essay from 1976. "He asked the Epsteins to work in some vignettes which would point out the plight of refugees and allow him to make good use of Rick's café." Innumerable members of the cast either had, like Curtiz, relatives still stranded in Europe or had themselves experienced the horrors of Nazi Germany directly. Quite a few of them, including Sakall, Dalio, and Palfi, would lose family in the camps. When shooting the Paris flashback scene of Rick and Ilsa at the French sidewalk café, in which the pair asks themselves how long it will be until the Germans storm the capital, one of the female extras burst into inconsolable tears. Curtiz had to halt the production temporarily. A small bearded man, another extra on the set, purportedly walked over to the director and tapped him on the shoulder. "I am very sorry, sir," he said to Curtiz. "But that is my wife. Please pardon her. You see, our home was in Paris. And we went through that awful day."

Even an actor like Conrad Veidt, who left Germany of his own accord in 1933 (the same year he married the Jewish-Hungarian Lily Prager), was essentially a refugee by the time of the production. To express his opposition to the regime, the non-Jewish actor is said to have listed "JEW" in large block letters for his religion on a form he was required to submit with National Socialist authorities. The Nazis responded in kind, keeping his films from being shown anywhere in the Third Reich. "When I went back to Germany from Hollywood in 1929," commented Veidt with startling prescience, "I felt a strangeness in the air. It was like the agitation before a terrible storm." By 1941, after spending his initial exile years in England, Veidt found himself living comfortably with his wife as new transplants in Beverly Hills. Even if he was repeatedly expected to play one on screen, he enjoyed the distance from the real Nazi officials that had previously threatened his existence.

Having arrived in Los Angeles around the same time, Paul Henreid and his wife, Lisl, traveled in social circles composed largely of other successful, well-known émigrés, including Veidt. "It seemed to us that Hollywood, in those days, was a gathering place for some of Europe's most intriguing people," Henreid notes in his memoir. "There were the novelists Lion Feuchtwanger, Thomas Mann, and Vicki Baum. There was Bruno Walter, who had conducted and directed the Vienna Opera, and Arturo Toscanini, and Gregor Piatigorsky, the cellist—the list seemed endless, and they were all old friends or friends of old friends." He also notes his standing get-togethers with the Prague-born actor Francis (Franz) Lederer, who had played opposite Louise Brooks in G. W. Pabst's *Die Büchse der Pandora* (*Pandora's Box*; 1929) and who at Warner Bros. earned star billing in *Confessions of a Nazi Spy*, and with Bertolt Brecht, whose Viennese-Jewish wife, Helene Weigel, would bake delicious *Gugelhupf*, a sweet delicacy from the Old

Country, for their regular guests, and even of the occasional pool party with director Fritz Lang and his latest female star.

Although Peter Lorre felt as if he'd changed countries, quoting Brecht, "oftener than our shoes," he shared much of Henreid's enthusiasm for his adopted country. By 1935, he was living on Adelaide Drive in Santa Monica. "I love the water and sunshine and fresh air and flowers," he told a journalist from the *New York Post*. "I am delighted to be here, because I can have a home." Yet both Henreid and Lorre encountered prejudice that they'd hoped to leave behind on the other side of the Atlantic. Henreid writes, for example, of a startling sign he found posted outside a Miami hotel during his 1942 tour to promote *Joan of Paris*: "Jews and Dogs Not Permitted." As he comments further in his memoir, after pondering the hypothetical question of whether what was happening in Germany could ever occur on American shores, "I had never realized there was so much vicious anti-Semitism under the cover of warmth and pleasant smiles." When Lorre had a similar experience, vacationing in a hotel in the White Mountains of New Hampshire, the notorious prankster responded by spilling the ink blotter on the reception counter and sending the hotel, which proudly espoused the same restrictive policies, a three-year subscription to the Jewish newspaper *The Forward*.

An article by the German-born critic and philosopher Hannah Arendt appeared in *The Menorah Journal*, another preeminent Jewish publication of the era, the same month that *Casablanca* went into general release. In "We Refugees," she offers an unvarnished account of what Hollywood could merely allegorize and depict by way of cinematic illusion and ellipsis. "In the first place," Arendt declares, using the collective pronoun throughout, "we don't like to be called 'refugees.' We ourselves call each other 'newcomers' or 'immigrants.'" She assigns herself the task of advocate, increasing popular awareness of the émigré's plight—to tell, as she puts it, "the story of our struggle" so that it can "finally become known."

> We lost our homes, which means we lost the familiarity of daily life. We lost our occupation, which means the confidence that we are of some use in this world. We lost our language, which means the naturalness of reactions, the simplicity of gestures, the unaffected expression of feelings. We left our relatives in the Polish ghettoes and our best friends have been killed in concentration camps, and that means the rupture of our private lives.

She goes on to assert, after describing her experiences in Gurs, the French concentration camp in which she was temporarily held, "We were expelled from Germany because we were Jews." Although serious in tone, Arendt's account includes yet another St. Bernard anecdote ("You don't know to whom you speak," one man tells her soon after she arrives in the New World, "I was section-manager in Karstadt's [a great department store in Berlin]"). Like the lucky ones in *Casablanca*, after her internment, Arendt managed to secure passage from Lisbon to America. "Refugees driven from country to country," she concludes in her essay, "represent the vanguard of their peoples."

This does not in any way deny the Hollywood gloss. Sure,

there's the telegenic Bulgarian couple Jan and Annina Brandel—played by Austrian-born actor Helmut Dantine and the Warner family member Joy Page—and their fairy-tale victory as they win the money for the otherwise prohibitive costs of exit visas at the roulette table. There's also Paul Henreid's performance as Victor Laszlo, the concentration camp survivor in the perfectly ironed double-breasted, cream-colored suit, who gives the audience a freedom fighter as European leading man (Hal Wallis expressed his reservations, largely unheard, in a memo about the choice of costumes: "they are refugees, making their way from country to country, and they are not going to Rick's Café for social purposes"). "He is central casting's idea of the kind of refugee you wouldn't mind having in your living room," suggests filmmaker Mark Rappaport. "He's not always complaining about his destroyed life, his devastated country, and the loved ones he's lost."

Despite the artificial nature of the film—it's a fiction, after all—it still somehow speaks with uncommon poignancy to the exile condition, not only during the war years of the 1940s but at later historical moments and in different settings. "The atmosphere of *Casablanca*, specifically the waiting, is so reminiscent of my experience in Egypt, waiting for the exit visas," explains André Aciman, who fled Alexandria with his Jewish family in the mid-1960s. "Everyone among our peers was stuck, waiting to get out of Egypt, trying to get money and property out with them. It is a narrative that speaks to anyone who wants to get out, who is trying to escape, and the refugee cast (Dalio, Lorre, Sakall) speaks to that. They were all exiles themselves." In 1992, for the fiftieth anniversary of *Casa-*

blanca, a group of Moroccan Jews met at Temple Em Habanim in North Hollywood, to discuss the bearing that film's story had on their own experience of flight. "The American forces landed on November 8—just one week before they were to take us all away to Germany," one man commented. "If they had waited two weeks later, we would have all died in concentration camps."

This interpretation of the film, as having real historical, political, and personal implications, was not lost on audiences of its day. On December 4, 1942, just eight days after the film's premiere in New York, *Aufbau*, then edited by Manfred George—himself a Jewish refugee and the former editor of numerous Berlin newspapers—published a trenchant review of the film. "Today more than ever coincidence, fate, intrigue and politics are the agents that dress up a film story," begins the review. "Those in the know—you and me—people from a Europe that has gone to pieces, now have a duty to enlighten those for whom such moments may seem unbelievable from their political or spiritual standpoints." The unnamed reviewer continues:

> Can the average American moviegoer imagine the importance of an exit visa? Especially if it's meant for a persecuted Czech who has been hunted by the Gestapo all the way to North Africa, along with his wife, both prominent members of the anti-Nazi underground movement? The scene is the "Café Américain" from an American adventure in Casablanca, where in between roulette and whiskey, Negro jazz and Arabic music, Vichy police and

> the Gestapo, a black market for exit visas flourishes—reserved mainly for refugees with money or jewels.
>
> Michael Curtiz has magnificently brought to life the African witches' cauldron: the atmosphere is dense, the story line breathtaking, and many moments—above all, one in which the Czech incites the Café patrons to drown out the clamor of "Die Wacht am Rhein" sung by Nazi officers with the "Marseillaise"—unforgettable.

European émigrés in America, so the review suggested, had an obligation to translate the story of *Casablanca*, especially the exodus thread woven into its plot, to a native-born audience. From their vantage point, the famous and widely prized "Marseillaise" scene was ultimately a celebration of resistance among the many refugees that populate the screen. Rick and his Hollywood-confected oasis in the desert speak for all of them.

AFTER THE WAR—despite the oft-harrowing circumstances of the journey to America, and the challenges the émigrés faced after arriving in Hollywood—many of these *Casablanca* actors were eager to return to Europe. In fact, the poignant review of the film in *Aufbau* almost seems to have anticipated this. "There are so many former German and Austrian actors concentrated in this film," the final lines of the piece have it, "that one can make a prediction: if some day films are to be freely shown again in a Germany that is rid of Nazis, then they will be made in Hollywood. For Hollywood has at its disposal the elite of German-language actors (and screenwriters and directors)." The prediction was only half right: while Hollywood continued to make films utilizing the refugee talent, within the next decade, quite a few of *Casablanca*'s actors—especially those who were either underutilized or confined to undesirable stereotyping—took the first opportunity they had to return to Europe. They often took with them the bittersweet memories of Hollywood and, over the years, an increased awareness of the storied film production in which they had participated.

Curt Bois was among the early ones to return. In 1945, the year that *Casablanca* had its European debut, in Portugal—mentioned fleetingly in the intriguing fictional account "Émigré Hotel" by Argentine writer Edgardo Cozarinsky—he was still playing obscure bit parts in movies like *Saratoga Trunk* for Warner Bros. His final roles in Hollywood were largely offered to him by German-speaking émigré directors like Max Ophüls (*Caught*), Richard Oswald (*The Loveable Cheat*), and Robert Siodmak (*The Great Sinner*), all three pictures from 1949, who still admired his earlier work in German theater and film between the wars. "For thirteen years," writes his German biographer, Gerold Ducke, of Bois's years in American exile, "he subsisted on very small, even the tiniest of film roles. He was often unemployed for weeks or months between roles. No way to live when one is still young and wants to work. But he knew that others were worse off, and often thought about the many who were murdered." Bois had hoped in vain that he would be able to revitalize his theater career in the United States; he was never given the chance to demonstrate the strengths for which he was best known in Germany and

Austria. At the last social gathering he attended before leaving Hollywood, a studio costume party, he is said to have shown up wearing his street clothes with a handmade sign hanging around his neck: "Just a Tourist."

Upon his return to Berlin in 1950, Bois was immediately celebrated by Herbert Jhering, one of the most prominent theater critics from the Weimar era, who, like Bois, would continue to work professionally in the German Democratic Republic. "A Berliner comic has returned from America," announced Jhering from his perch in East Berlin. "He came back from the United States without having enjoyed the enduring impact he deserved, after his early success. For Curt Bois of all people—a true Berliner in essence, in accent, a Berliner in his entire relationship to the world—is anything but a regional comic. His coolness, his perspicuity, his wit are indeed that of a quintessential Berliner [*urberlinisch*], and yet comprehensible to the entire world as articulated through gesture." Jhering goes on to explain that what Bois really needed is not "America's commercial theater or TV series," but rather the "repertory" and "ensemble" theater that was now in the process of rapid redevelopment in East Berlin by the recently returned Bertolt Brecht, who had arrived in the East German capital the year before. "Curt Bois can play Gogol and Goldoni," Jehring concludes, "Lope de Vega, Shakespeare, and Brecht, Glasbrenner and Ostrowski"—in other words, something he was never able to do while living in the United States.

In the unpublished German-language typescript of what later became the memoir of Lotte Palfi, the diamond seller in the film, there is a short epilogue that did not appear in the published English text. In it, she describes how in 1982, she and her then-husband, Paul Andor (né Wolfgang Zilzer)—who in *Casablanca* played the wily refugee carrying expired papers and Free French pamphlets, the man in the panama hat who fails to elude the Vichy police and is shot dead beneath the massive poster of Marshal Pétain in the first reel—were invited as honorary guests of the Berlin Film Festival. They were to be celebrated along with fellow émigré actors Elisabeth Bergner, Curt Bois, Dolly Haas, Franz Lederer, and Hertha Thiele. "Not only was our joy about this honor immense," she writes, "but we were even more moved by the noble attitude to which the invitation testified: the desire 'to make the crooked straight again.' Of course, one's lost career can never be replaced; we had to resign ourselves to that long ago. But it feels good realizing that, fifty years after Hitler's seizure of power, 'You haven't been forgotten.'" By that point in time, West Germans were becoming increasingly interested in coming to terms with the Nazi past, and part of that process meant recognizing, even honoring, those who had been forced to flee.

The director of the Austrian Film Museum, Alexander Horwath, recently described watching *Casablanca* as a teenager around 1980 at the Burgkino in Vienna and being completely moved. He was far more affected by it than by any of the other Bogart films shown at that same time in their original English versions. "From the very beginning, *Casablanca* was naturally a critical touchstone," he commented. "It's a film that conveys within a popular medium the story of exile and is well suited to do so, because it takes up the fictional story lines and then folds in the biographical truths represented by the émigré cast and crew. Despite being a perfect Hollywood studio product, it has a true-to-life quality that is otherwise quite rare. Even if one doesn't know the background of these actors, one somehow feels it in their accents and speech." He remarked further how in 1993, when working as the director of the Vienna International Film Festival, he helped to organize a two-month series devoted to the exiled film professionals, many of whom made guest appearances in Vienna. While planning this series, Horwath often returned to *Casablanca* as a key film for understanding that same time period.

Over the years, the film has been shown with considerable frequency in Austria, both in repertory cinema houses (in the original English) and on television (dubbed into German). In 2012, in Vienna's central square, Horwath had a hand in programming a popular outdoor summer screening series, "The Casablanca Connection," devoted to the many detour-laden paths taken by Austrian émigrés that lead to the film. "Michael Curtiz's *Casablanca* serves as a point of departure," observed the series co-organizers Brigitte Mayr and Michael Omasta in their introduction, "for a cinematic journey toward remembering the homeless in exile about whom one otherwise knows so little today."

In West Germany, the initial release of the film in 1952 was a heavily edited, dubbed version (also shown during the early years in postwar Austria), stripped of all scenes that might disturb the delicate, halfhearted process of de-Nazification—Major Strasser is completely cut out, as are all references to the Third Reich, creating a film that's some twenty-five minutes shorter. Gone is the singing of the "Marseillaise"; gone, too, all anti-Nazi jokes and dialogue. The old Czech partisan Victor Laszlo becomes Victor Larsen, a Norwegian atomic physicist hunted by Interpol. Two decades later, the uncut version became something of a cult film—it played, in English, in art-house theaters and was first shown dubbed in its entirety on German TV in 1975—among those born during and after the war. Journalist Stefan Volk, who has written on postwar German film censorship of Hollywood movies, claims that although the abridged 1952 version earned a lukewarm reception in the German press, by the mid-1970s the full-length, original *Casablanca* had earned an ardent following, and today is regarded by many as "*the* Hollywood classic par excellence."

In a scene in Peter Härtling's 1979 novel *Hubert oder Die Rückkehr nach Casablanca* (*Hubert, or The Return to Casablanca*), the title character, Hubert Windisch, who is sent to battle during the Third Reich, leaves Germany behind for Paris sometime in the early postwar years. There he has his first chance to watch the film, whose reputation has long preceded it, at a makeshift cinema near Montparnasse. "He'd heard of the legend of this film," writes Härtling, "but until now had not been able to see it. Besides, the warning that the German dubbed version bastardized the plot had acted as a deterrent. Here, however, it was shown in the original." Hubert proceeds to buy himself a ticket and a glass of wine, and he takes a seat in the back row of the dark theater.

Amid the flickering lights and the slightly distorted sounds coming from the theater's shabby old speakers, Hubert experiences a complete transformation. "He encountered himself, found himself in someone else's memory, in one that had never existed for him before, that had actually never been, that some Misters Epstein and Koch had contrived, a story about somebody, about Rick, not about himself and yet very much about himself—made for him alone." Hubert suddenly hears himself deliver the voice-over narration, "in English, as if it were his mother tongue": "With the coming of the Second World War many eyes in imprisoned Europe turned hopefully or desperately toward the freedom of the Americans [*sic*]." Much like Woody Allen's character in *Play It Again, Sam* (1972), Hubert abandons reality for the celluloid universe of the film, imagining himself as an omniscient character seated opposite—even mirroring—Rick as he plays chess. Hubert finally leaves the theater, clammy with sweat and almost in a mild narcotic trance, and makes his way to a tiny hole-in-the-wall bar near his hotel, where he imagines a voice bidding farewell to the old Monsieur Windisch, quoting a line from the film uttered by Rick during the Parisian flashback (and which serves as the epigraph to the novel): "Who are you really? And what were you before?"

French anthropologist Marc Augé, in his personal account of the film, *Casablanca: Movies and Memory* (2007), tells the story of first watching it as a young boy with his parents in Paris sometime in the late 1940s, soon after it was first shown on that side of the Atlantic. Although the adults took some issue with the Hollywood depiction of France on the eve of German occupation, they were particularly moved by the "Marseillaise" scene. "My father had told me of another 'Marseillaise' in another film, *La Grande Illusion*, and also of the anthem he and his student friends had sung in the reserve officers' school at Auvours near Le Mans, where they were taking classes when the announcement came of the Germans' imminent arrival." For Augé, who later in life indulged in multiple repeat viewings of the film at Paris's revival houses in the Latin Quarter, *Casablanca* is bound up with the wartime memories of his childhood, of flight and return.

"The movies give us a child's vision," he remarks elsewhere in his book. "To see a film again is to recover a past that retains all the vivacity of the present." *Casablanca* came out at a time in France when people were still rejoicing the end of the war. Augé recalls approaching American soldiers on the street, hitting them up for chocolate and chewing gum. These memories, the joy of the late 1940s as well as the pain of being forced with his mother to seek shelter in the French provinces during the war, are somehow tied to the memories conjured in the film: "the essential scenes of the film illustrated insistent, recurring, obsessive themes—waiting, menace, or flight—which by dint of the hazards of history, were imposed upon my childhood." The refugee story, coupled with the story of Nazi and Vichy oppression, struck a profound resonance in Augé, as it no doubt did in other French moviegoers of his generation. The critic André Bazin, for example, called Bogart "the actor/myth of the war and post-war period."

In postwar Hungary, the country that once served as home to Curtiz and Sakall, *Casablanca* managed to assert its presence as well. It took a bit longer than in France, until sometime in the 1960s, after the Hungarian revolution of 1956, but viewing the film became an annual ritual for many of its citizens. "You know, December 25, Christmas Day, was a holiday and there was one television channel only and in the afternoon they would broadcast *Casablanca*," explained Hungarian filmmaker Gyula Gazdag. "It became a tradition to screen it, and for people to watch it. I don't remember anything about any national pride [in the director or actors]; it was just the popularity of the film. They just loved watching it. And of course I loved watching. It was dubbed into Hungarian." It didn't much matter that the native actors and actresses who did the dubbing were less than ideal (the woman who provided the voice for Bergman, in Gazdag's recollection, "made the character just, so, so whiny and weepy"), families would gather around the television after Christmas lunch and enjoy the Hollywood fantasy.

"If I think back," Gazdag added, "it was probably more the fact that at that time it was quite rare to be able to see a classical American movie." Hollywood films were not available during the Nazi occupation, nor were they made accessible immediately afterward under Soviet rule. "So in a way, that was something that was very exceptional that it was an American movie, I think that was a big part of it. That it had some connection to Hungary in the 1930s as well. But, there was nothing really written about it, and again probably for that reason: if something had been written in the newspaper, it would become something that all of a sudden the authorities would have seen in a different light and may not have encouraged it anymore." As it was, *Casablanca* managed to fly under the radar. Although some might have considered it contraband, and although the connection to Hungarian culture before the war would go largely unnoticed, the Hungarians continued to replay the film into the late 1980s, after the country's borders were flooded with refugees in the run-up to the fall of the Berlin Wall.

More recently, in Sweden, where the film was long shown in a truncated, censored version released during the war, *Casablanca* has gained a new prominence in the wake of Stig Björkman's 2015 documentary *Ingrid Bergman in Her Own Words*. Mårten Blomkvist, the film critic for *Dagens Nyheter*, was asked to contribute a piece on *Casablanca* to Swedish national radio while he was in Cannes covering the 2015 festival. At that particular moment, Sweden was engaged in a fiery debate about the Syrian refugee crisis and how to accommodate the enormous number of new immigrants. "Then it struck me, for the first time" Blomkvist remarked, "it's a film about migrants, which is so very timely right now. But you never think of it as a film about migrants, because of the luxurious settings."

Casablanca may now, more than ever, be considered "everyone's favorite émigré film" or even "the best refugee film of the war years," as a critic in the *Wall Street Journal* recently hailed it. It was certainly the all-time favorite film of my Czech-born father-in-law, who survived the war with his family under an assumed name and as a teenager fought alongside his father in the partisan resistance against the Nazis (a plaque of recognition he received from the Czech government hangs in our dining room). He later helped arrange for his family to migrate to Canada after the war, and eventually made his way to New York City. Like many of the players in the film, he had a noticeable accent—in fact, he had one in every language he spoke. And he had a Middle European charm that came out in both manner and speech. Although it would seem to make most sense that he would harbor a deep personal identification with Victor Laszlo, given their shared partisan commitments and national origins, it was Rick Blaine, and Bogie in particular, who served as his ultimate hero (he wore a trench coat to the end of his life). For him, it was not merely a matter of telling time fluidly—or sketchily, as the film would have it—that would ensure assimilation in America. Rather, it was the ability to cultivate the sartorial habits, the idiom, and the sensibilities of the stars that his newly adopted country also held so dear.

Chapter 5

WE'LL ALWAYS HAVE PARIS

Roughly a third of the way into the picture, while Rick grumbles drunkenly into his whiskey glass, tugging on a cigarette, and Sam reprises "As Time Goes By" after hours in a darkened back room at Rick's Café, we're treated to a nine-minute flashback—nowhere to be found in the original *Everybody Comes to Rick's*—of the long treasured, long repressed Parisian romance between Rick and Ilsa on the eve of Nazi occupation. The room is, quite fittingly, drenched in menacing shadows projected onto the walls by intermittent beams from the airport watchtower. Michael Curtiz has cinematographer Arthur Edeson's camera dolly in on Rick, as thick swirls of smoke dissolve to a static shot of the Arc de Triomphe, and several bars of the "Marseillaise" fill out the space on the audio track previously occupied by Sam's piano. Suddenly, Rick is shown with an uncharacteristic smile on his face, seated next to Ilsa, also grinning, as they make their way from the Champs-Élysées to the countryside—images flitting by, as if in a dream, thanks to studio-confected rear projection—driving in a convertible touring car. In a rapid succession of short, compressed shots, a travel album of sorts, we then see the happy couple on a boat ride down the Seine, laughing and sharing a bag of peanuts as if at a baseball game; Ilsa cheerfully arranging a bouquet of flowers in the windowsill of Rick's Paris apartment; then Rick ceremoniously popping the cork of a champagne bottle, a cigarette dangling from his mouth, and the two of them seated on a couch raising their goblets.

"Who are you really? And what were you before? What did you do and what did you think? Huh?" Rick asks Ilsa after an otherwise dialogue-free segment. (Curtiz either botched the sync sound when shooting the sequence, as Hal Wallis later recalled, or opted to have the montage of images M.O.S., "mit out sound," in the witty designation that German-speaking émigrés contributed to the technical jargon used in Hollywood). Reestablishing the ground rules of their romance, Ilsa replies: "We said 'no questions.'" Acquiescing to that provisional arrangement, Rick abandons his questions, chuckles a bit, and makes one of his signature toasts, "Here's looking at you, kid."

One of the great triumphs of *Casablanca* comes from its subtle, ambiguous, often oblique handling of love, sex, and romance. Throughout the film, what is left unsaid is every bit as important as, if not more important than, what's said. Rather than granting instant gratification, the kind of intricate storytelling employed by the film's writers, director, producer, cast, and crew relies on deferred and largely denied satisfaction. This of course only heightens the intense longing and invites narrative participation from the viewer's imagination, perhaps more than in most other classic Hollywood films, to help fill in the gaps of a story that remains otherwise incomplete.

As the string of flashback scenes continue to unspool, we see Rick and Ilsa dancing rhumba cheek to cheek to the seductive rhythms of "Perfidia"—Wallis insisted on this song, which he'd just made use of in *Now, Voyager*, since Warner Bros. held the rights—in the swank ballroom of a Parisian nightclub (a scene that Bogart purportedly dreaded, for fear of the awkward height differential between him and Bergman and his known lack of skill as a dancer). Then Curtiz cuts back to the apartment, where Rick, seated on the couch, resumes the basic line of questioning he'd begun earlier. He wonders aloud, "Why I'm so lucky. Why I should find you waiting for me to come along." Ilsa quickly translates Rick's questions into what she presumes he must mean ("Why there is no other man in my life?") before giving a direct answer. "That's easy," she says matter-of-factly. "There was. He's dead." And just like that, the no-questions rule has to be temporarily suspended. Ilsa needs her chance to inform Rick, and the audience with him, of her past and then go on to insist, as the generic rules of a Hollywood romance would seem to demand, that the single best answer to all their questions is an extended passionate kiss.

In depicting these snippets of Rick and Ilsa's Parisian romance, *Casablanca* faced the same challenges of any major motion picture made in its day, when the Production Code Administration (PCA), the self-regulatory censorship body

Bergman and Bogart dancing on the set, as director Curtiz looks on.

introduced in 1934 by the Motion Picture Producers and Distributors of America, was operating in full swing. Initially spearheaded by Will Hays, the former postmaster general and onetime chairman of the Republican National Committee, the PCA grew out of the Hays Office and the National Legion of Decency and was ultimately put in the hands of the hard-nosed Catholic moralist Joseph I. Breen. Its main charge was to see to it that American movies adhered to three general principles:

1. No picture shall be produced which will lower the moral standards of those who see it. Hence the sympathy of the audience shall never be thrown to the side of crime, wrongdoing, evil or sin.
2. Correct standards of life, subject only to the requirements of drama and entertainment, shall be presented.
3. Law, natural or human, shall not be ridiculed, nor shall sympathy be created for its violation.

The PCA also issued guidelines on how to apply the Code to twelve specific areas, from "Crimes Against the Law" (murder, illegal drug traffic, among others) to "Special Subjects" (actual hangings, the sale of women, miscegenation, liquor, and drinking). Under the category of "Sex," one of the Hays Office's favorite whipping posts, the PCA insisted, "The sanctity of the institution of marriage and the home shall be upheld. Pictures shall not infer that low forms of sex relationship are the accepted or common thing."

Most essential for the Parisian flashback, then, is the sliver of information that Ilsa airdrops into the conversation early on in those nine minutes of reminiscences, when she attests to her steadfast and appropriately noble belief that her husband must be presumed dead when meeting Rick. Without that important admission, any such depiction of Rick and Ilsa's romance would surely have been unacceptable to the Code. "The main thing that affected our work in those days was that we were so handcuffed by censorship," recalled Julius Epstein of his time at Warners in the 1930s and '40s. "The nation shook when Clark Gable said 'damn' in *Gone With the Wind*." At the very top of the PCA's long list is "Adultery," which may, as the strict dictates of the Code had it, "sometimes [be] necessary plot material," but (and this is a rather big but) "must not be explicitly treated or justified or represented attractively." In other words, those flickers of pleasure-filled romance in Paris could not be shown with the clear knowledge that Ilsa's husband, and her marriage, could somehow still be alive and well during Rick's courtship of her and the final consummation of their relationship.

Casablanca was made at a critical time for movie censorship. The day after the Japanese attack on Pearl Harbor, the same day that a bound copy of *Everybody Comes to Rick's* arrived in the mailroom at Warners, Will Hays reasserted his unwavering position that Hollywood should "maintain the continued flow of wholesome entertainment as an essential contribution to military and civilian moral and national spirit." Six months later, in June 1942, when Breen returned to his position as head of the PCA—after a yearlong hiatus as general manager at RKO—the federal government established the Office of War Information (OWI), its specific charge to ensure that films did their part to promote the war effort. Breen, however, did little to change course. He echoed Hays in his general view and reemphasized what he saw as the continued urgency of the PCA at the precise moment that *Casablanca*'s production was in full swing. "The war simply does not affect the Code or its application," he told an interviewer that summer. "It has raised no issues or questions that were not present and covered by the Code in peace time."

The Parisian flashback is a particularly fascinating case in point, as its dueling narrative strands of love (the wholesome variety, of course) and glory (in the service of the Allied war effort) would have to appeal to the dueling censorship bodies, the PCA and the OWI. After Rick and Ilsa are shot in close-up, in their passionate locked embrace, the flashback proceeds *not* with a string of additional suggestions of their amorous affair but with an evocative medley of newsreel images—Nazi tanks, bomber jets, and streams of German troops encroaching on the French capital. The camera thus turns our attention to the Parisian streets, frantic newspaper salesmen hawking the latest news of the German invasion. (The studio's production notes, prepared by the Warners publicity office, claim that the newspaper "prop" they used in this scene was an authentic copy of the June 11, 1940, edition of *Paris Soir* that technical advisor Robert Aisner smuggled out with him while fleeing Nazi-occupied France.) As Rick and Ilsa, now seated at a sidewalk café, try to make sense of the newspaper headlines, a loudspeaker announces, in French, that the Germans will soon arrive, a statement that Rick translates for the audience in case anybody should miss it. Pivoting seamlessly from romance to wartime heroism, the brief exchange between Rick and Ilsa helps to underscore the vital transformation in Rick, which fits rather neatly within OWI policy. "Richard, they'll find out your record," remarks Ilsa. "It won't be safe for you here." Accepting his fate, and the increasing call for partisan commitment, Rick admits: "I'm on their blacklist already, their roll of honor."

Although elsewhere in the picture he may intermittently feign a kind of Renault-like neutrality, or his own brand of uncaring political opportunism, the Rick who is revealed during the flashback—which is to say, the Rick who is madly, incorrigibly in love with Ilsa—shows no signs of equivocation regarding Nazism. In fact, like Laszlo, he is a favored target of the regime and a marked antagonist. Consider for instance the penultimate scene in the flashback, in which Rick and Ilsa hurriedly guzzle down champagne with Sam at a Montmartre café known as La Belle Aurore ("Henri wants us to finish this bottle and then three more," announces Rick, "He says he'll water his garden with champagne before he'll let the Germans drink any of it"). Sam helps narrate the story as it plays out for the audience, singing the final stanza of "As Time Goes By": "It's still the same old story / A fight for love and glory," he begins, highlighting the delicate, yet eternal nature of love. Rick's reprise of his earlier champagne toast is interrupted by the loudspeaker announcement, in German, that the Gestapo will arrive in Paris the next day. The offscreen sounds of battle punctuate a third round of questions about Rick and Ilsa's respective pasts. As if to rehearse the earlier observation made by Ilsa, Sam declares, "The Germans'll be here pretty soon now, and they'll come looking for you. And don't forget there's a price on your head."

Rick and Ilsa's romance is thus threatened, and temporarily undone, by the war. Although Ilsa, by this point in the flashback visibly nervous and either aware that her husband has suddenly resurfaced or simply aware of that prospect, urges Rick to leave Paris, he does all that he can—recalling the desperate pleas that Yvonne makes to him early on in the film—to deepen their relationship. Yet, as seasoned devotees of the film know all too well, the moment Ilsa professes her love for Rick one last time and steals a final kiss, the denouement of the flashback catapults us from La Belle Aurore to the rain-soaked Gare de Lyon train station (conjured by Curtiz using a set repurposed from *Now, Voyager*). "Kiss me," Ilsa insists in the café, a blustery, dewy-eyed utterance that would win Bergman legions of fans, "Kiss me as if it were the last time." In an early draft of the script, the line had a far less romantic, more overt wartime ring to it: "Hitler or no Hitler, kiss me!" The fleeting champagne-fueled optimism at La Belle Aurore is just as quickly replaced with Rick's devastating realization that he's been stood up, jilted by Ilsa on the train platform. Ilsa's farewell note, left behind for Rick, its ink running down the page with each drop of rain, does the crying for a man not able to shed tears.

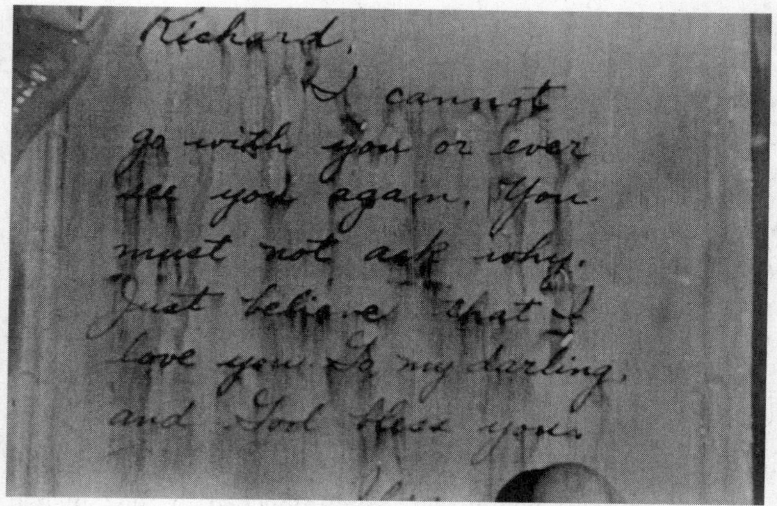

Richard,
I cannot
go with you or ever
see you again. You
must not ask why.
Just believe that I
love you. Go my darling,
and God bless you.

Ilsa's farewell note.

Although there is no extant paper trail from the Office of War Information—it's hard to imagine there would be much opposition to *Casablanca*'s espousal of patriotism and its strident championing of the Allied war effort—there are more than half a dozen pages of evaluative commentary left behind by Joseph Breen and his censorship staff at the Production Code Administration. For several straight weeks, Breen and his script readers, Geoffrey Shurlock and Charles Pettijohn, combed through various drafts and revisions. On May 19, 1942, just under a week before principal photography was to commence, Breen sent Jack Warner a memo warning him of possible red flags. "We have read Part I of the incomplete script for your proposed picture CASABLANCA," his letter began. "While of course we cannot give you a final opinion until we receive the balance of the script, we are happy to report that, with the exceptions noted below, the present material seems to meet the requirements of the Production Code." He went on, however, to underscore several bawdy formulations, incendiary language that in his eyes was in need of urgent attention.

All of the lines initially flagged by Breen—each branded "unacceptably sex suggestive" and demanding either revision or excision—concerned Captain Renault and his objectionable sex-for-visa exchange program. In the first instance, the line stems from the explanation that the pickpocket (Curt Bois) gives to the naïve English couple as they witness a band of suspects being rounded up in the first act ("Of course, a beautiful young girl for M'sieur Renault, the Prefect of Police")—a line that, amazingly enough, was left untouched in the finished picture. In the second instance, the line in question ("The girl will be released in the morning") was removed altogether, as was an additional line that was to be spoken by one of the cooperative young girls, stating the terms of the deal when in Renault's claws ("It used to take a Villa at Cannes, or the very least, a string of pearls—Now all I ask is an exit visa.").

In the final instance noted by Breen, taken from the scene in which Rick and Renault are seated outside the café, as Sascha heeds Rick's instructions to escort Yvonne home, only a single word had to be changed. The draft script had Renault's line as "How extravagant you are—throwing away women like that. Some day they may be rationed." By the time filming was complete, "rationed" had been swapped out, in accordance with Breen's suggestion, for "scarce," thereby mollifying things ever so slightly. In the end, it was left to the studio to bargain and plead with the PCA, trying assiduously to retain original wording or have things doctored as unnoticeably as possible.

On May 21, Breen sent an additional memo to Warner, this time a little less optimistic in tone. "The present material contains certain elements which seem to be unacceptable from the standpoint of the Production Code," he wrote using the same boilerplate language employed in many a memo with his name attached to it. "Specifically, we cannot approve the present suggestion that Capt. Renault makes a practice of seducing the women to whom he grants visas. Any such inference of illicit sex could not be approved in the finished picture." The material in question contained dialogue between Strasser and Renault, presumably penned by the wisecracking Epstein twins and excised from the script by the time production began, in which the Nazi officer confronts the French prefect about his illicit habits:

Strasser: Don't you think that with so much important work to be done, you could devote a little less time to personal matters?
Renault: Well, you enjoy war. I enjoy women. We are both very good at our jobs.
Strasser: I think the German viewpoint is a much healthier one.
Renault: You are probably right. At least your work keeps you outdoors.

Also included in the draft material, prompting more red flags from the Hays Office, was a scene in which Renault faces a vexing decision between two attractive young women, a blonde and a brunette, who come to see him about resolving their visa problems. "Which one?" he asks himself. "Ten years ago there would have been no problem. Oh, well, tell the dark one to wait in the private office and we'll go into the visa matter thoroughly." In his account of the production, Harlan Lebo notes yet another prickly add-on to the scene whose pruning was all but inevitable: Renault tells his aide, as a greedy afterthought, "And it wouldn't hurt to have the other one leave her address and phone number."

Despite these excisions, the Renault of *Casablanca* remains a man of lecherous habit. There are plenty of glimpses of this, even after cuts and final changes were made for the release print. We might recall, for instance, the scene in which the young Bulgarian Annina comes to see Rick for advice, confessing to him her plans to do "a bad thing" in order to secure the coveted exit visas from Renault for her and her husband. When she explains at the start of that scene that she's come to the café accompanied by Renault, and that she's brought her husband with her, Rick responds with the faint suggestion of a ménage à trois. Additionally, when asked by Annina what kind of man Renault is, Rick replies, with a wink and nudge: "Oh, he's just like any other man, only more so." As Roger Ebert aptly noted in his audio commentary prepared for the 2002 special-edition DVD release, "The film implied a great deal more than it was able to say."

An unintended consequence of the Code was subtlety. Instead of showing Renault bed each of the desperate visa seekers, it's merely hinted at and often in the sliest of ways—gestures, glances, nods that might fly beneath the PCA's radar. When studying the film today, young college students often comment on the power of suggestion, demanded in the 1940s, and its advantage over the current modes of more explicit representation. They observe this especially in Renault and Rick, the film's "charming scoundrels," as Umberto Eco calls them; they also pick up—this is the twenty-first century, after all—on the homoerotic bonds between the two men.

Watching *Casablanca* today, it's hard to miss certain cues in which mere suggestion almost seems to carry an army of exclamation marks with it. For example, when Ilsa and Victor come to see Renault in his office, in the company of Strasser, to talk about their own visa problems, they end up leaving in a huff. One of Renault's aides then abruptly enters the room and announces, "Another visa problem has come up." Claude Rains very demonstratively reveals an impish grin, walks over to the mirror, tightening his necktie and primping himself as he gives his trademark response: "Show her in." Despite all official recommendations to the contrary, Renault's anticipation, let alone his chosen series of gestures, couldn't be any more transparent. "After a meeting between Breen and Wallis," explains Aljean Harmetz, "a number of lines that referred to Renault's womanizing were removed from the script, but Claude Rains's performance left no doubt that Renault traded exit visas for sex."

Michael Curtiz had considerable experience making movies both before and after the Production Code. His racy little B picture of 1934, *Mandalay*, starring Kay Francis and Ricardo Cortez, dealt unflinchingly with white slavery, one of the many iterations of sex that were strictly *verboten* under the Code (that particular film was released a few months before the PCA had taken root). Yet, just as Curtiz knew how to smooth over the rough patches of an unfinished script, he knew how to finesse the scenes that might otherwise scream out to the censors. His breathtakingly efficient direction—"keeping scenes moving, crowding them with atmosphere and suspense," as Hal Wallis put it—made it possible to fudge, or at least to render sufficiently elliptical and ambiguous, scenes involving any breaches in morality. Together with Wallis and studio head Jack Warner, he was able to negotiate, even to push the envelope on, the fine line of moral respectability demanded by Breen and his censorship staff. Kenneth Tynan may have given *Casablanca* its most backhanded compliment when he called it "a masterpiece of light entertainment," but part of its frothiness came from the need to brush over—or, following Curtiz's jaunty lead, to flit past—the areas that might otherwise spark the ire of the chief arbiters of the Code.

A DAY AFTER the first PCA report arrived, Hal Wallis received "Notes on Screenplay Casablanca," the detailed commentary prepared by Casey Robinson. The best-paid writer at the studio, and someone whose talents Wallis especially prized, Robinson was known for adapting love stories, frequently emotionally wrenching melodramas, and for handling controversial, otherwise untouchable themes in ways that were palatable to the censors and to mass audiences. In the case of *Kings Row* (1942), an adaptation of Henry Bellamann's bestselling novel—with Claude Rains in a supporting role as the deranged, possessive Dr. Alexander Tower—Robinson had managed to convince Geoffrey Shurlock of the Hays Office that the litany of hot-button issues addressed in the novel (incest, sadism, terminal illness) could be adapted and revised in an acceptable way for the screen. "'Look, the sin is punished,'" he and Wallis had argued to Shurlock. "And that," Robinson later told an interviewer, "took care of that." That same year, in *Now, Voyager,* Robinson prepared a script that, despite its patently taboo subjects (insanity, adultery), proved to be a terrific hit for the studio and a major vehicle for its stars, Bette Davis and Paul Henreid. Robinson served as more than a writer on that film; he was also Wallis's technical consultant, his confidant regarding the rushes prepared by director Irving Rapper, and a general fixer of sorts.

Born to Mormon parents, and raised in a college town in rural Utah, Robinson was politically and socially more conservative than the three principal writers assigned to *Casablanca*, the Epstein twins and Koch, all of whom were born and raised in New York City and embodied various shades of liberalism. Although Robinson's father taught in the theater and music department at Brigham Young University, young Casey went east to attend Cornell—a decade before playwright Murray Burnett arrived there—and had been working in Hollywood for fifteen years by the time Wallis tapped him for three weeks' work on *Casablanca*. Robinson had started his career writing subtitles for silent pictures ("as good a way for a new writer to begin as any," he later recalled) and sold his first story to Columbia before following producer Harry Joe Brown to Warners in the mid-1930s.

When Wallis contacted Robinson about *Casablanca*—he had already begun sketching the script for *Passage to Marseille* (1944), another Hal B. Wallis production that, with much of the same charmed ensemble cast and Curtiz as director, would prove to be an unanticipated sequel or a cinematic reunion—it was again in something of a fixer's capacity. Robinson wasn't so much expected to write new material for *Casablanca* as to prop up the sagging romance and to do so in a tasteful way that would elude the wrath of the PCA. Harmetz suggests that Robinson may have drafted a complete version of the flashback, though Julius Epstein repeatedly disputed that claim. For his part, Robinson insisted to Joel Greenberg, in a 1974 interview, that it was Bogart, by then disillusioned with the existing script, who had approached him during the production. "'This is no love story,' he said. 'It ought to be a great love story.' And the reason Hal came to me is that they had promised Bogart that I would write it. Hal said, 'If Casey will write the love story, will you come back and go to work?'" The truth of the matter is that Bogart was already signed and committed, the script was in draft, and much of the love story already existed. What Robinson provided were mostly tweaks to the script, tightening things up here and there. Even in his notes, written only days before the first takes were filmed, he mentions the existence of the final scene in which Ilsa departs for Lisbon with her husband.

In his focus on the romance between Rick and Ilsa, and the list of recommendations he gave Wallis, the one character that Robinson seems almost unwittingly—and possibly against his own personal prejudices—to have strengthened is Sam. Indeed, the knowing expression on Sam's face when he spots Ilsa entering Rick's Café is the audience's first hint at the past romance between Rick and Ilsa. When she approaches Sam, betraying their former acquaintance by asking him to play some of the old songs, Robinson saw an opportunity. "Play up very strongly Sam's trying to avoid playing this ["As Time Goes By"]," he wrote to Wallis. "I'm sure the material will tell the audience that there is something of great significance to this music, and something of romantic significance." He also encouraged Wallis to amplify Ilsa's desperation to get to Rick through Sam; without revealing specifics, she is to convey a deep sense of urgency. As he put it, "this business serves as a very good buildup for the love story and will pique the audience's interest and make the first meeting between Ilsa and Rick tremendously effective." Finally, in the scene between Rick and Sam just before the flashback, Robinson made another firm recommendation: "You must heighten here the great fear that Sam has, the almost superstitious darky [*sic*] fear, and also heighten his pleading with Rick to get out of town until the woman is gone. The audience will get from this the fact that the woman has done terrible damage to Rick, but also that this woman is of terrific importance to Rick, and is a very effective lead-in to the flashbacks."

Not everything that Robinson suggested, however, was incorporated into the final script. For instance, he felt that Rick and Ilsa's first encounter, when they become reacquainted in North Africa, should occur alone at night at his café ("much along the lines of the scene I wrote for the test"), and that the second scene at Rick's apartment should be filmed in the afternoon. Wallis and Curtiz decided to do things differently, having Victor and Ilsa show up at the café together, and having Ilsa return to Rick's apartment late at night only after she's run out of options for securing the letters of transit.

Regardless of his seemingly misguided idea to shoot the scene in daylight, Robinson's notes do an impressive job of capturing the emotional and moral turmoil of Rick and Ilsa's past romance—much of which is ultimately worked into the film—and the initial motivation that brings them back together again:

> She comes, as she tells Rick, because she was angry last night and even this morning, but she has been thinking

> it over and she can easily see why he thinks of her as he does. She wants to clear that up, because she loves Rick, because the days they had together in Paris were the most beautiful in her life. She does clear it up. She tells him Laszlo is her husband. She tells him all the background of their marriage, and tells him the real reason she didn't come to the train in Paris. She tells him she loves her husband and explains the quality of that love—her admiration, respect, even veneration. To her [Laszlo] is the personification of the best ideals of her nature, of honor, of sacrifice for a great cause. Rick understands, softens, is ashamed of himself. . . .

Robinson's main role, as advisor and script doctor, was as much aimed at Wallis and Curtiz as it was at the actors in front of the camera. He may not have been handpicked by Bogart to work on the love story, but he certainly understood the stakes.

One of the most significant points in his extensive notes and suggestions concerns the scene when Ilsa returns to Rick's for the letters of transit, a scene that existed in the Epsteins' version but that he felt needed further work. "I would play the beginning of the next scene between Rick and Ilsa pretty much as it is," Robinson advised Wallis, "but greatly alter the finish." He proceeds to give the following story analysis:

> Ilsa comes for the visas. She tries to be hard-boiled. She can't be. She breaks down completely. But completely. She tells Rick that she loves him and will do anything he wants. She will go anywhere, stay here, anything. She is

> absolutely helpless in the great passionate love that she has for him. She will leave Victor. Rick can get him out of Casablanca. She knows that she's doing wrong, she even says so. She knows that in a way it is a violation of all the high idealism and honor of her nature. She knows she is being wicked but she can't help herself. This is a great scene for a woman to play.

His shameful views concerning the perceived nature of women notwithstanding, Robinson helped to unbury the lede, as it were, to uncover the romance and melodrama that he felt should help anchor the story and drive viewers to the box office. Attributing sole authorship to Robinson would be a mistake, just as it would be to give exclusive credit to any one of the three credited screenwriters. Faint traces of influence, however, can surely be detected nonetheless.

Unsurprisingly, the romance between Rick and Ilsa is what ultimately got the attention of Breen and his staff at the PCA. Especially worrisome is the scene Robinson describes, when Ilsa visits Rick at night in his apartment above the café and offers both him and the audience the terrifying chance that their romance might be rekindled again, even though Ilsa is officially known to be a married woman. Several weeks into production, Breen wrote Warner one of his more sternly worded memos. "The present material seems to contain a suggestion of a sex affair which would be unacceptable if it came through in the finished picture," Breen began. "We believe this could possibly be corrected by replacing the fade-out on page 135 [i.e., the scene in Rick's apartment], with a dissolve, and shooting the succeeding scene without any sign of a bed or couch, or anything suggestive of a sex affair." Savvy audiences knew to read a fade-out as Hollywood shorthand for steamy copulation, and Breen's henchmen at the PCA saw it as their prerogative to stamp out all such intimations of immorality. "If shot this way," Breen continued, "we believe the finished scene would be acceptable under the provisions of the Production Code. However, great care will be needed to avoid anything suggestive of a sex affair. Otherwise it could not be approved."

Even so, the sequence as it was shot makes the intimation relatively easy to recognize. Once Ilsa succumbs to pent-up desire, collapsing in Rick's arms after attempting in vain to secure the prized letters at gunpoint and lifting her face to receive a fulsome kiss, the dissolve to the watchtower does little to dispel fantasies of what may have occurred off screen. "Bogart is smoking the standard-issue postcoital cigarette," writes film historian Richard Maltby in his meticulous examination of these 3½ seconds of the film, "the airport tower is recognizably phallic, and the shot sequence of embrace/dissolve away from scene/return is a conventional device for signaling an offscreen—a censored—significant act." Maltby draws our attention to the great paradox that lies at the heart of the scene and, more generally, at the heart of movie censorship of the time: "Rick and Ilsa *must* have slept together, *and* they *can't* have done so."

In his analysis, Maltby sees *Casablanca* as emblematic of "the intricate and intimate relationship between movies and their viewers," the crux of fandom and something that has long preoccupied moviegoers and critics. The place in which this becomes most acute is in viewers' understanding of the sexual relationship between Rick and Ilsa. An audience naturally indulges the impulse to speculate, even (or especially) moviegoers in the 1940s. In his influential 1944 book, *The Hollywood Hallucination*, Parker Tyler writes:

> A pale, rational, dead-gray, blushlessly journalistic problem of the movies has been whether the act of fornication did or did not take place. Whenever this much-shunted problem appears, it is but an indication that the true importance of the sexual act and its biological secrets is being underrated. The conventional nature of theatrical representation, its ambiguity in regard to this alternative of did or did not, has consistently been exploited by the movie city as propaganda to get us to believe in the honor of hero and heroine.

For his part, Richard Maltby quotes a poignant passage from F. Scott Fitzgerald's posthumously published novel *The Last Tycoon* (1941) to further illustrate the fine line between sexual suggestion and breach of Code that movies like *Casablanca* had to walk. Monroe Stahr, the mogul protagonist of the novel, describes the ways in which audiences are expected to understand a heroine's putatively sexualized modus operandi: "At all times, at all moments when she is on the screen in our sight, she wants to sleep with Ken Willard. . . . Whatever she does, it is in place of sleeping with Ken Willard. If she walks down the street she is walking to sleep with Ken Willard, if she eats her food it is to give her enough strength to sleep with

Ken Willard. *But* at no time do you give the impression that she would ever consider sleeping with Ken Willard unless they were properly sanctified."

Throughout *Casablanca*, Paris serves as a stand-in for the utopian, unsustainable erotic bliss alluded to in the flashback, and suggested even earlier. The first time we see Rick and Ilsa together is also the first mention of Paris, signaling to the audience its latent significance. The mysterious love story between Rick and Ilsa initially lies behind a tissue of intentionally vague references: when Ilsa somewhat naïvely asks Renault who the café's namesake is, he responds, serving as Rick's wingman, "well, if I were a woman, and I . . . were not around, I should be in love with Rick." Similarly, Rick storms over to the table after Ilsa persuades Sam to play "As Time Goes By" and demands that he stop the forbidden song. His cheeks trembling, an expression of pain working its way to the surface, Rick is almost conjured by Ilsa's imagination ("Well, you were asking about Rick," Renault tells Ilsa, "and here he is"). After some awkward fumbling, the couple recalls La Belle Aurore and the fateful day that the Germans arrived in the French capital. "I remember every detail," Rick says with a bit of swagger, intensified in the staccato tone of Bogart's voice: "The Germans wore gray, you wore blue." Later on, during their after-hours tryst in Rick's apartment, Rick cynically refers to the feeling of being "back in Paris," insisting that the very mention of that city's name in Ilsa's sly negotiations for the letters of transit would amount to "poor salesmanship."

Film scholar Thomas Doherty, who devoted a book-length study to Joseph Breen and his career as Hollywood's chief censor, has suggested that the very line "We'll always have Paris" is coded language—or, rather ironically, language used to elude the iron fist of the Production Code—to suggest the sexual past of Rick and Ilsa. If we think of "Paris" as a substitute for "sex," then Rick's speech on the rain-soaked tarmac in the movie's final scene can be heard in a different register: "We'll always have Paris. We didn't have it, we'd lost it, until you came to Casablanca. We got it back last night." Despite the absence of their actual encounter from the movie, the erotic charge laces Rick and Ilsa's dialogue.

As for the significance of that final scene, Rick serves as a mouthpiece for both the romance and the glory. "He is not just solving a love triangle," wrote Casey Robinson in his notes. "He is forcing the girl to live up to the idealism of her nature, forcing her to carry on with the work that in these days is far more important than the love of two little people. It is something they will both be glad for when the pain is over." That very sacrifice of love for glory is what also made it possible for the film to meet the requirements of the Code and of the newfangled Office of War Information: for Ilsa to stay with Rick would have not only been tantamount to the sanctification of an adulterous affair but also undermined the greater, righteous cause of the war effort. "Given the restrictive morals and self-imposed film industry censorship of the day," writes Harlan Lebo in his critical account of the film, "any other ending for *Casablanca* remains the stuff of Hollywood fairy tales." Rick's final resolution on the tarmac, to choose patriotic duty over personal libido, might be seen—at least in terms of its implications for the Production Code—as a variation on what a 1930 article in *The Nation*, "Virtue in Cans," branded "the perfect formula" for Hollywood dramas: "five reels of transgression followed by one reel of retribution."

In some cases, the PCA almost appears to have recognized that a game was being played between it and the studio. For instance, in a third memo, issued on June 21, Breen foregrounds an area that elicited special concern in his office: "The suggestion that Ilsa was married all the time she was having her love affair with Rick in Paris seems unacceptable, and could not be approved in the finished picture. Hence, we request the deletion of Ilsa's line 'Even when I knew you in Paris.'" That line, however, remained untouched in the film that went into the can and earned the final approval of the PCA (certificate 8457), issued on Will Hays's letterhead on September 2, 1942. "Joe Breen called me yesterday after he and his staff had seen *Casablanca*," reported Wallis to his publicity man Charles Einfeld. "I have never heard him rave about a picture as he did about this one. He told me he thought it not only one of the most outstanding pictures to come off the lot in some time, but one of the best he had seen in some years."

By that point, with the war raging in Europe and in the Pacific, puritanical concerns with sexual and social mores may have become, at least temporarily, subordinate to the Allied commitment. After its New York premiere in late November 1942, *Casablanca* went into general release and was shown to thousands upon thousands of civilians and enlisted men with the approval of the state censor boards in Massachusetts, Maryland, Ohio, Kansas, and then onward to Canada and Ireland. When the film was released a year later in Bergman's native Sweden, officially a neutral nation but one with lingering trade and diplomatic ties to Germany, it wasn't so much the sex that concerned the censors as it was the defamation of the Nazis (Rick's shooting of Strasser and Renault's kicking of the Vichy bottle were removed, as was Renault's wry comment on trashing Rick's Café after its doors are closed for business, "You know how that impresses Germans"), something that the OWI likely wouldn't have lost much sleep over. Even for the American release of the film, Bogart's original line when shooting Strasser ("All right, Major, you're asking for it") had to be changed ("I was willing to shoot Renault, and I am willing to shoot you"), as Wallis instructed Curtiz in a memo of July 22, 1942. It had to be made clear that Rick shoots in self-defense and not in cold blood. "This should be delivered with a little more guts," wrote Wallis, "a little more of the curt hard way of speaking we have associated with Rick."

IN HIS 1987 SHORT STORY, "You Must Remember This," the novelist Robert Coover essentially undoes the Production Code altogether and in its place offers a wickedly lurid depiction of all that we don't see during those precious seconds in Rick's apartment. After incorporating much of the original dialogue and re-creating the general atmosphere, up to the moment when Ilsa pulls a gun on Rick, Coover takes things into the realm of the imaginary, often with subtle or not so subtle comic effect: "'Holy Shit' he wheezes, pushing his hand inside her girdle as her skirt falls. His cheeks too are wet with tears. '*Ilsa*!' '*Richard*!'" Coover continues:

> They fall to the floor, grabbing and pulling at each other's clothing. He's trying to get her bra off which is tangled up now with her blouse, she's struggling with his belt, yanking at his black pants, wrenching them open. Buttons fly, straps pop, there's the soft unfocused rip of silk, the jingle of buckles and falling coins, grunts, gasps, whimpers of desire. He strips the tangled skein of underthings away (all straps and stays—how does she get in and out of this crazy elastic?); she works his pants down past his bucking hips, fumbles with his shoes. "*Your elbow!*—"

Things get more explicit from there—resplendent with the kinds of similes and metaphors one might encounter in mass-market erotica (with Ilsa "easing him into her like a train being guided into a station"). "He heaves upward," writes Coover of Rick, "impaling her to the very core: 'Oh Gott!' she screams, her back arching, mouth agape as though to commence 'La Marseillaise.'"

Still later, with Rick's "own buttocks bouncing up off the floor as though trying to take off like the next flight to Lisbon," Ilsa—perhaps more befitting of an homage to Madeline Kahn's Lili von Shtupp from *Blazing Saddles* (1974) than to Bergman's role—cries out, "Gott in Himmel, *this is fonn*!" Coover never lets go entirely of the film's moorings or its imaginary frame of reference, even while expanding the realm of sexual pairings: "This is not Victor inside her with his long thin rapier, all too rare in its embarrassed visits; this is not Yvonne with her cunning professional muscles." Ilsa eventually tells Rick, in a moment of postcoital exhaustion, "It was the best fokk I effer haff," and goes on to borrow a page from Paul Henreid's playbook in *Now, Voyager*: "She fits two cigarettes in her lips, lights them both (there's a bit of fumbling with the lighter, she's not very mechanical), and gazing soulfully down at Rick, passes him one of them. He grins, 'Hey, where'd you learn that, kid?'" Some of the moves they rehearse are no doubt meant more as a parody of the film—or, perhaps, a sly satire of the puritanical values of 1940s America. "He raises his glass. 'Uh, here's lookin'— She gulps it down absently, not waiting for his toast. 'And that light from the airport," she goes on, batting at it as it passes as though to shoo it away. 'How can you effer sleep here?'"

Two years after Coover, in the script that Nora Ephron wrote for Rob Reiner's romantic comedy *When Harry Met Sally*, the two title characters, recent graduates of the University of Chicago, furiously debate the ending of *Casablanca* while driving cross-country from Chicago to New York City in 1977. "Wouldn't you rather be with Humphrey Bogart than that other guy?" asks Harry Burns (Billy Crystal) incredulously, as if to suggest that any other option would be some kind of unforgiveable betrayal to human instinct. In her practically minded retort, Sally Albright (Meg Ryan) insists: "I don't want to spend the rest of my life in Casablanca married to a man who runs a bar." To which Harry, increasingly perplexed, responds, "You'd rather have a passionless marriage—" (qualified by Sally's interjection, "—and be First Lady of Czechoslovakia") "—than live with the man . . . you've had the greatest sex of your life with, just because he owns a bar, and that's all he does?" Sally ends the debate, "Yes, and so would any woman in her right mind. Women are very practical. Even Ingrid Bergman, which is why she gets on that plane at the end of the movie."

Later on in the film, when the deep friendship between Harry and Sally begins to blossom, there's a scene of them in their respective New York apartments, shown in split screen, watching *Casablanca* in bed on late-night television while talking on the telephone; they have both tuned in their sets at the moment that Rick is about to trigger the Parisian flashback. (By the 1970s, *Casablanca* had become the movie most frequently broadcast on American TV, and even as late as 2007, in Pixar's hugely popular animated comedy *Ratatouille*, there is a scene in which the lovable rat Remy relaxes watching *Casablanca* on television.) Without recounting their earlier disagreement over the film while on the road ten years ago, Harry simply launches in: "Now, you're telling me you would be happier with Victor Laszlo than with Humphrey Bogart?" Fully forgetting, or perhaps merely repressing, their earlier conversation, Sally asks, "When did I say that?" Harry explains it was while on their cross-country journey. "I never said that," declares Sally with apparent conviction. "I would never have said that." Content with this change of tides, a small victory for his team, Harry acquiesces: "All right. Have it your way."

Just months before her death in June 2012, screenwriter Ephron wrote a short Valentine's Day piece for *The Daily Beast* in which she listed her all-time favorite love stories, including Frank Capra's *It Happened One Night* (1934) and Billy Wilder's *The Apartment* (1960). Naturally, *Casablanca* ranks high up on her list, but unlike the other wordier entries, her commentary on the film is limited to just two short, revealing lines: "How many times can you see it? Never enough."

OF COURSE, the film would be unthinkable today without its infectious theme song "As Time Goes By." Originally written by Herman Hupfeld, an American-born composer who had studied in Germany, it was first featured in a 1931 Broadway musical called *Everybody's Welcome.* It was a long-standing favorite of Murray Burnett's before he inserted it years later into *Everybody Comes to Rick's.* Impossible as it may seem today, given the song's extraordinary success, Max Steiner, the film's composer, was disinclined to use it in the movie. "They have the lousiest tune," he told his wife, Louise, when he started work on the score, "they have it recorded, and they want me to use it." Steiner, who wrote the music for such classics as the original *King Kong*, *Gone With the Wind*, and *The Searchers*, had only recently finished his score for *Now, Voyager*, which would earn him an Academy Award and bountiful royalties for his song "It Can't Be Wrong." He wasn't pleased with the arrangement of the Hupfeld tune. "None of us likes having to use somebody else's schmucky song," observed composer David Raksin, who wrote the highly successful score for Otto Preminger's *Laura* (1944), which was initially slated to use "Sophisticated Lady" by Duke Ellington. "Even before he started work," recalled Wallis, "[Steiner] told me he hated the song 'As Time Goes By,' obviously upset because he had to use someone else's theme."

Although rumors circulated that Steiner managed, rather

miraculously, to persuade the studio to reshoot the scenes in which "As Time Goes By" is sung—and that this, ultimately, was prevented only because Bergman had trimmed her hair to play Maria in her next film, *For Whom the Bell Tolls,* and the retakes wouldn't match—they are likely little more than just that: Hollywood rumors. Instead, Steiner worked in twenty-four versions of the song, an array of highly evocative paraphrases and quotations, in the score he provided. "In the best Wagnerian manner," writes music scholar Peter Wegele, "Steiner reminds the audience that the song is the leitmotif binding Rick and Ilsa."

Little did he know that his subtle, recurrent variations of Hupfeld's tune would make it one of the all-time most memorable songs in the history of motion pictures. When the film went into general release in winter and spring of 1943, "As Time Goes By" enjoyed a twenty-one week run on the radio show *Hit Parade*, spending four of those charmed weeks, in March and April, at number 1. Even Steiner had to admit, in a newspaper interview from 1943, "'As Time Goes By' must have had something to attract so much attention." A musician's strike that coincided with the production kept the song from being recorded anew—it was only much later that Dooley Wilson's rendition became a classic—and so the slower, tinnier, less throaty 1931 version sung by Rudy Vallee was re-released. In her profile of Wilson from 1944, Dorothy Kilgallen remarked, "There's only one explanation of why Dooley and the old torch are a dynamite combination and it's fairly simple. It's his number, that's all. A lot of people will sing it with better voices, but nobody will ever sing it as well as Dooley sings it." (In 2004, when the American Film Institute ranked the top 100 songs in American cinema Wilson's version of "As Time Goes By" was number 2, topped only by "Over the Rainbow" from *The Wizard of Oz*.)

When considering Steiner's score, it's the music in the flashback in particular that is arguably richest in complexity, conveying both the romantic and political strands of the story. For each segment, he arranged a medley of disparate sounds and compositions: "As Time Goes By," the "Marseillaise," "Romance," "Perfidia," "Gracioso" in one instance; "As Time Goes By," "Nazi Spy," and "Menace" in another. He even worked in fragments of the so-called "Deutschlandlied," the German national anthem, to cast the music in a specific historical register. Ronald Haver suggests that Steiner's use of "As Time Goes By," which bookmarks the flashback, echoes the visual presentation as a whole. His final rendering of the music in that scene, Haver adds, "rolls, strides, bounces, and mourns its way through the film, echoing on a celesta, reprised by muted trumpets, and underscored by harp. It is by turns tender, brooding, ominous, stately, and triumphant. It ties the disparate elements of the film together with a romantic patina. In truth, *Casablanca* would not be the classic that it is without Steiner's accompanying score."

The music and cultural critic Jody Rosen, author of *White Christmas: The Story of an American Song*, observes, "The thing about that song is like 'White Christmas' before it, and like many other songs that were clogging up the Hit Parade at that moment, the context was the war. And the theme of these songs is wistful longing. So they're not songs about romantic satisfaction in the present or even the kinds of heartbreak songs that were on the charts at other times before and after. They really are about a certain built-in nostalgia." The most successful songs of the day were indeed ballads of romantic longing, not war songs along the lines of what the Office of War Information had urged composers to make, but simple love songs, even songs of doomed love, written at the time or rearranged. "Love is being able to dream about it forever," notes David Thomson, "instead of actually turning it into everyday reality. So the song fits the 'same old story' of desire being the lasting light."

Steiner was acutely aware, perhaps too aware, of the cliché-ridden nature of Broadway show tunes, and yet in his score he melded pop and classical compositions in a way that is almost unparalleled in music history. At the same time, he incorporated songs that spoke to audiences in a language otherwise forbidden by the Code: when Ilsa and Victor enter Rick's Café, Sam taps away at the keys playing Cole Porter's "Love for Sale," an early hint of the illicit romance between Ilsa and Rick. "Two clichés make us laugh," writes Umberto Eco in his essay on *Casablanca*, "but a hundred clichés move us because we sense dimly that the clichés are talking among themselves, celebrating a reunion."

Just as the opening line from the song, extracted from Hupfeld's original chorus, instructs us, "You must remember this," so too the film invites viewers to indulge their memories. One of the chief ways it does this is by replaying images, in the flashback sequence, over music. This effect has been adopted and advanced in the age of YouTube, when mash-ups and

Composer Max Steiner conducting, in 1939.

movie collages often form the backdrop of music videos. Bertie Higgins's 1982 hit ballad "Casablanca"—whose Japanese cover version topped the charts—is now posted on YouTube amid a sea of sentimental clips from the film, starting with the Parisian flashback; it has received more than three million views to date. The opening line of Higgins's Vegas-style lounge lyrics, "I fell in love with you watching *Casablanca*," conjures up a level of schmaltz that is occasionally associated with the film. His refrain offers little relief: Higgins riffs incessantly on Hupfeld's original lyrics, recognizing a kiss as something more than just that and reasserting his enduring love by citing the original song's title. (A karaoke version of the song also exists, suggesting a degree of popular appreciation that cannot be ignored.) More recently, in 2012, British deep-house performer Low Deep T released the video for his catchy electronic dance single titled "Casablanca," with its own film-inspired refrain, "I think I left the love of my life behind in Casablanca." It has enjoyed over twenty million views since it's been posted on YouTube.

Although the film never attained the kind of cult status in Sweden that it did elsewhere in Europe, in the 1970s a stage production there featured a Swedish version of "As Time Goes By," written by the popular comedy duo of Hans "Hasse" Alfredson and Tage Danielsson. It was performed by jazz singer Monica Zetterlund, with lyrics describing the basic political setting and plotlines of the film. Swedish film critic Mårten Blomkvist explained to me that the song—coinciding more or less with the Swedish release of Woody Allen's *Play It Again, Sam*—helped to introduce the otherwise surprisingly neglected classic into popular discussion.

Over the years, as a direct tribute to the film, Dooley Wilson's version of "As Time Goes By" has been reincorporated into Hollywood features. As recently as 2013, in John Carney's romantic comedy *Begin Again*, we essentially have the twenty-first century version of Harry and Sally lying in bed watching the film on TV in split screen. The film's two leads, music producer Dan Mulligan (Mark Ruffalo) and songwriter Gretta James (Keira Knightley), stroll the streets of New York on a warm summer night, eventually sitting on the steps in Union Square, listening to Wilson croon Rick and Ilsa's torch song—what actor Johnny Depp once called "the national anthem for broken-hearted lovers" —from an iPhone through a shared set of ear buds. Before playing it from her iTunes library, Gretta announces her fear that Dan "might find this cheesy," perhaps an unintended nod to Steiner, but asserts that it's still one of her all-time favorite songs from one of her most cherished films. "It's such a great song," the Irish-born director Carney said in an interview soon after the film's release. "I think that kids don't know that song and younger people don't quite know that song. I think it's great to try and sort of keep those things alive a little bit."

Perhaps the greatest coda to "As Time Goes By," however, were the two recent auctions of Sam's pianos: the one he played at La Belle Aurore and the more elegant, center-stage piano from Rick's Café. In December 2012, Sotheby's in New York City sold the fifty-eight-key mini upright that Dooley Wilson played at the Montmartre café for $602,500, nearly four times the price it last received on the auction block when it was sold to a Japanese collector in 1988. Auction house vice chairman David Radden insisted that this piano, even though it isn't the one he played in Rick's Café, remains among the world's most precious pieces of movie memorabilia. "The piano is a star of the film," he said, "the music is so emotive, so moving, and the piano really becomes a symbol of the love story between Bogart and Bergman." In his official statement before the sale, he asked potential bidders, "How can anything say 'I love you' better than the piano from 'Casablanca'?"

Two years later, in November 2014, the golden-yellow upright piano from Rick's Café in which Rick hides the letters of transit (its hinged lid reversed so that Rick could open it from the back), sold for a whopping $3.4 million at Bonhams on Madison Avenue. On that same day, the auction house sold the letters of transit ($118,750), and its entertainment director, Catherine Williamson, described the deep connection between the two items. "Fifteen minutes into the movie, he tucks them in there," Williamson said of Bogart's clever move. "They're under there while Sam plays; they're there for all of the activity that happens in the café. It represents the way out for them. That's what made it so important." The piano's previous owner, a Los Angeles dentist named Gary Milan, who also owns the famous statuette from *The Maltese Falcon* ("the stuff that dreams are made of"), had lent American cinema's most precious upright for various celebrations. In the mid-1990s, he allowed Warner Bros. to include it in a makeshift museum on its studio lot, and in 2006 he lent it to the Hollywood Bowl Orchestra to play a suite from *Casablanca* (the piano came with its own full-time security guard). These days Sam's piano is every bit as iconic as Dorothy's ruby slippers from *The Wizard of Oz*, which are housed alongside other prized possessions of American folklore in the Smithsonian Institution; its value, cultural and monetary alike, has only accrued with time.

In the seven and a half decades since the film's release, "As Time Goes By" has been performed by such legendary singers as Chet Baker, Perry Como, Bing Crosby, Billie Holiday, Frank Sinatra, Jimmy Durante (whose rendition was later used, over the opening credits, in Nora Ephron's *Sleepless in Seattle*), Tony Bennett, Rod Stewart, Johnny Nash, Engelbert Humperdinck, the Carpenters, and Sammy Davis Jr. Even Bob Dylan has played a cover, as have ZZ Top, Liberace, Bryan Ferry, Kenny G, Barbra Streisand, and the Muppets. Few songs have such illustrious afterlives, and few convey so well the achingly timeless romance first introduced in *Casablanca*. Today, every single movie released by Warner Bros., whether on DVD or one of the current digital streaming platforms, has those same indelible notes of Rick and Ilsa's song, so thoroughly evocative of *Casablanca* and of movies more generally, play as its trademark theme over a stock photo of the old Burbank studio and its company logo.

Chapter 6

PLAY IT AGAIN

When *Casablanca* premiered in New York City over Thanksgiving weekend 1942, and then made its way into general release in the early months of 1943, critics couldn't contain their enthusiasm. In the *New York Times*, Bosley Crowther hailed it as "one of the year's most exciting and trenchant films," while theater critic Howard Barnes of the *New York Herald Tribune* called it "impressively topical" and "an excellent film." In the industry trade papers, the chorus of affirmation grew with each review. *The Hollywood Reporter* judged it "Academy Award caliber" and "a drama that lifts you right out of your seat," and the review in *Daily Variety* concluded by branding it "a film with as many top performances as individual evidences of top production."

Not all critics were in lockstep unanimity, however. Writing in *The New Republic* in December 1942, Manny Farber considered it among the many "epic phonies" churned out by Hollywood's major studios. "Before Allied troops made it more famous," he wrote with characteristic irony, "Casablanca served as a jumping-off spot to America for many of Europe's refugees—therefore a timely place to carry on Warner's favorite cops and robbers." In his unflattering assessment, "the picture has more acts than it knows what to do with for truth and beauty—and gives too much time to less important ones." Two months later, in *The Nation*, James Agee said in his mixed review that while he enjoyed the picture, he snickered at a few of its lines, which he then singled out for ridicule in his piece—including "Oh, Victor, please don't go to the underground meeting tonight"—making sure to note that had a friend not reminded him of these clunkers, he wouldn't even have been able to criticize them. "*Casablanca* is still reverently spoken of as (1) fun, (2) a 'real movie,'" he wrote in his 1943 end-of-the-year roundup on Christmas Day. "I still think it is the year's clearest measure of how willingly, *faute de mieux*, people will deceive themselves." Agee's skepticism echoed in some of the dissenting voices that followed. Pauline Kael summed up the collective objections in a short piece on the film in the mid-1960s: "One's tender sentiments will probably still be stirred, but in the cool night air afterward one may wonder a bit that this received the Academy Award as Best Picture of 1943, and that awards were given to Michael Curtiz as Best Director, to Julius and Philip Epstein and Howard Koch for the Best Screenplay, and the Thalberg Award to producer Hal Wallis."

The film's success, as measured in its vast popular appeal and the numerous awards it received, made a different impression inside the industry. From the first moment that the mountains of box-office receipts were tallied, thoughts quickly turned, as they had after other major commercial successes in Hollywood, to the idea of a possible *Casablanca* sequel. As early as the spring of 1943, Warners contract writer Frederick Faust, who had written a number of pulps and westerns under the nom de plume Max Brand, prepared his "Report on Suggested Sequel to *Casablanca*" for Hal Wallis. Around that same time, Wallis declared, in a letter to one of the many *Casablanca* enthusiasts writing in to suggest a redux, "some consideration is being given to doing a sequel to *Casablanca* and this may materialize." Faust's idea was based on a thirty-one page treatment called *Tangiers*, submitted to the studio by Fredrick Stephani, the same playwright who—to close the *Casablanca* circle—would go on to write *Hickory Stick* with Murray Burnett the following year. In it, the story shifts locale to Algeria, where, at the same moment that the armada of Allied troops lands on the North African beach, Rick reveals himself to be a secret agent and Renault is revealed as a champion of the Free French.

Faust expressed immediate concerns about Stephani's proposed changes, and especially took issue with Rick's character evolution. "There is no necessity, of course, to repeat the action of *Casablanca*," he assured Wallis, "but the emotional drive, which succeeded before, could be repeated or increased in the new picture. The main point is that Rick made the first picture. I would stick to the original lines of his character and keep him the same man." What Faust goes on to describe in his report turns out to be, in many ways, the basic formula for many if not all of the other Bogart pictures made in the years immediately after *Casablanca*. "Here is our country at war, and in a far-off corner of the world there is a hard-boiled American with such a past that he can't return to his country. He can't put on an American uniform by enlisting, either. Criminals aren't allowed to serve."

The idea of a romantic outsider, an outlaw, or a self-imposed exile who harbors a strong moral compass and who knows, when the time comes, how to do the right thing remained highly seductive throughout the war years. Yet, even at the outset, Faust recognized the difficulty of adapting Stephani's scenario. He held serious doubts about having Rick supported by two women, as the narrative outline had it, including Ilsa ("Madame Laszlo") who returns after the death of her husband; about the order of events in the new rendition; and about the proposed tweaks to the film's original backdrop. "Good sequels," he maintained, "almost always try to repeat the chief characters *and* the setting." In the end, Faust's summary evaluation of Stephani's efforts didn't leave a lot of room for optimism: "His sketch seems to me to be about twenty per cent possible and eighty per cent overboard." Unsurprisingly, the plan for the film—which was to take the title *Brazzaville* from the brief mention, in the final lines of *Casablanca* of a Free French battalion stationed there—got shelved.

With an eye toward other possible sequel ideas, Warners hastily sent out a press release even before their prize film went into general release, hoping to draw further attention to its hit: "Popularity of North African pictures since American troops moved in on the Axis, and *Casablanca* started setting box-office records, has boosted the acting price of camels from 15 dollars a day to 25." Publicity offices were notorious for stretching the truth—recall the misleading announcement that Ann Sheridan and Ronald Reagan were slated to costar in *Casablanca*—and this may merely have been a matter of marking its new territory. It didn't take long, in any case, for a series of pictures with striking affinities to *Casablanca* to be made at the studio.

First, Curtiz directed *Passage to Marseille*, written by Casey Robinson and starring much of the same ensemble cast (Bogart, Rains, Greenstreet, Lorre, and Helmut Dantine), billed as, if not a bona fide sequel, a studio-bred cousin of sorts. The film's trailer announced in outsized bold script, superimposed over snatches of its predecessor's soundtrack, "LAST YEAR WARNER BROS. ELECTRIFIED THE WORLD WITH *CASABLANCA*. THIS YEAR, WARNER BROS. ANNOUNCE *PASSAGE TO MARSEILLE*." Remaining essentially in character, Claude Rains dons an eye patch and a new affiliation as Free French Captain Freycinet, while Bogie plays the heroic French bomber pilot Jean Matrac, a born leader and staunch anti-Vichy partisan willing to sacrifice his own life for freedom. In an elaborate yarn told as a flashback within a flashback, the rugged outcast Matrac, bearing a standard-issue scruffy beard, world-weary eyes, and a hidden tender heart, mounts a dramatic prison break from a French penal colony—a thinly veiled Hollywood allegory of a Nazi concentration camp—enabling his fellow inmates to return to the valiant fight for France. To endow the film with proper patriotic fervor, standby composer Max Steiner repurposes the same medley of favored notes of the "Marseillaise" used in *Casablanca*.

Warners had already tried to apply the same basic formula when, two years earlier, it took most of the principal cast and director John Huston of *The Maltese Falcon* to make a war movie called *Across the Pacific*. Like *Passage*, it was a relatively anemic spin-off, trading on the names of Bogart and Mary Astor in the service of the war effort. Soon after *Passage* came *The Conspirators* (1944), starring Paul Henreid and Hedy Lamarr (once thought of as the ideal candidate for Ilsa), with Greenstreet and Lorre in tow. "It was a mishmash of leftovers from *Casablanca* and *Passage to Marseille*," recalled veteran Warners film editor Rudi Fehr, "so we retitled it *The Conspirators*, starring Headache [*sic*] Lamarr and Paul Hemorrhoid [*sic*]. But Hal Wallis liked it; that was enough." Frederick Faust noted in his earlier communication with Wallis that a rough draft of *The Conspirators* was being written at the exact same moment that the studio was mulling over sequel ideas. "Every film is a preview of the next," wrote German émigré sociologists Max Horkeimer and Theodor W. Adorno in Los Angeles in the mid-1940s, "which promises to unite the same heroic couple under the same exotic sun: anyone arriving late cannot tell whether he is watching the trailer or the real thing."

Among the other films with a certain *Casablanca* touch, or at least a waft of its early glory, is Howard Hawks's *To Have and Have Not* (1945)—a film that James Agee called "the kind of tinny romantic melodrama which millions of cinemaddicts [*sic*] have been waiting for ever since *Casablanca*." Set in Martinique, in an exotic café run by the upstanding proprietor Frenchy, played by Rick's former croupier Marcel Dalio, the film further dramatizes the clashes between the pro-Nazi Vichy authorities and the Free French resistance. The hulking Dan Seymour, who had previously used his imposing figure to powerful effect guarding the door to Rick's in *Casablanca*, serves as the Vichy prefect in Martinique, his fake French accent as shaky as his control over the partisan underground. The film's action is confined to the same summer after the fall of France depicted in *Casablanca*'s Parisian flashback, when a hard-bitten, cynical American fisherman named Harry "Steve" Morgan (Bogart) is lured, reluctantly, into the cause of French resistance. Bogie barks more than a few lines that help the audience recall his signature zingers as Rick ("I can't afford to get mixed up in your local politics," he tells Frenchy, and when asked where his true political sympathies lie, he snarls, "Minding my own business!"). When Harry is finally praised for joining in the good fight ("I'm glad you're on our side"), he claims pure monetary interest, not genuine political allegiance as his motive, echoing Rick Blaine's explanation of his early anti-fascist efforts: "I'm getting paid." Even Harry's romance with the youthful pickpocket and nightclub singer Marie "Slim" Browning (a nineteen-year-old Lauren Bacall) has to be temporarily deferred, set aside for the larger cause.

It's hard to blame Warners for trying so persistently to recapture the magic of *Casablanca*. Most of the early attempts, like *Passage* and *The Conspirators*, have been buried in the annals of motion-picture history or simply overshadowed by the enduring success of the original. However, *To Have and Have Not* is a major exception—not as a simple redux of the

1942 hit, but rather as a deeply cherished, widely appreciated film in its own right. It was also the start of one of Hollywood's great romances: Bogart and Bacall, the same fairy-tale couple whom Hawks would famously recast in *The Big Sleep* a year later. (Late in life, Hawks purportedly told an interviewer that he'd "swapped assignments with Michael Curtiz, exchanging *Casablanca* for *Sergeant York*," but that was at best a faulty memory or perhaps merely another embroidered tale of glory from an industry famous for generating self-serving myths.)

With television's steady rise in popularity during the 1950s ("How can anyone watch a big picture on that little box?" Jack Warner once quipped ruefully), Warners attempted to make inroads in the new medium, releasing an hourlong *Casablanca* series that ran with limited success for seven months in the 1955–1956 season. Actor Charles McGraw, a square-jawed, gravel-voiced detective type who was relatively unknown (he played one of the hired assassins in Robert Siodmak's 1946 noir *The Killers*), stood in for Bogart as Rick; Marcel Dalio got to try his hand as Renault; and Clarence Muse, once thought of as the ideal Sam, was given a second chance because Dooley Wilson had passed away a couple of years before. The role of the witty, accented waiter Carl, played by S. Z. Sakall, who had also recently died, was reprised by fellow émigré and *Casablanca* alum Ludwig Stössel, who had played the America-bound refugee Herr Leuchtag whom Sakall so memorably toasted. Finally, Dan Seymour stepped in for Fat Man Sidney Greenstreet—who, like Wilson and Sakall, had also died—as Signor Ferrari. As part of the "Warner Brothers Presents" series, the studio tried to capitalize on the existing sets, props, and plot points of the film. But viewers never took to it, and it died almost as quickly as it had been hatched.

Already in the early 1950s, the idea for a *Casablanca* musical had circulated, although it didn't find any takers. The following decade, after Jack Warner sold the controlling interest of his studio to Seven Arts Productions, screenwriter Julius Epstein teamed up with composer Arthur Schwartz to give the idea another go. Among the collected papers of theater producer Leland Hayward, there is a flurry of correspondence about the potential of the Epstein-Schwartz musical that extends over November and December 1967: prospective investors express their enthusiasm for what "promises to be *the* major musical hit of the next season"; reservations soon emerge about Epstein's proposed Parisian prologue; the new untitled script is sent out to talent agents, casting offices, and prospective directors, including Otto Preminger; screenwriter Howard Koch files a request for partial credit, even though he, Burnett, and Alison are ultimately kept from terms of the deal outlined in the contract. Conceived just a year before Mel Brooks would make a splash and stir up plenty of controversy with *The Producers* (1968), the *Casablanca* musical was to feature a rather tasteless scene in which the languishing refugees do a chorus number harmonizing about their worries of getting to America. It was also to include Rick and Sam singing a duet in hushed tones. Unimpressed, Seven Arts balked at the idea.

Far more successful in reaching new generations of moviegoers, and movie lovers, were the revival screenings that soon began to occur with staggering frequency across the United

States and the globe. It all started on April 21, 1957, at the Brattle Theater in Cambridge, Massachusetts, perched on a lonely corner just north of Harvard Square. Functioning as Harvard's local art-house cinema since 1953, the Brattle first earned a name for itself by programming the European auteurs (Ingmar Bergman, Federico Fellini, Michelangelo Antonioni, among others) that were then being lionized by the critics in such influential magazines as *Cahiers du cinéma*. Its main programmer, Cyrus Harvey Jr., had studied for a year in Paris on a Fulbright fellowship after the war, where he spent many hours watching movies at the Cinémathèque Française. When he returned home, he brought with him some of the tastes he acquired abroad.

In January 1957, after Bogart passed away, Harvey and his partner Bryant Haliday—the pair had also founded Janus Films, the pioneering American distributor of foreign films, a year earlier—began to think of paying tribute to his work by doing a Bogart series. "I think *Casablanca* was the first one we played," Harvey recalled many years later. "It was my favorite. I thought that Bogart was probably the best American actor who ever lived. And the picture caught on very rapidly. The first time we played it, there was a wonderful reaction. Then the second, third, fourth, and fifth times it took off. The audience began to chant the lines. It was more than just going to the movies. It was sort of partaking in a ritual."

Every year after that, during reading period and exam week, in the winter and once more in late spring, the Brattle would schedule its Bogart series with *Casablanca* as its centerpiece. In his recent biography of Bogart, Stefan Kanfer describes the scene in Cambridge in the spring of 1957:

> Final exams were coming up at neighboring Harvard, and students needed a break from the strain of cramming. Warners' morality play in the desert, complete with Nazi villains, compromised refugees, and a love triangle, provided a perfect escape at an ideal time. Imbued with romantic agony, the undergraduates identified with Rick Blaine's noble misery as he forsook Ilsa for the Greater Good. Again and again they returned to the Brattle, wearing trench coats and dangling cigarettes from their lower lips, singing "La Marseillaise," shouting lines of dialogue on cue.

Students had their individual favorite scenes, and they would deliver them as sermons on the mount, committed to memory and filled with conviction. Writer Jean Strouse, who attended Radcliffe in the 1960s, recalls a boyfriend of hers at Harvard who, when they traveled together in Europe the summer of their sophomore year, would incessantly cite Bogart's dialogue from the film. Along similar lines, critic David Denby reports in his 2012 reappraisal of the film in *The New Yorker*, "Sometime in the sixties, a mythic event occurred in Harvard Square. At the Brattle Theatre, during a showing of *Casablanca*, the sound failed in the last scene, and the assembled worshipers, speaking as one, intoned the famous last line: 'Louis, this could be the beginning of a beautiful friendship.'" Forget for a moment the actual wording of that final line ("Louis, I think this is the beginning of a beautiful friendship"). It's the story that matters, a firm testament to a kind of unparalleled movie love.

"To be at the Brattle when *Casablanca* was playing," Brattle programmer Harvey commented as he shared his memories many decades after the first Bogart series launched, "was, in a small way, like being at a theater in ancient Greece watching *Oedipus*. Some people came twenty-five and thirty times. The film was almost mythical, and audiences would repeat lines the way they did in Greek amphitheaters." That sort of intense cult-film response, not unlike midnight screenings of *The Rocky Horror Picture Show* decades later, contributed immeasurably to the deeper, often obsessive connection that the film elicited in audiences over the years.

"Our whole little crowd would go and sit together in the balcony, and when Victor Laszlo said, 'You fought against the Fascists in Spain,' we would cheer," recalled cultural critic Todd Gitlin of his years as an undergraduate at Harvard in the late 1950s and early '60s. His initial attraction to the film had to do with how well it spoke to the young-activist zeitgeist, providing a kind of mythic bedrock to the students that filled the 300-seat auditorium of the Brattle. "If you were to diagram the moral density of the film," he told me, "it's very thick." Its core question, as he sees it, remained hauntingly relevant: "What does it take to be a good person in a monstrous age?" Poet Honor Moore, who attended Radcliffe in the mid-1960s, recounted seeing *Casablanca* at the Brattle around those years. It was the era of the civil rights movement, the beginning of the peace movement. "Everybody would pile into the theater, and there was a great air of excitement," she told me. "When the moments came, there would be a kind of vibration, and then we would all cheer and clap and sing along." Her classmates, not all of them cinephiles or activists, would shout out their favorite lines; given that the films were shown during reading period and exams, there was a lot of pent-up energy. "It was a kind of exuberance," Moore added, "I think that the 'Marseillaise' moment got connected somehow to the emergent spirit of the '60s. It was a defining and defiant moment." Inside the Brattle Theatre, there was a popular student haunt called the Blue Parrot Café and a Club Casablanca cocktail bar, which marked the beginning of other such *Casablanca*-themed establishments that popped up across the globe, from Philadelphia and Berlin all the way to Panajachel, Guatemala.

On the West Coast, at Stanford University, a sampling of student observations on the film during the late 1960s and early '70s was gathered by a recent graduate of the college named Walter Bougere. Screenwriter Howard Koch incorporated excerpts of these student comments in the epilogue that he wrote to his 1973 *Casablanca* anthology, which offered for the first time the published screenplay and an assortment of essays, reviews, and related materials. "When Captain Renault, after that long pause, tells his troops to round up the usual suspects," notes Jack Kenealy, an eighteen-year-old student who had seen the film twice, speaking as if he could have been describing the student audience at the Brattle, "it was impossible to keep back a wild applause. It was just engulfing. There was ecstatic joy. The whole theatre at that point went up in a large cheer. It was a kind of universal thing." Koch goes on to cite a quip made much earlier in the century by Havelock Ellis, "Art is the recreation of the world after the heart's desire," to explain how "the young people of today are obviously searching for a new set of values nearer to their 'heart's desire.'"

At a time when the war in Vietnam was still smoldering, and when opposition to America's military aggression was continuing to build, especially among students, the unsullied patriotism expressed in the film came across as startlingly fresh and completely removed from the toxic political culture of the day. After watching the film for the first time, a twenty-four year-old nursery school teacher named Myrl Manley offered the following observation:

> The thing that bothered me most in the whole film was that I felt a real surge of fervor when they started singing "The Marseillaise." I really wanted to stand up with all of them. [. . .] It would be nice if I could stand up with them and sing with them but I can't because I know what they're singing is out of key with what I hear. The need is to have something outside of ourselves that we believe in, that we're willing to come together for and share that sense of brotherhood. And I guess that is what feeds into the counter-culture. The feeling is that we're working toward something that we mutually believe in and that we can work together for. Even if we don't know where we're going, we know the direction is good.

Young moviegoers of the 1960s and '70s found in the film what was absent in their world. "Maybe it's an emotion we're starved for," says one student, "a luxury other generations have been able to afford but we have to go without." Likewise, a political activist, who had watched the film three times, observed: "*Casablanca* is the kind of film that makes a radical feel he's part of the mainstream."

Although in the epilogue to his anthology Koch does not mask his general lament for what he sees as the lost art of storytelling, and the lack of emotional investment that moviegoers of the early 1970s seem to have in their films, he expresses nothing short of glee that students and other young people are discovering *Casablanca* for the first (or even for the twelfth) time. "Like pilgrims, they go back time and again to a film made thirty years ago, a simple melodrama," he writes in his concluding lines, "to find an emotional release and to renew their hope for a more humanistic society of the future. Perhaps they are telling us something important."

While the film may have spoken—and continues to speak—to viewers across generations, it hasn't escaped its share of criticism along the way. In March 1979, the writer and critic Dwight Macdonald and his filmmaker son Nick, then ages seventy-two and thirty-four, spent a memorable evening at the Thalia, an old movie house on New York's Upper West Side, taking in a revival screening of *Casablanca* on a double bill with *The Big Sleep*. After watching it, the two got into a fierce debate over the film's merits. For Nick Macdonald, who had spent his college years at Harvard in the 1960s attending the occasional Bogart festival at the Brattle and who in the meantime had committed himself to a career of independent filmmaking, the movie was little more than standard-issue Hollywood product, "unoriginal and lots of cornball." His father, however, who liked to play devil's advocate, thought of *Casablanca* as "a good, bad movie with style." That sort of critical qualification, a "good, bad movie"—emphasizing entertainment value over aesthetic achievement, a guilty pleasure of sorts—has become a relatively common rhetorical reflex among critics, even those who cherish it deeply. "Though not the best movie ever," wrote *The Philadelphia Inquirer* film critic Carrie Rickey in 1992 on the eve of the film's fiftieth-anniversary celebration, "*Casablanca* is the best friend among American films."

AROUND THE SAME TIME that the Brattle screenings became such a remarkably popular tradition, on the other side of the Atlantic, critics from *Cahiers du cinéma* were beginning to rediscover American cinema, particularly the work of renegade directors who fit into their newfangled conception of *la politique des auteurs*, a somewhat romanticized notion of the filmmaker as singular artist. The Bogie cult soon took effect—the *Cahiers* circle was especially fond of his work with directors Howard Hawks and John Huston—and yet the French critics were less inclined to embrace the films he made with Curtiz, who was widely viewed as more of a factory assembly-man than an artist. In 1968, adapting the *Cahiers* model in his enormously influential work *The American Cinema*, Andrew Sarris branded *Casablanca* "the most decisive exception to the auteur theory," a work that, as one of Hollywood's "happiest of happy accidents," lacked a deliberate and definitive signature style. "*Casablanca* achieved its cult status through the public rather than the critics," contends Peter Wollen, highlighting its exceptional status, "whereas *Vertigo* (1958) or *The Searchers* (1956) were made into cult films by the *Cahiers* team themselves." In other words, *Casablanca* was much more a matter of popular taste than that of a rarefied group who saw themselves as the true arbiters of the cinematic vanguard.

When French filmmaker François Truffaut, who began his career writing for *Cahiers du cinéma,* was living in Los Angeles in the summer of 1973, he was approached by a representative at Warners about doing a remake of *Casablanca*. He responded:

> It's not my favorite Humphrey Bogart film, and I rate it much lower than *The Big Sleep* or *To Have and Have Not*. So, the thought of directing a new version should logically scare me less and I realize the film would take place in a French ambience. However, I know that American students adore this film, especially the dialogue, and they know every line by heart. I would be equally intimidated by the actors; I can't imagine Jean-Paul Belmondo or Catherine Deneuve succeeding Humphrey Bogart and Ingrid Bergman. I know that people see these things differently in America. The idea of directing a remake doesn't shock me, provided it's a very good, bold story which could be treated with greater candor today, and a title that doesn't carry too much weight in the history of American cinema.

Needless to say, Truffaut never took on the project for Warner Bros., and there never would be a French remake.

Back in Paris, from 1947 onward, *Casablanca* was regularly shown in the city's grand picture palaces and even as part of occasional retrospectives and classic Hollywood series at the Cinémathèque Française. It quickly garnered wide admiration among the masses, earning yet another wave of ardent appreciation. In his slender volume of aphoristic musings on the film, *Casablanca: Movies and Memory*, French anthropologist Marc Augé, who first saw the film as a young boy soon after the war and watched it countless times in the Parisian revival houses as an adult, returns to *Casablanca* as an occasion to remember his childhood and, by extension, to recall the foundational myths of postwar France. Bound up in the film's story—and the experience of watching and rewatching it—is the story of Augé's uncle, who served under Vichy as an officer in the navy in Morocco and who, with fortuitous good sense and timing, shifted his allegiance to the Allies and Free France. (Augé remembers how a photo of Pétain was suddenly removed from his parents and grandparents' bedroom.) There, too, are the memories of hearing German airplanes, even seeing the black crosses on their wings, as they flew over the French countryside. "Today," he writes, "the city of my childhood dreams exists only in the Latin Quarter, in Curtiz's film." He then adds, commenting directly on his most recent of repeat viewings: "Louis Renault and Rick, the Frenchman and the American, had just concluded their friendship pact. I was the last to leave, lost in dreams and even moved as I always am when I see *Casablanca* yet again."

On both shores, over successive decades, *Casablanca* has invited intense personal identification, often brought about by habitual repeat viewing, which exceeds nearly all other film-viewing experiences. As Augé puts it elsewhere in his musings on the film, "It's because we need to believe in love, in heroism, and in self-denial that we instinctively adhere to the most romantic version of the story and, in the secrecy of our memory, give way to the intimate and personal montage of our film, this film whose title, *Casablanca,* flickers every time we pronounce it, that hereafter resonates in us as if it were a memory coming out of a distant past." Like those throngs of moviegoing pilgrims at the Brattle, Augé would return to it seeking spiritual communion or cinematic meditation. "To see a film again is to recover a past that retains all the vivacity of the present," he writes, adding, "it is always the same movie that the lover of film rediscovers, including the same characters and the same actors."

Augé was in his twenties by the time that the French new wave burst onto the scene. Bogie had died by then, but he was far from forgotten. "Bogart is a man with a past," wrote critic André Bazin in *Cahiers du cinéma* the month after the actor's death. "When he comes into a film, it is already 'the morning after,' his face scarred with what he has seen, and his steps heavy for all that he has learned." In Jean-Luc Godard's *À bout de souffle* (*Breathless*; 1960), the romantic lead played by Jean-Paul Belmondo spends much of his screen time fashioning himself after Bogie and mastering the movie star's gestures. Near the start of the film, after hot-wiring an American sedan and successfully escaping the cops, Belmondo's

Michel stops deliberately in front of a Parisian cinema. There he stares good and long at a poster of *The Harder They Fall* (1956), Bogart's final film, coolly intoning, "Bogie." He then blows a few drags of smoke at the lobby cards and production stills kept behind glass outside the movie house, and rubs his lips ever so languidly—a single hard-boiled gesture he repeats throughout the picture—as if to conjure a French reincarnation of Sam Spade or Rick Blaine.

Even in such foundational and formally unconventional French new wave films as Alain Resnais's *Hiroshima Mon Amour* (1959), a dizzyingly elliptical romance set in postwar Japan, there are subtle nods to the enduring classics of 1940s Hollywood, in particular *Casablanca.* In *Hiroshima*'s final minutes, the core themes and emotional architecture of the Bogart-Bergman romance somehow bubble up to the surface. "Here is an 'impossible' love story between two people struggling with the imagery of a distant war," writes James Monaco in his book on Resnais. "At the end of this romantic, poignant movie about leavetakings and responsibilities, the two fateful lovers meet in a café. Resnais gives us a rare establishing shot of the location. 'He' is going to meet 'She' for the last time at a bar called 'The Casablanca'—right here in the middle of Hiroshima!"

For the late Italian writer and literary critic Umberto Eco, who presented his extensive semiotic analysis of the film—after watching it over and over again throughout the 1960s, '70s and into the '80s—in "Casablanca: Cult Movies and Intertextual Collage," that is indeed the formidable power of *Casablanca.* In his critical estimation, the film both anticipates future films and builds on those of the past, forming a vital chain of what he calls "intertextual archetypes." While *Casablanca* may not be a work of art, it is very much a cult movie. It is beloved by its audiences in far-flung corners of the world. "The spectators quote the best lines before the actors say them," as Eco notes, underscoring a telltale sign of cinephilia. The film, he goes on to say, is far greater than the sum of its parts: "I think that in order to transform a work into a cult object one must be able to break, dislocate, unhinge it so that one can remember only parts of it, irrespective of their original relationship with the whole. . . . only an unhinged movie survives as a disconnected series of images, of peaks, of visual icebergs."

In laying out his definition of a cult movie, Eco extracts some two dozen archetypes from the film—the globe, the Promised Land, Purgatory, the Barbarians, the Magic Key, the Magic Horse, the Game of Life and Death, among many others—that reveal its intertwined, symphonic, and seemingly universal nature. Eco then arrives at his trenchant summation:

> *Casablanca* is a cult movie precisely because all the archetypes are there, because each actor repeats a part played on other occasions, and because human beings live not "real" life but life as stereotypically portrayed in previous films. *Casablanca* carries the sense of déjà vu to such a degree that the addressee is ready to see in it what happened after as well. It is not until *To Have and Have Not* that Bogey plays the role of the Hemingway hero, but here he appears "already" loaded with

> Hemingwayesque connotations simply because Rick fought in Spain. Peter Lorre trails reminiscences of Fritz Lang, Conrad Veidt's German officer emanates a faint whiff of *The Cabinet of Dr. Caligari*. He is not a ruthless, technological Nazi; he is a nocturnal and diabolical Caesar [i.e., Cesare from *Caligari*].

Eco goes on to state, in an oft-quoted formulation from the essay, "*Casablanca* became a cult movie because it is not *one* movie. It is 'movies.'" In other words, it is its "movie-ness" that helps to elicit a cult response. Without commenting directly on Eco's assertion, anthropologist Augé gives his own spin on this idea, suggesting in his meditations on the picture that "to remember one film also means remembering film itself, that is, remembering images, somewhat as if the technique of cinema had from the beginning operated the mental labor that selects perceptions in order to turn them into memories, as if in some way it had accomplished the labor of memory."

Perhaps the most extreme, if also most comical personal identification with the film and its cultic power came in the enormously successful 1969 Broadway production of *Play it Again, Sam*, written by and starring Woody Allen. The story of a maladjusted film critic who turns to Bogie for life lessons, Allen's work emerged from the same general climate of impassioned, youthful film culture as the Brattle screenings and their European counterparts. The action begins inside the Greenwich Village apartment of Allan Felix (Allen), "one of life's great watchers," who's gazing at *The Maltese Falcon* on television—by the time we get to the second act, we learn that Felix holds something of a local record for having watched the film twelve times in two weeks. Hailing from the same family tree that, over the course of Allen's film career, would produce a long line of urban neurotics, schlemiels, and endless variations on the Jewish nebbish, Felix is described in the stage directions as "a slight, bespectacled young man of about twenty-eight or nine who looks as if he stepped out of a Jules Feiffer cartoon." He spends his days, when not banging on the keys of his manual typewriter and filing film reviews, indulging in the assorted fantasies and daydreams of a *luftmensch* or perhaps a distant relative of Walter Mitty. Theater critic Brendan Gill called him "a cringingly miserable little twirp of an intellectual" in his otherwise affirmative review of the play in *The New Yorker.*

Inside his apartment, a large photo of Bogart adorning a prominent wall of his living room stares down at Felix. Soon enough, after Felix bemoans his spectacularly failed marriage, the ghost of Bogie (really actor Jerry Lacy doing his best to reanimate Bogie's spirit), appears before him. He delivers a few mildly contrived lines with cloying dramatic swagger ("There's no secret, kid. Dames are simple."), causing Felix immediately to cramp up. "I'm not like you," he protests. "At the end of *Casablanca*, when you lost Ingrid Bergman, weren't you crushed?" Bogart retorts, in hyperbolic Rick Blaine mode, "Nothing that a little bourbon and soda wouldn't fix." As the story continues, Felix attempts in vain to tap into his own inner Bogart. He goes on a series of disastrous dates, most of them mismatched set-ups by his dear friends the real estate hound Dick Christie (Tony Roberts) and his fashion art director wife Linda (Diane

Haunted by Bogart, Woody Allen in a still from the 1969 Broadway production of Play It Again, Sam.

Keaton), but remains chronically unattached. In his dreams, magically coached by Bogie and serenaded by Dooley Wilson's "As Time Goes By," he's far more successful ("Oh, Allan, you are fantastic," crows one of his imaginary lovers).

Throughout its three snappy acts, the play is shot through with a high-voltage current of 1960s cinephilia. Felix not only models his speech and behavior on his beloved film idol but organizes his life around an extreme form of movie worship. Left alone with Linda while Dick is out of town on a business trip, his first impulse is to suggest, "There's a new Godard film at the Sutton" (his ex-wife's major complaint in their divorce: "All we ever do is watch movies"). When Linda and Felix, two lonely neurotic hypochondriacs cut from the same cloth, finally kiss at the close of the second act, the music returns, following the by now widely appropriated misquotation from *Casablanca* that gives the play its infectious title: "Play it again, Sam!" When the moment arrives for Felix to own up to Dick about his indiscretions, he makes the scripted sacrifice, sending Linda off with her husband and reciting verbatim the famous speech Rick delivers on the fog-drenched tarmac. When Linda expresses wonderment, Felix admits sheepishly, "It's from *Casablanca.* I've waited my whole life to say it."

The show ran for more than a year. Owing to its success on Broadway, a British stage production—with Dudley Moore as Allan Felix and the setting moved from Greenwich Village to a flat in northwest London—opened at the Globe Theatre in September 1969. Soon after came a national tour stopping at cities across the United States, with Red Buttons starring as Felix at the Blackstone Theater in Chicago in September 1970, and Bob Denver taking his turn as the lead at the Playhouse on the Mall in Paramus, New Jersey, in September 1971.

A year later, the ultimate encore appeared in the form of Herbert Ross's film adaptation, with a screenplay by Allen. Rights to the play had been sold for the princely sum of $350,000 in 1968, before it had even hit the stage, and the film's commercial viability, hitched as it was to the enduring fame and fortune of *Casablanca,* was a foregone conclusion for its producers at Paramount. In addition to the obvious name recognition, the film, starring Allen and original cast members Keaton, Roberts, and Lacy, hoped to exploit the current hippie zeitgeist in the wake of the Summer of Love by switching the location from New York City to San Francisco, where Allan Felix now lives his movie-obsessed life amid the din of West Coast bohemia, miniskirts, long-haired bikers, groovy swingers and all. It worked. "The best compliment I can pay Mr. Allen's comedy," wrote theater critic Kevin Kelly in the *Boston Globe*, recognizing the pervasive tendency in the late 1960s to rebroadcast Bogie films on the little screen, "is to advise you to skip the late-late shows on television in favor of him, even if they happen to be *The Maltese Falcon*, *To Have and Have Not*, or even for that matter *Casablanca*."

As such, the late-show broadcast of *The Maltese Falcon* that sets off the theatrical rendition is crucially replaced by the final scenes of *Casablanca*, projected on a large repertory screen, with the slack-jawed Felix seated in the audience in a state of total rapture. While he watches, transfixed, the reflection of the film flickers in the lenses of his thick black glasses. He grins contentedly, mouths a few of the words, and raises his eyebrows nervously in approval. As he leaves the downtown theater, still under the spell of that most famous of classic Hollywood film finales, he tries to snap out of it ("Who am I kidding? I'm not like that. I never was. I never will be. That's strictly the movies"). He retreats to his nearby apartment, a veritable shrine of movie love littered with books on Godard and Bogart, lobby cards, production stills, and walls of film posters—many of them, like the oversize one of *Across the Pacific* that hangs above his bed, starring Bogie—where the unforgiving glare of his real life is compensated for by a fantasy world of shadow and light.

As in the play, a cresting wave of cinephilia and proto-film-geekdom washes over the movie. Felix works as a projectionist at Cinema 40, a fictional variation of Amos Vogel's renowned Cinema 16 film society in New York City, and plans his evenings around such late-show broadcasts as *The Big Sleep*. When he feels uneasy on one of his many ill-fated dates, in a hilariously desperate comfort-seeking gesture, Felix suggests checking out an Erich von Stroheim festival. And when Felix and Linda begin to kindle their adulterous romance, Linda proposes that they watch Ida Lupino's *The Bigamist* (1953). The plot of the film, like the play, hinges on Felix's ability to become Bogart, to internalize the language and set of codes he's learned in his fantasy conversations with that god of all film gods.

Even beyond the plot twists and set pieces, all paths eventually lead back to *Casablanca*. Felix's chance to prove himself worthy as a man, to assert himself, comes in his ability to recite Rick's famous lines on the tarmac, and to send Linda off on a plane to Cleveland—not quite as romantic as Lisbon, but this is the 1970s, after all—with her husband. The two stand together, drenched in thick fog and wearing their *Casablanca*-inspired garb, bidding farewell while a few sentimental notes from "As Time Goes By" and Dooley Wilson's throaty voice reverberate in the background. The passing of the three decades that both separate and connect the two films is almost palpable.

A year later, when the film of *Play It Again, Sam* premiered in London, where the cult of *Casablanca* had long since taken hold, critic Peter Buckley challenged the main Ross-Allen cinematic conceit. He wrote, "Perhaps the biggest error in judgment—and the one that shows up the weakness of the film—was to start and end *Play It Again, Sam* with clips and restagings of *Casablanca,* and thus align it totally with a perfection it could never hope to achieve." Rather than bolstering the loving homage, in his eyes, such scenes only point to the conspicuous deficiencies of the later film. "All that's left for *Sam* to do is to send up *Casablanca* (with affection of course) and that's so easy it's impossible," he asserted. "What is so fascinating, and sad, is that the straight scenes from the earlier film, the dialogue and the emotions are played full front and they send warm waves and chilly tingles up one's spine, yet when the same scene is done in the '70s version, it's played for cute laughs. A sad commentary on the decline of style and the way we make films now." The American film historian Leo Braudy made a similar point about the film in *The World in a Frame: What We See in Films,* his important book of 1976: "It works as nostalgia and even inspiration, but finally it is only 'played again,' not really re-created as a viable personal style."

When asked many years later about his choice to highlight *Casablanca,* Allen made it seem like something he'd merely done on a lark. "It's one of thousands of movies I've seen," Allen recalled in a 1990 letter, "and the use of Humphrey Bogart in my stage play *Play It Again, Sam* was accidental and arbitrary, undoubtedly inspired by one of the popular posters of him at the time and reinforced by the fact that he was one of a number of standard symbols of macho-romantic movie stars." As recently as 2014, when a first edition of his play was being auctioned at a PEN International benefit at Christie's, Allen disavowed the work altogether, telling a reporter from the *Wall Street Journal,* "*Play It Again, Sam* is a junky play. It is typical commercial claptrap and is nothing I'm proud of." He added, "I wrote it when I was younger and would not do it the same way—or any way again." The only redeeming feature of the play, as Allen characterized it, was the chance it offered him to establish his enduring personal and professional friendship with actor Tony Roberts and to initiate his romance with Diane Keaton.

The same year that Woody Allen debuted his rebellious play, Pauline Kael published an influential essay, "Trash, Art, and the Movies," in *Harper*'s magazine. In it, she offered sustained critical reflections on the current state of film culture, on the practices of moviegoing and moviemaking, on the hidden virtues of "bad movies"—her famously backhanded compliment of *Casablanca*, as "a movie that demonstrates how entertaining a bad movie can be," still relevant—and her unabashed distaste for some of the "good" ones. "Like those cynical heroes who were idealists before they discovered that the world was more rotten than they had been led to expect," she begins, as if offering a wink to Rick Blaine and other screen roles Bogart inhabited, "we're just about all of us displaced persons, 'a long way from home.' When we feel defeated, when we imagine we could now perhaps settle for home and what it represents, that home no longer exists. But there are the movie houses." Going to the movies, suggests Kael, not only may serve on occasion to lift the spirits, but offers us a chance to escape, temporarily, from the hidebound responsibilities that bog us down in the real world. "Movies—a tawdry corrupt art for a tawdry corrupt world—fit the way we feel," she observes. "The world doesn't work the way the schoolbooks said it did and we are different from what our parents and teachers expected us to be. Movies are our cheap and easy expression, the sullen art of displaced persons." It's no wonder that movies then had a special appeal to students (even if Kael had very little nice to say about *The Graduate*), who were still heading in droves to theaters like the Brattle.

Not far from Cambridge, on the campus of Brandeis University, in Waltham, Massachusetts, budding film producer Stan Brooks was a college junior and chairman of the campus Film Commission in the academic year 1978–1979. His chief responsibility was programming the Friday night film screenings that took place at the Levin Ballroom. During his first years at Brandeis, he had visited Cambridge to attend several of the Brattle screenings. He was already a zealous

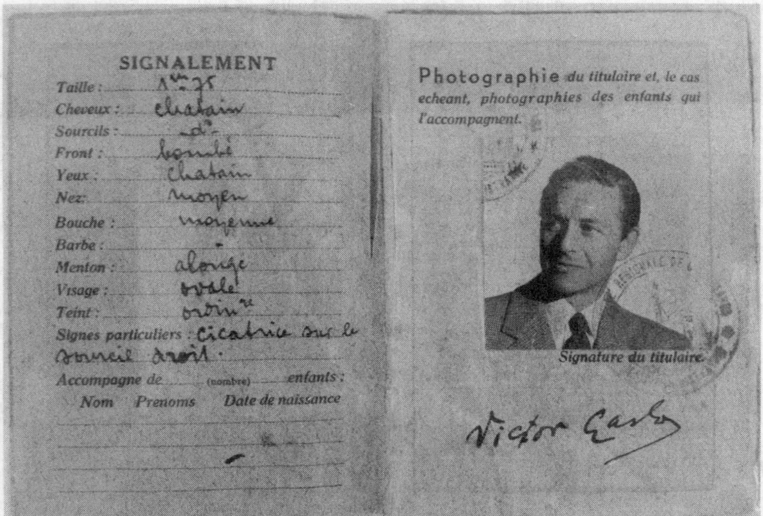

Laszlo's passport.

Casablanca devotee—later in life, at an auction at Sotheby's, he would even buy the studio-made passport used by Victor Laszlo in the film—and had also seen *Play It Again, Sam* several times. "It was during the second semester," he told me, "I just came up with this idea cutting together the two movies frame for frame so that it's one movie. It was amazing to me that at the beginning of *Play It Again, Sam* is exactly the end of *Casablanca*, and then you pull back and you see the credits, then you pull back, and you see Woody." For Brooks, this was nothing short of a cinematic coup—merging one of his all-time favorite films with one of the great recent tributes to it. That Friday night, the moviegoers who filled the seats of Brandeis's main auditorium may not have immediately noticed the clever sleight of hand ("I didn't get too many, 'Oh, wow, that was awesome' pats on the back," he recounted), the spliced reels flowing seamlessly into one another on the old Bell & Howell 16mm projector, but that didn't matter. Either way, they had the spell of *Casablanca* cast over them, as they witnessed an extraordinary mash-up reel decades before YouTube.

The spell continued into the next decade. In 1981, in a TV segment on CBS's *60 Minutes* called "The Greatest Movie Ever Made," commentator Harry Reasoner tried as best he could to sum up *Casablanca* in just four clipped, declarative sentences: "Boy meets girl. Boy loses girl. Boy gets girl back again. Boy gives up girl for humanity's sake." That simple formula may have been what drove the NBC executives to try, one more time, to launch a *Casablanca* TV series, this go-round with David Soul, who had recently starred as Hutch in the popular cop series *Starsky and Hutch* (1975–1979), as Rick Blaine. "I think it's a mistake, because *Casablanca* without Bogie, Bergman and Claude Rains just won't be *Casablanca*," original screenwriter Koch warned at the time, forgetting to mention that he himself was still toying with the idea of a sequel. The series, which premiered in April 1983, lasted just five episodes (and yet somehow picked up an Emmy award for cinematography that year).

Rather than writing a conventional sequel to the film, or a script of any kind for that matter, film critic and historian David Thomson cooked up the idea of creating a number of

David Soul as Rick Blaine in the 1983 television production of Casablanca.

written vignettes, fictionalizing the imagined afterlives of the film's three lead characters in his intriguingly cryptic novel *Suspects*. "It is film criticism and movie history," he tells his readers in a note that precedes the text, "but it is a fiction in which the material (the life) is the world created in a genre of movies. This is not just a way of warning readers of the rules of the game. It is a reminder that fiction has no hold unless we believe in it, and that movies use the exact poignant imprint of so many glances and faces to make a dream."

In Thomson's rendering, after departing from Casablanca in 1941, Ilsa Lund makes her way with Laszlo to New York City, where she becomes a foreign-language teacher, provides the subtitles for early Ingmar Bergman pictures, dates writer Delmore Schwartz, and eventually serves as the personal assistant of U.N. Secretary General Dag Hammarskjöld, in whose company she dies in 1961 en route to a humanitarian mission in the Congo. As if that weren't enough, in the same chapter on Ilsa, Thomson presents a fictionalized researcher named Gail Levin who speculates that Ilsa may have also posed, half nude, for Edward Hopper's 1949 painting *High Noon*. Thomson then offers some new backstory on Ilsa (she spent a year in Nazi Germany, teaching Swedish and doing her part to break up a few anti-Jewish street battles in Berlin, before transferring to a school in Paris), while revising a few of the film's narrative threads (Rick serves not only as a lover in Paris, but as a mentor teaching her the classics of Western Marxism, and as for her relationship with the underground leader: "In truth, she never warmed to Laszlo and had early misgivings about his genuineness"). Upon arriving in New York, Ilsa gets swept up in Laszlo's anti-fascist work, but they quickly grow estranged. "It was an undoubted relief for her when Laszlo died, of emphysema, in 1952," writes Thomson, returning us in the next clause to that enthralling blur of fiction and cinema, riffing on Henreid's famous trick immortalized in *Now, Voyager*: "He had kept up a vulgar society trick of smoking two cigarettes at the same time."

Thomson devotes a chapter each to Laszlo and Rick, explaining in the first instance how the freedom fighter continued his political engagement in the New World, becoming a suspect of the FBI, and eventually giving a quasi-Brechtian performance before the House Un-American Activities Committee, and in the second how Rick grew up in Nebraska, played quarterback, aspired to read Lenin in the original Russian, and fought in Spain with the Abraham Lincoln Brigade. Lazslo's relationship to Ilsa, as *Suspects* has it, was as theatrical as his relationship to the anti-fascist movement in America, where he received top billing for as long as he could. Rick wasn't much better off himself: "The affair with Ilsa was hopeless; she had all these causes, perhaps Rick used her to remind himself of all he'd lost." Rick eventually flees Paris for Casablanca, where he opens his café. The great plot twist comes with Louis Renault: "Apparently he took one long look at Rick and knew he was homosexual underneath all the brooding and the sneers about women." After the murder of Major Strasser, the two skip town for Marrakesh, where they live out the war years in a general state of romantic bliss, Louis caring for Rick, the two of them "laughing together over reports of the red scare in America."

Thomson's novel succeeds, in its lapidary, compressed

form, in capturing the raw essence of the three characters and then allowing that essence to spawn a set of new stories. These fictionalized characters could not exist without their cinematic counterparts, nor without the obsessively creative, film-saturated mind of their creator. "*Suspects* is a book that could have been written by the Woody Allen character in *Play It Again, Sam* or the title character in Walker Percy's *The Moviegoer*," asserted film biographer and critic Scott Eyman when the book came out in 1985, "hopeless addicts of the better-than-reality reel life of movies." We are all, on some level, seduced by the dream world of movies, by the neat story lines as well the mysterious gaps and omissions. In conversation with the *New York Post* film critic Lou Lumenick in 2012, Thomson said specifically of *Casablanca*, "Part of the reason the film is so popular is because the ending is so enigmatic." Whether that makes it necessary to launch a feature-length sequel, however, is another matter.

Around the same time that Thomson completed his novel, screenwriter Howard Koch was developing a new treatment, which by 1988 he would call *Return to Casablanca*. In that sketch, Victor and Ilsa search in vain for Rick after he and Renault have joined the Free French in their battle against Nazi Field Marshal Rommel and his desert battalions in North Africa. The big twist in Koch's version: "After leaving Casablanca for America, Ilsa learned she was pregnant. She gave birth to a boy who grew up in America. The real father of the boy, it turns out, was not Laszlo but Rick. He was conceived the night Ilsa came to Rick's place to plead for the Letters of Transit." The boy is given his father's name, carries his legacy ("he grew up to be a handsome, tough-tender young man reminiscent of his father"), and as a twenty-year-old returns to Casablanca to retrace his father's steps, aided by a waiter who once worked at the Café Américain. Young Rick learns of a new movement, a local citizens' brigade with an Arab woman known as Joan at the helm. She leads a fight to hunt down the remaining "Nazi-led outlaws." In 1989, Koch's treatment was rejected by his old studio. When he died in 1995, it was left behind with his papers, silent testimony to his unremitting passion for the film.

In 1992, to celebrate the fiftieth anniversary of *Casablanca*, television mogul Ted Turner, who by then held the rights to the film, presented a high-profile screening at New York's Museum of Modern Art. In his introduction he mentioned, among other things, his past efforts in 1988 to colorize, as he had done with other black-and-white classics, a new print of *Casablanca* in the hope of having it reach a new audience. "*Casablanca* is art," insisted director Martin Scorsese on the colorization question, lifting it above its status as mere cult movie. "You don't mess around with it." (When the process was first initiated, in 1988, the head of colorization for Turner remarked: "We're doing everything except [Mickey Mouse's] *Steamboat Willie*. There are some things you just can't touch.") Bogart's son Stephen, who was present for the MoMA screening, later suggested, in a similar spirit to Scorsese, that if one is intent on colorizing a film like *Casablanca* one may as well add arms to the Venus de Milo. Also at the screening was King Hassan of Morocco, invited to represent the country that Warner Bros. had attempted to re-create on its sound stages in summer 1942. Near the close of the gala, he was given the chance to speak. What he asked, innocently enough, was whether it might not be a bad idea to try a sequel, maybe a *Casablanca 2*.

Despite the many failed, if valiant, efforts of others before him—the shelved screenplays, failed television series, and experimental fiction—former *Time* magazine music critic Michael Walsh wrote a sprawling novel, *As Time Goes By*, published in 1998 by Warner Books. When the idea was first conceived, Walsh's project was thought of as another chance to redevelop the original story—both prequel and sequel—for further Warner screen adaptations. Instead, it turned out to be a relatively conventional story, much less playful or experimental than *Suspects*, in which Rick and Ilsa reconnect in England, after having left North Africa. There they become involved in the plot to assassinate Nazi official Reinhard Heydrich, the Reich Protector of Czechoslovakia and one of the chief architects of the Final Solution. The real plot, successfully undertaken in June 1942 by British Special Operations and members of the Czech government-in-exile, had been fictionalized in Hollywood films like Fritz Lang's *Hangmen Also Die!* (1943) and Douglas Sirk's *Hitler's Madman* (1943). In Walsh's handling, it aspires to be a taut spy thriller but often falls flat.

"In today's popular culture," wrote *New York Times* critic Martin Arnold soon after Walsh's novel was published, "the journey between fast buck and sheer greed has a stopover called the sequel. Book publishing, alas, is no different from movies or television." With a colossal first printing of 250,000 copies and rights sold to fifteen separate foreign translations,

As Time Goes By had serious ambitions. "It's a great story of very brave people doing extraordinary things," commented Maureen Egen, the president of Warner Books. "It's one of the greatest unfinished love stories ever." That, however, does not guarantee success. Even before Walsh, a German novelist and screenwriter named Cornelius Fischer, who had met Julius Epstein at a film festival in Munich in 1992, had tried to peddle the idea of a novel as sequel. "Letting a German author write an update of *Casablanca*, the most Hollywood film of all time, might seem ironic," Fischer observed in 1998, after Walsh's novel had appeared. Arnold pointed to the inauspicious odds of success, given that most sequels, both literary and cinematic, tend to bomb. "It's a tough business, making a sequel work, no matter how astounding the writer."

As recently as 2012, independent producer Cass Warner, granddaughter of studio cofounder Harry Warner, announced plans to adapt the synopsis *Return to Casablanca*, based on the treatment that Koch had written in the late 1980s. Warner took a screenwriting class from Koch in Santa Barbara in 1988, and she began interviewing him for her documentary project *The Brothers Warner* (2007). Despite the countless obstacles she has faced, including lack of sufficient backing and widespread skepticism, Warner continues to hope the film will be made by her company, the aptly titled Warner Sisters. Admittedly, not everyone is bold enough like Cass Warner or Michael Walsh or David Thomson—or even Fredrick Stephani, at the start—to offer up their own version of what happens after that famous walk, rain-soaked runway still glistening, into fog and mist. "I don't want anybody messing around with my favorite movie in any way, shape or form," critic Leonard Maltin told Lou Lumenick after Cass Warner announced her plan. Similarly, in her recent book, *I Do and I Don't: A History of Marriage in the Movies,* film historian Jeanine Basinger asks, "Did anyone want to imagine that Ilsa and Victor Laszlo's plane would crash? That they would divorce? That Captain Renault would step on a land mine and Rick would go back to America and open a hot dog stand in Jersey? Of course not. Everyone wanted to leave them in all that glamorous fog on the Casablanca tarmac, fat brims pulled down low, morals ramped up high, no future necessary."

Chapter 7

A BEAUTIFUL FRIENDSHIP

Casablanca remains, intriguingly and seductively, a story without an ending. That, after all, is what Ilsa tells Rick when trying to explain what happened before she jilted him on that Paris train platform. It's also what he later tells her when he tries to come up with the right narrative of their romance. But most crucially, it's what we, as viewers, are faced with after Bogie utters the film's last line about "the beginning of a beautiful friendship" and then disappears with Claude Rains into a thick blanket of fog and mist. This open-ended quality makes us all that much more inclined to return to the film, which plays on in our minds, the same way we return to other cherished stories told among close friends, lovers, and family members.

Part of the great appeal of rewatching the film—"one of those rare films that actually improves with repeat viewings," as Roger Ebert once observed—is to indulge in the satisfying, childish pleasure of repetition: to relive and recite the comforting lines of dialogue, and to indulge in the fantasy of the characters as our dearest companions. "My first response to it," remarks Leonard Schwarz, one of the interviewees in the survey of *Casablanca* viewers done at Stanford in the late 1960s and early '70s, "is like greeting an old friend. My mother always forgets how good it is until I make her watch it on the late show. She never sees the point to start watching it and then she can't leave it." Writing in *The New Republic* in 1992, Stanley Kauffmann offered his affectionate reflections on the film upon watching it fifty years after its debut: "One more reward, not unique to *Casablanca*, but certainly part of its pleasure—a peculiar familiarity. As I watched the actors take their places in the story . . . I felt a sense of community. I *knew* those men. They used to visit me every four or five months, in films called by one name or another, but the titles didn't matter—I knew *them*." Even for viewers without a deeper acquaintance with the film, an uncannily familiar attachment can quickly take hold. "When I think of it, I feel warm, like when I think about a good friend of mine," commented a first-time viewer in the Stanford survey.

For more seasoned scholars and critics, the friendship may stretch back considerably further in time. "At age twelve I was deeply impressed by Ingrid Bergman, walking toward an airplane on a misty runway, the tears on her face just glimpsed beneath the large hat that shadowed her face" observes James Card in his "Confessions of a *Casablanca* Cultist." He continues, "At age twenty seeing it again in a theatrical revival, I thought it was as good as I had remembered, not something I had outgrown. Later, in graduate school I saw it at the old New Yorker theater on Broadway in a showing memorable for a curious interaction of film and audience, who applauded the first appearance of each major performer, as if the film were a live stage presentation. Perhaps that response should have identified the reaction of a cult, but at the time I had never heard the term associated with film." Vaguely akin to the protagonist of Shel Silverstein's famous children's book *The Giving Tree*, Card grows old with the film, returning to it at each phase of his life (unlike Silverstein's protagonist, however, he doesn't demand of the film the tragic sacrifice demanded of the tree). "Later, as a college professor," he adds, "I have enjoyed introducing the film to students who whoop with gleeful surprise at lines like, 'Major Strasser has been shot. (Pause.) Round up the usual suspects.' Finally after repeated viewings on television, I realize it is a film of which I, like so many others, never tire."

Born the year that the film went into general release, sociologist and critic Todd Gitlin has also matured with *Casablanca*. "This is a film from my parents' generation," he told me, "and I'm aware of that. So in some way it's a bridge." He continued, "Their world became more palpable, richer, and more significant to me as a result of this stylized, incandescent representation of it. And that must have been something going on generationally. My classmates had parents who had been in the war." Not only its function as steady companion, but also its overall artistic significance has increased with time. "*Casablanca* is at the very peak of American cultural achievement in the twentieth century," Gitlin asserted. "It certainly is as definitive of a core American fable as *Gatsby*." In his incisive chapter on the film, in *A Certain Tendency of the Hollywood Cinema*, film historian Robert B. Ray fleshes out the *Great Gatsby* comparison. "Like Jay Gatsby (another hero with mysterious origins)," observes Ray, "he [Rick Blaine] was obsessed with a past that he sought simultaneously to obliterate. In maintaining this ambiguous relationship, Rick represented not only typical frontiersman, but also America itself."

In 1976, writing in *American Film* magazine, Ron Haver, film programmer at the Los Angeles County Museum, struck a similar chord when trying to describe the profound impact of the film over time: "It provides tangible evidence of not necessarily the way we were, but more important, the way we wanted to be. It is this sense of the more positive beliefs and virtues of another time that gives the film its timelessness. *Casablanca* bridges the generations, giving us a sense of the hopes of an earlier decade and reminding us that a heritage need not be lost to the passage of time."

It's the kind of movie one welcomes back each time it's broadcast on television or plays on the big screen. Critic Leonard Maltin, who first watched the film as a young boy at the Eighth Street Playhouse in New York City ("in a darkened theater, on a big screen, larger than life, with a sympatico audience," as he recounted for me), regards *Casablanca* in a class of its own. "To me, it remains the perfect movie. It's no wonder that it's held up as a model screenplay; but it's not just a great screenplay, it's a great movie." Quite fittingly, the third edition of Maltin's *Classic Movie Guide*, published in 2015, has an iconic shot of Rick and Ilsa in tender embrace on its cover.

In 1998, when the American Film Institute polled fifteen hundred industry leaders, film critics, artists, and studio professionals to choose the one hundred greatest American films ever, *Casablanca* was topped only by Orson Welles's masterpiece *Citizen Kane* (1941). Although the two Hollywood classics could not be formally more different—one the collective reward of the studio system, the other a virtuoso performance by an ambitious, young auteur—they frequently vie for the coveted top spot in the American motion-picture pantheon. At the close of his audio commentary made for the 2002 DVD release of *Casablanca*, Roger Ebert made the apt observation: "When asked what is the greatest film of all time, I say *Citizen Kane*. When asked what is the movie you like the best, I say *Casablanca*." A decade later *New Yorker* critic David Denby flatly asserted, "*Casablanca* is the most sociable, the most companionable film ever made." He added, "In the entire history of American cinema, only a few other movies—*Gone With the Wind*, *The Wizard of Oz*, *The Godfather*—have been loved as much and as well as *Casablanca*." Such views are not unique to Denby, nor to those critics who have come before or after him. That same year, director Steven Spielberg remarked in *"Casablanca": An Unlikely Classic*, the short documentary feature by Gary Leva made for the 2012 DVD release: "*Casablanca* is one of the best-told narratives I've ever witnessed as an audience [member] and as a fan."

For a number of years now, scholars and critics, not to mention the legions of fans, have tried to grasp what makes *Casablanca* endure. "People who have never seen the movie know the lines," commented film historian Jeanine Basinger. "For a film to be like *Casablanca*, it has to be both deeply of its own time and very loosely outside of its own time." She added, "There's a quality there that the thing it's about is so totally 1942, 1943, and yet the way those '42, '43 things are being presented to us is very much 2016. The nostalgia of loss, of cynicism, dying to be romantic, romantics having to be cynical because of the times they're in—all those things last. There really is no other film like it." Or as critic Kenneth Turan, who first watched *Casablanca* in the 1960s as a student at Swarthmore College outside Philadelphia, writes in his 2014 encomium included in *Not to Be Missed: Fifty-Four Favorites from a Lifetime of Film*, "The finished film manages the feat of being as political as it is romantic, a story where humor, idealism, cynicism, espionage, melodramatics, and even deadly gunplay all play a part. It's almost like a whole season of films crammed into a single 102-minute package." Elsewhere in the book, he quotes German filmmaker Werner Herzog on the power of a memorable film: it "sticks to you forever. It never leaves you. It becomes part of your existence."

Naturally, for those with familial ties to the storied production, the connection is that much more profound. Television screenwriter Anya Epstein, granddaughter of Philip and grandniece of Julius, grew up with the film in her family history and lore. Her father, Leslie, the director of the creative writing program at Boston University, has mainly carried the torch, incorporating strands of the film in his own writing (his current novel in progress bears the working title *Hill of Beans*) and carefully preserving the Oscar that his father received in 1944. Growing up in Los Angeles, Leslie Epstein used to hear his father and uncle laughing uncontrollably while crafting screenplays in their home library. "To a young boy," he once remarked, "it seemed, this writing, to be an attractive way to live one's life."

For years, Anya Epstein avoided the career path she seemed almost destined to take. "It was more of a deterrent than anything," she said of her illustrious family past. "When you have held over you this greatest movie of all time, why try?" But, having already written for successful television shows like *Homicide*, she inherited a number of leather-bound screenplays after her grandmother passed away; in them, she saw more than a few affinities between her work at NBC and that of the Epstein twins at Warners. Similarly, Monika Henreid, Paul Henreid's daughter who is a former film actress and current documentary filmmaker, continues to feel linked, both professionally and personally, to the film's legacy. "I think as far as the film itself is concerned," she told me, "people, over the generations, are attracted to it and will go back to watch it a second time, because it tells a very noble story."

"Ask the man on the street today to name a Hollywood picture," writes David Thomson in his 2012 *The Big Screen: The Story of the Movies—And What They Have Done to Us*, "and *Casablanca* will be there in the first list." Even for the millions who aren't related to the movie by blood, its hold on the imagination remains so powerful that it's become the go-to picture for any film-centered celebration. In the autumn of

2010, a screening of *Casablanca* ushered in opening night of the Dallas Film Society's outdoor series at AT&T Performing Arts Center in Texas. Two years later, at the open-air venue of the Academy of Motion Picture Arts and Sciences, the jury responsible for the "Oscars Outdoors" series selected it for its inaugural screening. For the film's introduction at the Academy open-air event, Monika Henreid did the honors. "One of the first things I always ask is 'How many people have seen this film before?'" she explained. "And in the case of that particular evening, I would say half, and there were probably four hundred people there." She sees her role today as something of an ambassador for the film, preserving the legacy of her father and helping to recruit new fans while also satisfying the expectations of the old. "You're sharing a double honor," she said. "You're initiating one group, and you are sharing a love of [the film] with another. It feels genuinely wonderful."

A little over a year later, on a chilly Sunday evening in November 2013, more than a thousand people streamed into the newly opened United Palace of Cultural Arts (UPCA) in the Washington Heights section of New York. Formerly home to the Loew's 175th Street Theatre, one of New York City's most sumptuous picture palaces, the UPCA opened its doors with a screening of *Casablanca*. Many guests arrived that night in costume or in the kind of retro party attire, tuxedos, and gowns patrons might have worn when the place was still known as Loew's, posing for pictures in the lobby in front of a life-size cardboard cutout of Bogie dressed in full *Casablanca* garb.

Once the audience took its seats, Mike Fitelson, UPCA's executive director, greeted the packed house (a live performance of "As Time Goes By" cued his arrival onstage). Finding the massive crowds a welcome surprise, he quipped: "And I thought that movies were dead!" In recognition of the largely Dominican neighborhood, the 35mm print screened that evening came complete with Spanish subtitles. *New York Post* film critic Lou Lumenick introduced the film—many members of the audience, like those at the open-air venue in Hollywood, were seeing it for the first time—talking about its colorful production history at Warners and its wider significance today.

Lumenick had published a two-page reappraisal of the film in November 2012 on the occasion of *Casablanca*'s seventieth anniversary. Soon after, he noted in a follow-up article that it was possibly the most popular piece he'd ever published at the *Post*. Using the metrics of the day, he observed that twenty-six hundred "likes" and fifty comments were posted on the newspaper's website (and more than a thousand on the Facebook page of the Humphrey Bogart estate). "I've seen *Casablanca* projected more often than any classic film in the United States," Lumenick recounted.

> I first showed it in college, at a film society at City College in New York, in 1969–1970. I've seen it at Lincoln Center, they showed it at the Smithsonian for the seventieth anniversary, and I saw it there. What really strikes me about *Casablanca* is that the audience, for the last fifty years, reacts pretty much the same to the film no matter what the audience composition is. [. . .] People laugh at the same things, everyone goes misty at the "Marseillaise," everyone breaks into laughter when Claude Rains says

> "I'm shocked, shocked to find that gambling is going on here." I can't think of another film that plays so consistently, no matter who you show it to, no matter when you show it.

He added, with particularly sharp emphasis: "It's a film that's very much of its time, but it's also utterly timeless."

I saw this phenomenon myself in the fall of 2012, when I taught my first-ever seminar on *Casablanca* to undergraduates at the New School in New York City. Most of the students in the class had never seen the film. But they all *knew* of it; they knew the iconic lines; knew the vague contours of the Bogie-Bergman romance; and had long heard about it from their parents, grandparents, friends, and relatives. Watching it in class, they laughed and cried almost on cue, they cheered and expressed occasional disbelief, and generally found themselves enraptured. They became, in some cases reluctantly and against their twenty-something intentions, fans of the film. When Leslie Epstein visited the class, bringing with him the Oscar that his father and uncle won in 1944, they greeted him like a dignitary from a magic kingdom.

Lloyd Clark, a lifelong collector of movie memorabilia and *Casablanca* fan of a singular order, used to teach courses on the film in Arizona. In 1992, for the fiftieth anniversary, he hosted an elaborate costume ball, counting playwright Murray Burnett and actor Leonid Kinskey among his distinguished guests. Over the decades, he collected articles that addressed the issue of colorization, the AFI rankings, auctions of memorabilia, copyright lawsuits, and all manner of allusions to the film (among them, the grand opening of a frozen yogurt shop in Scottsdale, Arizona, called Humphrey Yogart), as well as his correspondence with Howard Koch, Aljean Harmetz, Leonid Kinskey, and even with Conrad Veidt's grandnephew. He held on to the syllabus of the class he taught for years at Rio Salado Community College, actor and crew obituaries, and assorted interviews.

Born in 1923 in a small town in central Texas not far from Fort Hood, Clark joined the U.S. Army in 1942, the year that *Casablanca* went into production. By the time he retired from the service, he was a colonel. He also obtained a degree in journalism and worked in civilian life as a newspaperman, first at the *Dallas Morning News* and later for the *Phoenix Gazette*. In his final years, he wrote a weekly column for the *Daily News-Sun*, in Sun City, Arizona, which he called "As Time Goes By." Unable to shake his obsession with the movie, up until his death in 2014, he devoted entire columns to *Casablanca*. In August 1997, he voiced his opposition to the depiction of Humphrey Bogart in the "Legends of Hollywood" stamp series from the U.S. Postal Service ("Of all the portraits by all the artists in all the world, they had to pick that one—a sanitized version of a make-up artist's creation.") A column from March 2009, "'Play It Again, Sam' Fallacy Remains in Lore," aired his grievance over the continued misrepresentation of the title of Woody Allen's play as an actual line from the film, noting as a casual aside that he had recently watched the film for the eighty-eighth time. In March 2010, a few years after the AFI announced its selection of the most memorable quotes from motion pictures, Clark published a column praising its selections, five from

Casablanca in the top fifty alone, but criticizing the omission of Renault's prized "shocked, shocked" line. "The inclusion of more quotes from 'Casablanca' than from any other film on the roster," he wrote, "reinforces my assertion that it is the all-time best motion picture and that it will be viewed and studied by future generations of cinema educators and fans much as Shakespeare has been and continues to be."

Although Clark surely ranks among the most passionate fans of the film, he is far from alone. In 1999 a columnist in the *Long Beach* (Calif.) *Press-Telegram* told the story of Erroll Parker, cohost of the cable-access show *Inside Long Beach*, who by that point had watched the film more than six hundred times. When Parker was temporarily bedridden after breaking his leg at the age of fourteen, his sister suggested watching *Casablanca* on TV to pass the time ("You might like this movie," she said nonchalantly). "You have to understand, I'm an African-American (and former Black Panther) who has become absolutely intrigued by this movie," Parker commented many years and many viewings later. "I didn't live in the era of the Second World War or the Depression, but I've romanticized about that era and about how the world seemed so different in those days." He became so absorbed by the film as a young boy that as soon as could, he hitchhiked to the Academy of Motion Picture Arts and Sciences offices in Beverly Hills to learn all that he could about it. He eventually bought a copy of the VHS tape and kept it in his recorder, playing it once or twice a month. In recent years, he's even lectured about the film to high school students. As he remarked, describing how his faith was restored after speaking with students about

Casablanca and asking them what they might do if they were in Rick's shoes, "Doing the right thing is what this movie is all about."

In the twenty-first century, viewing options for true fans have become even more immersive. In 2013, the Troxy Theatre in London's East End was transformed into Rick's Café Américain as part of Secret Cinema, a British company that specializes in "live cinema." Like the screening in Washington Heights, only more so, spectators were asked to come in costume. Once inside, they mingled with other spectators and with actors, also in costume, filling out the interior of Rick's: playing cards at the roulette table; having a cocktail at the bar; dancing to the film music; watching as various scenes, like the arrest of Ugarte, were reenacted in front of their very eyes. Eventually the lights went out, and the film was screened for the audience of actors and filmgoers. The result, as one critic put it, has pushed the "boundaries of cinema culture." It offers the opportunity "to not only see a classic, but to live it."

Casablanca's power is such that even decades after working on *Round Up the Usual Suspects*, her highly detailed, exhaustively researched account of the film's production history, writer Aljean Harmetz recently told me that the movie still makes the final cut when it comes to selecting the precious handful of films she'd take with her to a desert island. Her chief criterion for such a fantasy selection: "These are movies which you'd want to rewatch over and over. There are certain movies that I admire, and even love, but I wouldn't take them because I wouldn't want to watch them over and over." She explained further, "I myself am drawn to bittersweet nostalgia, to the loss of innocence," and all the films she would take with her, but especially *Casablanca*, speak to this.

Even in times of crisis, people turn to the film as a trusted reference point and a beacon of stability. When actor Anthony Perkins lay on his deathbed in 1992, he issued a statement: "I chose not to go public about [having AIDS] because, to misquote *Casablanca*, I'm not much at being noble, but it doesn't take too much to see that the problems of an old actor don't amount to a hill of beans in this crazy world." That same year, in the heat of civil war in the Balkans, a screening of *Casablanca* was held in Belgrade. A notice in *The Hollywood Reporter* announced, "There will be a simulation of the black market where visas, gasoline coupons and airline tickets to Lisbon can be obtained."

During the past decade or more, the love of *Casablanca* has moved outside of the Anglo-American arena, reaching far-flung corners of the globe and forging new friendships among viewers. In China, as part of the Third Beijing International Drama Festival in 2005, a musical adaptation of *Casablanca* was successfully staged at the Great Hall of the People. Blending classical ballet, opera, and musical theater, the production starred Romanian Simona Noja, a principal dancer with the Vienna State Opera Ballet, as Ilsa and Italian Giuseppe Picone, a principal dancer with American Ballet Theatre, as Rick. John Clifford, who choreographed the piece, had originally proposed a theatrical adaptation to Warner Bros. in 2003. "The idea of other actors trying to say the great dialogue and be compared to the legends, Bogart and Bergman, is ridiculous," Clifford, the founder of the Los Angeles Dance Theater, told a journalist from *China Daily* in the days leading up to the production. "But the idea of dancers and singers portraying these characters was interesting to them." He insisted that his version was not simply a theatrical re-creation of the film, but rather a multimedia mix of pantomime, dance, and visual and sound effects. "A film is different than a performance," observed the dancer Noja. "You can watch it and watch it, it stays the same. But a live performance has something unique." As choreographer Clifford added, "I hope the Chinese audiences will enjoy all of our efforts and I have every confidence that the basic message of *Casablanca*, which is love, honor, forgiveness, and sacrifice, will be easily understood by all." Whatever else the production may have achieved, it presumably has also inspired the Chinese audience to watch the original film.

Not long after the Beijing production, the Takarazuka Revue, an all-female theater ensemble known for its glitzy productions of Western-style musicals, staged a Japanese version of *Casablanca* in its 2009–2010 season. The Japanese troupe, which celebrated its one hundredth birthday in 2013, has become known for its elaborate and inventive adaptations of Hollywood movies, among others, *The Sound of Music*, *West Side Story*, and *An Officer and a Gentleman*. An English-language review of their *Casablanca* musical suggests that the actress Yuhi Ozora, who plays Rick, is in certain regards more romantic and more sympathetic than the embittered Bogie; in one scene, the Japanese musical shows Rick, in a flashback, fighting as part of the anti-fascist forces in Spain. While the script was otherwise faithful to the English original, the Takazuka production used a revolving set to move between the main room of Rick's Café

Américain, its casino, and the market. Even if earlier attempts to stage a *Casablanca* musical in the English-speaking world were often greeted with skepticism, the Japanese version included a crowd-pleasing chorus number with lines of refugees singing outside the French embassy, perhaps a nod more to the contemporary refugee problem than that in French Morocco during World War II (where there would be no such embassy). "A large component of the Takarazuka romantic dream," notes the unnamed critic, "is about the romanticism of Europe."

Although a Hollywood movie like *Casablanca*—even a musical version—could not possibly reach an audience in North Korea, where Western pop culture is forbidden, Adam Johnson's wonderfully inventive, Pulitzer Prize–winning novel *The Orphan Master's Son* (2012), set in the land of Kim Jong Il, uses the film as a vital plot point. When faced with the rare chance to acquire a contraband DVD of his choice during a special mission to America, the novel's protagonist, the loyal citizen, soldier, and spy Jun Do, selects *Casablanca* ("They say that one is the greatest"). Later, back in Pyongyang, he—having taken on the identity of Commander Ga—and the North Korean actress Sun Moon curl up in front of the screen to watch the DVD on a privately kept laptop computer. Sun Moon finds minor quibbles with the film ("Where are the common people?" "There is no magic letter that gets you out"), even striking a similar position to Sally (Meg Ryan) in *When Harry Met Sally*: "Why doesn't she settle down with the nice husband?" "Why does she gaze at the immoral Rick that way?" However, near the close of the novel, when Jun Do is devising an elaborate escape plan for Sun Moon, *Casablanca* almost serves as an instruction manual. "This is your letter of transit," he tells her, in a moment of self-sacrifice, handing over the precious laptop. "The golden thing that gets you to America."

As for the North African city depicted in the film, former U.S. embassy staffer Kathy Kriger left behind a career in the foreign service to become the proprietor of Rick's Café, which opened its doors in 2004. In the early days of fund-raising, after establishing a small company she called The Usual Suspects, Kriger struggled to find people who would support her plans for transforming a dilapidated mansion on the edge of the Old Medina into a shrine to classic Hollywood's most beloved movie. No one understood what she was hoping to achieve, especially in the wake of terrorist attacks that the city had endured in May 2003. In addition, the bureaucracy for establishing a business seemed impenetrably opaque. Then one day, her luck turned. The president of a local bank, a Mr. El Alami, came to see her. "Some of my fondest memories I owe to the Ancienne Médina and the film *Casablanca*," he told her. She soon had the backing she needed, and opened her business with great success.

During the first year of the bar's operation, Monika Henreid journeyed to Rick's Café to celebrate her birthday. When they met at the door, Kriger introduced herself: "I'm Madame Rick." Henried replied, "And I'm Victor's daughter." Meanwhile, the café continues to maintain its abundant popularity. "We're known all over the world," Kriger commented in 2016. "The Japanese minister of economy is coming here for dinner tomorrow. J-Lo's been here. *Casablanca* the movie is so famous that it brings people in from everywhere. They all know of it. Some people come from Europe just to have dinner, spend the night and go back."

DESPITE THE UNPARALLELED ARDOR that the film has garnered over the years, or perhaps because of it, *Casablanca* has also received its share of playful ridicule and affectionate mockery. In January 2015, in the midst of its fortieth season on television, NBC's *Saturday Night Live* ran a spoof ending of the film (three decades earlier, they had done a spoof with John Belushi and Candice Bergen as Rick and Ilsa). The pipe-chomping host of what's billed as "Cinema Classics," Reese De'What (Kenan Thompson), is seated in his stodgy, mahogany-paneled study. He presents a clip of the "alternate ending" that begins at the Casablanca airport, with J. K. Simmons, that week's host, standing in as Rick and *SNL* cast member Kate McKinnon as Ilsa. They utter a few choice lines from the original film's finale, adding some hilarious amped-up protestations from McKinnon's Ilsa ("Oh, Richard, no, no, please not without you, *nooo*!"). Much of the ensuing humor then derives from Ilsa's urgent wish to hightail it onto the flight to Lisbon while Rick, utterly tone-deaf, steamrolls through his speech.

Rick recites variations on the original screenplay while Ilsa—in her new late-night comedy incarnation—frantically tries to break out of his grip and get onto the plane. "Wow, you give me a lot to think about when I'm on that plane," she says in the dry, sardonic tone she uses throughout, "regrets, concentration camps, *ooooh*, it's a lot." The bullishly determined Rick can't see Ilsa's behavior as anything other than stalling

J. K. Simmons and Kate McKinnon in a 2015 Saturday Night Live *spoof.*

tactics, a ploy to delay getting on the plane, even though of course the opposite is the truth. "I'll wave at you through one of the little windows," she tells him. "It'll be *our* thing." By the time Rick pronounces his "We'll always have Paris" line, all Ilsa can say, hurriedly, is "Ah, Paris. Paris is the best. It's such a *cool* place." She has almost ripped free when he gets to the "hill of beans" segment, when she humors him one last time ("Beans are crazy—the crazy beans!"), and then beelines for the staircase to the plane the second she hears her cue: "Here's lookin' at you, kid."

The point of the *SNL* spoof—and this is true more generally of the place that *Casablanca* occupies in the collective imagination two decades into the twenty-first century—is that you don't need to have seen the original movie to know the lines. They're so completely saturated in humor, in political and cultural commentary, that a spoof is bound to work, even with an audience that is seventy-five years removed from the original. The operating assumption of any parody is that its intended audience will at least be slightly familiar, intuitively or through sustained exposure, with the work that is being skewered. Indeed, this was already the case in 1946, when the irreverent Marx Brothers made their feature-length comedy *A Night in Casablanca.* Originally planned as more of a direct spoof of the Warner Bros. film—they purportedly hoped to have characters with names like "Humphrey Bogus"—the finished film was far less of an explicit parody than the *SNL* skit. But it was enough to exploit both the name recognition and the widespread familiarity with the Warners hit. In the run-up to the production, Groucho Marx, in what may merely have been a shrewd publicity stunt, claimed to have received sharp threats from the Warner legal department.

Inside the studio, there may already have been anger brewing over what seems to have been an errant 16mm print of *Casablanca*, which Harpo was allegedly screening at his home. Jack Warner wrote an irate note to Roy Obringer, his general counsel, in January 1946. "According to Colonel Levinson," he reported to Obringer, "there are a number of prints missing from the ones that were given by our Company to the War Activities Committee. No doubt the print Harpo Marx has is one of these missing prints. Therefore, we can legally serve notice that we have been informed that he has a print of the picture calling his attention to the fact that it is a copyrighted

A production still of Chico, Harpo, and Groucho Marx in A Night in Casablanca *(1946).*

subject and he has no right to have a copy of this film, or any other of our pictures, without permission from us. Naturally, we would want to avoid stating that we actually know he has a print of this picture." The legal storm clouds thus began to gather in Burbank, just months before the Marx Brothers would release their film.

In turn, and far more publicly, Groucho Marx wrote a series of letters, a kind of meta-commentary on the film and Hollywood false pieties, which he sent to Warner Bros. "Apparently there is more than one way of conquering a city and holding it as your own," began his first mordant salvo. He cheekily plays ignorant when it comes to the studio's claim on the city of Casablanca, and suggests that the very moment that he and his brothers announced the proposed title for their film, they were issued a stern warning from the studio's legal watchdogs to avoid using the city's name in its title. Groucho goes on, in his inimitable style, to lampoon the studio for its arrogance and self-importance and for the suggestion that it alone is responsible for the discovery and ownership of Casablanca. How can anyone be so pigheadedly proprietary, Groucho seems to ask, before asserting that even if the two films were in theatrical release at the same time, your common American moviegoer would surely be able to recognize the difference between Ingrid Bergman and Harpo.

As he rips rhetorical holes in the Warner case, he goes on to question whether the studio feels it has the rightful ownership of "Brothers" in its name as well. "Professionally, we were brothers long before you were." Groucho gloats about their early days at the start of the century, before the founding of the Burbank studio. He goes on to challenge the originality of the names Jack and Harry, and even Burbank. Groucho admits the fact that his missive might be construed as a "bitter tirade," but insists it's not. Making nice, he asserts, "I love Warners. Some of my best friends are Warner Brothers." He ends his letter with a final comedic, mildly manipulative embrace: "We are all brothers under the skin," he insists in his overture to unity, hoping for amicable relations until *A Night in Casablanca* hits the screen.

The remaining exchange between Groucho and the Warner legal department, or what we have of it in Groucho's two additional letters, follows the anarchic plotlines of a Marx Brothers skit. When the studio asks to know more about the story of *A Night in Casablanca*, Groucho writes: "Paul Hangover, our hero, is constantly lighting two cigarettes simultaneously. He apparently is unaware of the cigarette shortage." Groucho assures his reader that there's much more to the story, but he doesn't want to ruin it for the legal team. "All this has been okayed by the Hays Office, Good Housekeeping and survivors of the Haymarket Riots." With any luck, the film might usher in a new global crisis of its own. When Warner Bros. asks for still more plot details, he all too happily obliges: "In the new version I play Bordello, the sweetheart of Humphrey Bogart. Harpo and Chico are itinerant rug peddlers who are weary of laying rugs and enter a monastery just for a lark." Groucho's well-known penchant for pushing the authorities' buttons and for quick-witted, naughty double entendre prevails. As if that weren't enough to wrinkle the suits in the studio legal department, Groucho concludes, "Humphrey Bogart's girl, Bordello, spends her last years in a Bacall house."

Half a century later, in 1995, Looney Tunes released an eight-minute Bugs Bunny cartoon titled *Carrotblanca*. Produced by Warner Bros. Animation, it was later included on the sixtieth-anniversary special edition DVD release of the feature film in 2002, and has been shown over the years theatrically and on television. Much like the classic, the short is set in Rick's Café, known here as the Café au Lait Américain. As we are introduced to the main hall, Daffy Duck is busy banging the keys of his upright piano singing his own lispy rendition of "Knock on Wood." Bugs soon appears on the scene in Rick's white dinner jacket (chomping on a carrot and uttering a Bogie-inspired, hard-bitten "What's up, doc?"), while Tweety Bird, playing Ugarte, known here as Usmarte, does an uncanny Peter Lorre impression ("You despise me, *don't you*?"). When Silvester Slaszlo and Kitty Ketty arrive, the well-wrought chords from the "Marseillaise" are played. Pepé Le Pew, doing his best to channel Renault's most lecherous side, practically mauls Kitty, planting a few wet kisses on her whiskers when she arrives at the café: "My little Swedish meatball, it is love at first sight, no?!" Yosemite Sam offers his high-voltage take on Strasser as the menacing General Pandemonium. There's even a flashback sequence to the days when Bugs and Kitty were madly in love, driving in their convertible, dancing, drinking, and ending with the waterlogged farewell letter.

Of course it wouldn't be *Carrotblanca* if Bugs himself didn't have a chance to give his own cartoonish spin on some of the old film hero's signature lines: "Of all the juice joints in the world in all the towns in all the countries of all the worlds, she picks this one" and "I stick my cottontail out for no one!" and "In this crazy world, the lives of three people don't amount to a hill of greens" and, finally, "Here's lookin' for you, Kit." It's hard not to think that these are lines aimed at parents, or even grandparents, sitting with the children watching the cartoon as well, but that, subconsciously, these same lines planted the seeds for the next wave of *Casablanca* fans.

Alternate endings have long been a source of pop-culture fascination, and in 1998, *The Simpsons* did its own rendition in "Natural Born Kissers," the finale of their ninth season on television. In that episode, complete with a title cribbed from the Oliver Stone movie *Natural Born Killers*, Bart and Lisa unearth a mystery film canister while playing with an old mine detector from the war they find in Grandpa's room at the Springfield Retirement Castle. The canister, unambiguously labeled "Casablanca Alternate Ending," contains an old reel that they promptly thread through a projector, beaming the black-and-white cartoon onto a portable screen, while Grandpa reclines in his La-Z-Boy in rapt attention.

Rick and Louis stand on that same old tarmac, with Rick uttering a copyright dodge of a final line ("Louis, I think this could be the start of a beautiful friendship"), just as Louis suddenly pulls a gun. "Look out, Rick, he's packing heat," warns Sam from his upright piano, which has somehow been transported onto the tarmac. Sam flattens Louis with his piano, wheeling over the French prefect ("Good work, Sam, I'll buy you a falafel," says Rick). Not quite done with its stream of filmic, cultural, and historical references—this is *The Simpsons*, after all—Hitler climbs out from underneath the hinged lid of Sam's piano, the same space formerly reserved for the letters of transit. "Not so fast, you *schmattenheimer*," barks Hitler, pulling another weapon, a grenade launcher of sorts, on Rick. Ilsa then drops from the sky in a parachute, stuffing Hitler back into the piano, as if returning a genie to its bottle, just in time for an explosive to detonate inside. Rick lights Ilsa's cigarette and tells Sam coolly, "You know what to do." This cues Sam to play *not* "As Time Goes By," but Hoagy Carmichael's "Heart and Soul," cutting to a church where Rick and Ilsa are married, the final title card "The End?" superimposed over the scene.

Rick and Renault in a 1998 episode of The Simpsons.

The focus then pulls back from the screen and returns to the room at the retirement home, allowing the three Simpsons to indulge in a little postviewing banter. "Unbelievable," says Lisa. "I'll say," Bart chimes in. "Wasn't it great?" He quickly adds, with an extra dose of self-conscious irony, "And the question mark leaves it open for a sequel." Grandpa, the self-avowed *Casablanca* loyalist, offers: "I've seen that movie ten times, and I *never* get tired of that ending." Suddenly, a character known as Old Jewish Man enters the room, chastising Lisa in a Yiddish-accented patois, "Oy, oy, oy, ver did you get zis, you shrunken old hag?" He proceeds to explain that he worked as a studio executive in Golden Age Hollywood ("My studio produced *Casablanca*, alright!") and had tried to tack on a happy ending to the picture. "Back zen, studio execs," he continues to explain, with a rather emphatic wink and a nudge, "vi vere just dopes in suits. Not like today." Finally, he offers Bart and Lisa a twenty-dollar bill to rebury the canister, along with another one he hands them labeled "It's a Wonderful Life—Shooting Spree Ending."

Naturally, America's longest-running, most wildly referential, and wickedly funny animated series could not possibly limit its inclination to parody classic Hollywood's most quotable film to just one episode. "A show like ours that has to turn out so much product will return to it again and again. We'll drink at the well of *Casablanca* many times," writer and executive producer Matt Selman, who is credited with the alternate ending spoof of "Natural Born Kissers," told me. "I don't know that I've ever seen the movie start to finish," he admitted, and yet its world-renowned dialogue demands to be quoted and requoted. "The iconic look and feel, and lines and scenes and moments from the movie, have been imitated and reincarnated in goofy pop culture for every generation."

Ten seasons after "Natural Born Kissers," which Selman looks back at less as a spoof of *Casablanca* than as a satire of Hollywood's overwhelming propensity toward formulaic feel-good endings, there came an episode of *The Simpsons* known as "Apocalypse Cow." In it, Bart becomes deeply attached to a calf while doing a brief summer stint working on a farm. When the calf grows older, and is ready for slaughter, Bart hatches a plan, with the help of Marge and Lisa, to send it off to India, "where your cow will be treated as a god," as *Simpsons* standby Kwik-E-Mart proprietor Apu assures Bart. On the tarmac of the Springfield airport, Bart delivers his heroic farewell speech: "If that plane leaves the ground, and you're not on it, you'll regret it. Maybe not today, maybe not tomorrow, but soon and *definitely* after they kill you and make you into Sloppy Joes." A few triumphant chords of the "Marseillaise" reverberate, as Bart intones, "Here's looking at you, cud." (On a top-ten list of *Casablanca* bad puns, near the top would have to be the one routinely used by crooner Dani Lubnitzki at Sammy's Roumanian Steak House on Manhattan's Lower East Side. His borscht belt refrain for "As Time Goes By" goes "A bris is still a bris.")

As recently as April 2016, *The Simpsons* drank at the well of *Casablanca* yet again. In its episode called "The Burns Cage" (yes, *The Simpsons* has a penchant for punning famed Hollywood movie titles), the Springfield Elementary School puts on a theatrical version of the Bogart-Bergman classic—a banner hangs across the school façade with the cheeky slogan "You must remember this: bring two pencils and a snack" emblazoned upon it. Lisa lands the part of Ilsa, and a new kid, a rebel named Jack—who has a voice that strikes a frightening resemblance to Bogie's despite his tender age—upstages the bespectacled Millhouse to play Rick. Demonstrating his natural coolness, Jack remarks, "Of all the schools in all the districts, I had to get transferred to this one." When he's banned from the show for fighting, awkward understudy Millhouse steps in for Jack and seemingly delivers all his lines with ease. It turns out it's actually Jack playing Millhouse playing Rick. "It's like a Xerox of a Xerox of a Xerox," Selman explained. "The episode we just did could be the final one [to riff on *Casablanca*]."

One can find *Casablanca* homages and parodies in a staggering variety of films: from the James Bond classic *Goldfinger* (1964), with Sean Connery donning the signature Rick Blaine white dinner jacket in an exotic locale, to the war movie *First to Fight* (1967), which folds in footage from the original film; from Peter Sellers's satirical direct citation, "Here's looking at you, kid," in *The Return of the Pink Panther* (1975) and the famous café scene of *Raiders of the Lost Ark* (1981) to the opening of Prince's *Under the Cherry Moon* (1986); from the atmosphere, characters, and casting of *Havana* (1990), the bold tribute to the original poster art, scattered plotlines, and airport scene of *The Good German* (2006), all the way up to the self-conscious naming of British spy Ilsa Faust (Rebecca Ferguson) and equally self-conscious choice of location, that fabled North African city, in *Mission: Impossible—Rogue Nation* (2015).

On the small screen, references to the film also proliferate wildly: from episodes of *M*A*S*H*, *Sanford and Son*, *The Bob Newhart Show*, and *The Muppet Show*, in the 1970s; *The Cosby Show*, *Three's Company*, *Miami Vice*, *Moonlighting*, and *Cheers* in the 1980s (the popular British series *Mr. Love* devoted an episode to the film in 1988); *Melrose Place*, *Baywatch*, *Murphy Brown*, *Frasier*, *ER*, and *Homicide* in the 1990s; and *The West Wing*, *Gilmore Girls*, *Will & Grace*, *Arthur*, *Law & Order*, and *That '70s Show*, in the twenty-first century. In the 2016 season finale of *Modern Family*, Rick's airport speech is taken out for another spin when four-year old Joe (Jeremy Maguire) tries to persuade his father to follow his mom on a trip.

When preparing her book on *Casablanca* in the 1990s, Aljean Harmetz noted that an Internet search engine drew 53,000 hits when typing in the search term "Casablanca Movie." That same search now yields close to a million hits; and in 2002 there was even a plan, a collaboration between the American Film Institute and Georgia Institute of Technology with funding from the National Endowment for the Humanities, to create a separate website known as "Casablanca: A Critical Edition." The unrealized project was meant to be "a prototype for a virtual cineplex containing interactive academic studies of classic movies" in which "clicking on 'flashback' might show Humphrey Bogart's Rick and Ingrid Bergman's Ilsa cavorting in Paris."

Rick as a building contractor in a 2015 New Yorker *cartoon by Bob Eckstein.*

Even if *The Simpsons* may be done making *Casablanca* a target of satire, other media outlets are not. Nearly a year after the recent *SNL* spoof aired, a cartoon by Bob Eckstein titled "If Rick Had Been a Building Contractor" appeared in the pages of *The New Yorker* (where previous *Casablanca* cartoons, like the one in 1981 in which a businessman arrives home to his wife reciting lines from "As Time Goes By," had appeared). Once again, we're in that evocative, familiar Casablanca airport. This time wearing a pair of workman's overalls and a plaid shirt, a carpenter's pencil behind his ear and baseball cap on his head, Rick looks directly at Ilsa; a small model of the Lisbon-bound Clipper flies off in the distance. His words, virtually unchanged from the script, now stand for all of those elusive contractors seeking to break the news to their unhappy clients that the work they commissioned isn't anywhere near done on time: "Maybe not today. Maybe not tomorrow, but soon and for the rest of your life."

As befits a movie that doesn't shy away from politics, *Casablanca* lives on in that arena as well. Writing in his *New York Times* column in late February 2016, when Republican Donald Trump's spectacularly rogue presidential campaign was no longer looking like it would simply go away, Paul Krugman observed the recurrent hypocritical, halfhearted professions of shock among members of the party elite, using one of Claude Rains's greatest lines: "As many have noted, it's remarkable how shocked—*shocked!*—that establishment has been at the success of Donald Trump's racist, xenophobic campaign." Such views needn't have a partisan dimension. A month later, Republican Senator John McCain published an op-ed piece in the same pages; in "Salute to a Communist," he paid tribute to recently deceased Delmer Berg, the last known living veteran of the Abraham Lincoln Brigade, which fought against the fascists in the Spanish Civil War. He likened him to Robert Jordan, the protagonist of Hemingway's *For Whom the Bell Tolls*, who dies fighting against General Franco's forces in Spain, and described his virtues as bearing an uncanny resemblance to those embodied in Rick Blaine. "You might consider them romantics," he wrote, "fighting in a doomed cause for something greater than self-interest."

Of course, not everyone would be quite so inclined to have you believe that *Casablanca* retains the same currency in 2017 as it did during the war years, or that references to it will continue to proliferate on a monthly, if not daily basis. In August 2015, in a short opinion piece in the *Boston Globe* provocatively titled "Don't Bogart Those Cultural Touchstones," writer Tim Cockey claimed that old Bogie and all his greatest performances—not to mention his greatest lines—had long been forgotten. His was a past era. "Humphrey's fifteen minutes are up," he quipped. As his chief evidence, Cockey told of a recent talk he gave to a large group, average people in their thirties, forties, and fifties, at which nobody seemed to get his references. Receiving a roomful of unexpected stares after rehearsing the otherwise world-famous line "round up the usual suspects," he pressed them, trying "A kiss is just a kiss," a foolproof reference to the hit song. "Other than a few nodding heads," he reports, "it was clear to me that I was not, as I'd assumed, referencing such a universally known cultural touchstone. Amazing but true: This crowd did not really know the movie *Casablanca*." Cockey is rather quick to resign himself to what he perceives as the natural progression of old icons—namely, that they die, and the masses move on. "Why should I be shocked, shocked that not everyone I encounter can identify the cultural genesis of 'shocked, shocked'?"

Yet the stubborn truth remains on social media—the preferred mode of communication for the same younger demographic that Cockey found woefully uninformed when it came to Bogart and *Casablanca*—there is no shortage of references to the film, the evocative publicity stills and poster art, and to the iconic lines of dialogue. On Twitter, the Bogart Estate tweets daily to its fifty-one thousand followers, and there are other feeds as well, including a large number of user groups associated with Turner Classic Movies (TCM), where *Casablanca* is the single most aired movie, with 125 showings as of 2015. As cultural critic Leon Wieseltier noted in a paean to TCM in *The New York Times Magazine*, "If watching old movies is a form of escapism, it is at least not an escape from the human world. It is, in fact, an escape to the human world."

On Facebook, there is yet another mass audience attentive to preserving—or at least discussing—classic films from Hollywood's golden age. To usher in 2016, Massachusetts Senator Elizabeth Warren posted a passionate New Year's Eve message: "Bruce and I will be celebrating the New Year tonight with just the two of us, pretty much the same way we've done many times before: lots of good cheeses, champagne, and *Casablanca*." (We might recall that more than seven decades earlier, on New Year's Eve 1942, FDR gathered a small group of guests at the White House for a private screening.) In the remaining three crisp paragraphs of her Facebook post, Warren showed her talents both as a film critic and political observer. "The movie gets to me every time," she begins:

> It's about love, loyalty, and courage. It's also about refugees. Casablanca was a stop along the route of people fleeing the terror of the Nazis. Young people on the threshold of building a new life, and old people hoping for a safe landing place. The movie was shot in early 1942 against a backdrop of Jews fleeing persecution and death, but the mix of people meeting in Casablanca speaks to the pain and vulnerability of all people forced to run from their homes in order to survive. *Casablanca* is about a very real threat to humanity, but also about how people survive, flourish and fight back.

She goes on to interpret the film not just in its original context but with an eye toward the debates swirling around the sociopolitical universe in 2016, with the Syrian refugee crisis and the rise of anti-immigrant sentiment. "The movie carries a double significance: it is a great story told about immigrants, but also a great story told by immigrants," she writes. The current refugee debate, taken up with great passion in today's opinion pages, is of course different from the one that *Casablanca* spoke to in 1942, and yet the parallels remain poignant. She hails the film as "a creative triumph—much like America—made stronger because it is woven together by people who are not a single race or a single religion, stronger because we choose to come together to build a new country based on our talents and energy and shared talents." Warren's final words, jotted down before wishing her friends and followers a happy new year, belong not just to her, but to millions of viewers who have watched the great Hollywood classic and who continue to watch it today: "Each time I watch it, *Casablanca* gives me hope."

Acknowledgments

While writing this book, I was fortunate enough to receive support from a number of individuals, institutions, and funding sources. First of all, I'd like to express my deepest gratitude to all of the generous souls who offered their time and wisdom when speaking with me about *Casablanca*: André Aciman, Jeanine Basinger, Mårten Blomkvist, Adrienne Burnett, Stan Brooks, Lloyd Clark, Anya Epstein, Leslie Epstein, Gyula Gazdag, Todd Gitlin, Aljean Harmetz, Monika Henreid, J. Hoberman, Alexander Horwath, Kent Jones, Karina Longworth, Lou Lumenick, Nick Macdonald, Leonard Maltin, Honor Moore, Saul Nirenberg, Jody Rosen, Matt Selman, Jean Strouse, David Thomson, Stefan Volk, and Cass Warner. During the extended stretch of research and writing, I also benefited from conversations with my extended family and with friends and colleagues, among them Eric Banks,

Doris Berger, Juliane Camfield, Thomas Doherty, Samantha Davidson Green, Stefan Grissemann, Rachel Harrison, Molly Haskell, Steve Incontro, David Joselit, Brigitte Mayr, Michael Omasta, Dominic Pettman, Carrie Rickey, Donna Rifkind, Joachim Schlör, and Dana Stevens. Both Gerd Gemünden and Dana Polan volunteered to read and comment on the entire manuscript, and I am most grateful to them.

At the New School, I would like to thank Dean Stephanie Browner for making it possible for me to take a full year's sabbatical, in 2015–2016, when I was offered a Public Scholar Award from the National Endowment for the Humanities in support of the project. Similarly, without the NEH grant, it's hard to fathom how the book ever would have been finished by its deadline. My gratitude also goes to my colleagues in the Department of Culture and Media and my students at the New School, especially my research assistants Diana McCorry, Logan Chappe, and Andrew Friedman, who helped with everything from transcribing interviews to cataloging and hunting down sources. At Dartmouth College, where I spent the summer of 2015 in residence at the Leslie Center for the Humanities, I owe my thanks to its director, Graziella Parati, and her assistant, Sean Delmore, for making that stint so productive. In the Dartmouth Media Lab, Chistopher Ivanyi helped me with some last-minute photo touchups. At the Warner Bros. Archives held at the University of Southern California's School of Cinematic Arts, the curator Brett Service deserves recognition for his kind assistance in guiding me through the studio's primary sources. At the Margaret Herrick Library, Kristine Krueger helped me immeasureably, both while I was on site and from afar. At Photofest, Ron and Howard Mandelbaum as well as Derek Davidson offered tremendous assistance in securing images for the book.

The first public presentation on *Casablanca* that I gave was at the Center for Jewish History in New York in 2012, on the occasion of the film's seventieth anniversary. I owe Judith Siegel, CJH's former director of cultural programming, a debt of gratitude for planning that event, which was scheduled soon after I published an op-ed piece on the film in the *Wall Street Journal*. I thank Gary Rosen at the *Journal* for the chance to write about the film. In October 2015, I had the opportunity to present portions of the book in a public lecture at the University of Vermont. Alan Steinweis deserves my gratitude for his generous invitation and his terrific hospitality. At Apexart in New York, I was honored to take part in the December 2015 Double Take series—in which two authors, in this case Molly Haskell and myself, present back to back on a subject (in this case, the final scene of *Casablanca*)—curated by my friend and colleague Albert Mobilio. In April 2016, I introduced a screening of *Casablanca* in Los Angeles at the Goethe-Institut. Thanks go to Paul Lerner, Fareed Majari, and Daniel Chaffey for making that event possible.

At Norton, I must express profound gratitude to my editor, Matt Weiland, for his abundant enthusiasm and support, not to mention his patience, as well as his talented assistant, Remy Cawley, for helping to guide the book into production. Also at Norton, ace copy editor Trent Duffy deserves a very hearty thank-you. The project never would have existed at all had it not been for my agent, Zoë Pagnamenta, who had great faith in the idea long before there was anything on the page. I thank her for her support and her friendship.

Finally, Melanie Rehak, my partner in crime and pretty much everything else, has read each word, often more than once, and offered the kind of expert advice that I never could have dreamed up on my own. She's also lived with the project for the past couple of years, as have our sons, Jules and Bruno. I dedicate the book to all three of them.

Notes

A NOTE ON THE SOURCES

While preparing this book, and telling the story that I attempt to re-create in the preceding pages, I have relied on several indispensable sources. For the production history of *Casablanca*, there is no single work that is more important than Aljean Harmetz's *Round Up the Usual Suspects: The Making of "Casablanca"—Bogart, Bergman, and World War II,* first published in 1992. In her wonderfully detailed account (reissued on the sixtieth anniversary of the film's release, in 2002, under the title *The Making of "Casablanca"*), Harmetz was able to include interviews with original cast and crew members, most of whom had long passed away by the time I began my project. I am therefore especially indebted to her for providing those personal testimonials. Similarly instructive are the primary documents—studio memoranda, production notes, correspondence, and the like—that Rudy Behlmer first collected in his 1985 anthology *Inside Warner Bros., 1935–1951.* However, in order to bring the story into the twenty-first century, I conducted dozens of new interviews and mined the archives in New York (at the New York Public Library, the Library for the Performing Arts, the Schomburg Center for Research in Black Culture, and the Center for Jewish History) and in Los Angeles (the Warner Bros. Archives at the University of Southern California and the Margaret Herrick Library of the Academy of Motion Picture Arts and Sciences). In the following notes, I provide only the sources for direct citations—quotations that I incorporate into my account—and thus wish at the outset to express my debts to those who came before me. All of the following citations from the Warner Bros. Archives are granted courtesy of Warner Bros. Entertainment Inc. The abbreviation WBA is used below to indicate that source.

INTRODUCTION

xiii **"picture that makes the spine":** Bosley Crowther, "*Casablanca*, with Humphrey Bogart and Ingrid Bergman," *New York Times*, November 27, 1942.

xiii **"not *one* movie":** Umberto Eco, "*Casablanca*: Cult Movies and Intertextual Collage" (1984), in *Travels in Hyperreality: Essays* (New York: Harcourt, 1986), 208.

xiv **"the most moving patriotic scene":** Leonid Kinskey, "It Lingers Deliciously in Memory as Time Goes By," *Movie Digest*, September 1972, 126.

xiv **"She will forever be":** William Grimes, "Madeleine Lebeau, Jilted by Bogart in *Casablanca*, Dies at 92," *New York Times*, May 16, 2016.

xvi **"genius of the system":** Bazin's words served as the epigraph to the magisterial study by Thomas Schatz, *The Genius of the System: Hollywood Filmmaking in the Studio Era* (1989; repr., Minneapolis: University of Minnesota Press, 2010), 1.

xvi **"Maybe there are better films":** Paul Whitington, "*Casablanca*, the Classic for All Generations," *Belfast Telegraph*, June 4, 2016.

CHAPTER 1. EVERYBODY COMES TO RICK'S

2 **"I had inherited $10,000":** Aljean Harmetz, *The Making of "Casablanca": Bogart, Bergman, and World War II* (New York: Hyperion, 2002), 53. In an earlier interview, conducted on July 7, 1983, Burnett told his story to Peter Lorre biographer Stephen D. Youngkin: see Youngkin, *The Lost One: A Life of Peter Lorre* (Lexington: University Press of Kentucky, 2005), 201–2.

3 **"an indescribable horror":** David Gritten, "You Must Remember

This: The *Casablanca* Story Began as a Play—and After 50 Years, Finds a Stage," *Los Angeles Times*, May 14, 1991.

3 **"a caricature of a Jew":** Harmetz, *The Making of*, 53.

3 **"It led from Marseilles":** Charles Francisco, *You Must Remember This: The Filming of "Casablanca"* (Englewood Cliffs, N.J.: Prentice-Hall, 1980), 37.

4 **"When we got on the train":** Harmetz, *The Making of*, 54.

5 **"a great contrast":** Youngkin, *The Lost One*, 202.

5 **"What a setting for a play":** Ibid.

5 **"No one can remain neutral":** Harmetz, *The Making of*, 54.

5 **"the white heat of anger":** Gritten, "You Must Remember This."

5 **"Joan nourished me":** Harmetz, *The Making of*, 55.

6 **"broken romances; desperate refugees":** Neill Lochery, *Lisbon: War in the Shadows of the City of Light, 1939–1945* (New York: Public Affairs, 2011), 1.

7 **"Joan Alison's favorite ploys":** Francisco, *You Must Remember This*, 40. See also Karen Moline, "The Dame Behind *Casablanca*," *Mirabella*, November 1989, 75.

8 **"The bar of RICK'S CAFÉ":** Murray Burnett and Joan Alison, "Everybody Comes to Rick's," unpublished manuscript (copy), Wesleyan Cinema Archives, Middletown, Conn. All citations of the play come from this source. In this excerpt, the brackets indicate that the ellipses are mine, rather than in the original; this convention is followed throughout.

13 **"himself and a college roommate":** David Margolick, "The Creator of Rick's Café Seeks Rights to *Casablanca* Characters," *New York Times*, October 10, 1985.

13 **"I always scream when he identifies":** Harmetz, *The Making of*, 55.

16 **"The play doesn't really need":** Francisco, *You Must Remember This*, 42.

16 **"as strongly as anyone":** Ronald Haver, "Finally, the Truth About *Casablanca*," *American Film*, June 1976, 11.

17 **"It was a cautionary tale":** Margolick, "The Creator of Rick's."

18 **"Five days after Pearl Harbor":** Hal Wallis with Charles Higham, *Starmaker: The Autobiography of Hal Wallis* (New York: Macmillan, 1980), 83.

18 **"The script needed a great deal of work":** Ibid.

18 **"Mr. Wallis would like you":** Wallis Office, memo of December 22, 1941, to Irene Lee, box 1, folder 1881A ("Casablanca" Story Memos 12/22/41–4/21/42), WBA.

19 **"we can get a good":** Aeneas McKenzie, memo of January 3, 1942, to Paul Nathan, box 1, folder 1881A, WBA.

20 **"It will be a tough job":** Wally Kline, memo of January 5, 1942, to Hal Wallis, box 1, folder 1881A, WBA.

20 **"I do not like the play at all":** Robert Buckner, memo of January 6, 1942, to Hal Wallis, box 1, folder 1881A, WBA.

20 **"We thought the play":** Harmetz, *The Making of,* 43.

22 **"They were just hack work":** Julius Epstein, "Interview with Patrick McGilligan" (1983), in Patrick McGilligan, ed., *Backstory: Interviews with Screenwriters of Hollywood's Golden Age* (Berkeley: University of California Press, 1986), 176.

23 **"would rather tell a bad joke":** Harlan Lebo, "A Conversation with Julius Epstein," in *"Casablanca": Behind the Scenes* (New York: Simon & Schuster, 1992), 12.

23 **"All of us at Warner Bros.":** Leslie Epstein, "Duel in the Sun," *The American Prospect*, November 16, 2001.

24 **"Those boys are always":** Ibid.

24 **"Read your contract":** Ibid.

25 **"Everybody at the studio":** Julius Epstein, "Interview with Patrick McGilligan," 183.

25 **"seventy to seventy-five writers":** Lebo, "A Conversation," 9.

25 **"How extravagant you are":** All citations of dialogue come from the film. The screenplay and all its iterations are kept in the Warner Bros. Archives, School of Cinematic Arts, University of Southern California, Los Angeles. The published script is available in Howard Koch, *"Casablanca": Script and Legend* (Woodstock, N.Y.: Overlook, 1973).

26 **"the single best use":** David Denby, "Everybody Comes to Rick's: *Casablanca* on the Big Screen," *The New Yorker*, March 19, 2012.

27 **"Round up the usual suspects":** Leslie Epstein, "Duel in the Sun."

27 **"that celebrated piece of patchwork picturemaking":** McGilligan in Julius Epstein, "Interview with Patrick McGilligan," 171.

28 **"They apparently see the situations":** Howard Koch, memo of

May 11, 1942, to Hal Wallis, box 1, folder 1881A ("Casablanca" Story Memos 4/22/42–5/21/42), WBA.

28 **"powderkeg of political tension":** Stephen Karnot, reader's report on "Everybody Comes to Rick's," December 11, 1941, box 1, folder 1881A ("Casablanca" Story—Play Script Summary), WBA.

29 **"Within the confines of a studio":** Harmetz, *The Making of,* 56.

29 **"my impression about *Casablanca*":** Casey Robinson, memo of May 20, 1942 ["Notes on Screenplay 'Casablanca'"], to Hal Wallis, box 1, folder 1881A, WBA.

29 **"Something very specific":** Casey Robinson, "Interview with Joel Greenberg" (1974), in McGilligan, *Backstory,* 307.

30 **"While we handle the foreign situation":** The entire letter is reprinted in Harmetz, *The Making of,* 48.

30 **"which I always thought was a terrible line":** Julius Epstein, "Interview with Patrick McGilligan," 185.

30 **"We were making changes":** Stephen Bogart with Gary Provost, *Bogart: In Search of My Father* (New York: Penguin, 1995), 87–88.

31 **"Today, that shameless get-off line":** David Thomson, *Humphrey Bogart* (London: Faber & Faber, 2010), 62–63.

31 **"The play provided an exotic locale":** Koch, *"Casablanca": Script and Legend,* 17–18; see also Howard Koch, "The Making of America's Favorite Movie: Here's Looking at You, *Casablanca,*" *New York,* April 30, 1973.

31 **"one of the world's worst plays":** James Agee, *Film Writing and Selected Journalism,* ed. Michael Sragow (New York: Library of America, 2005), 42.

31 **"When I sent down":** Koch, *"Casablanca": Script and Legend,* 25.

32 **"Koch has an awfully bad memory":** "Burnett-Alison Sue Adaptor Koch; Say His Bad Memory Injured 'Em," *Variety,* July 11, 1973.

32 **"When it was all over":** Howard Koch, *As Time Goes By: Memoirs of a Writer* (New York: Harcourt Brace Jovanovich, 1979), 82.

33 **"I've always liked Howard":** Julius Epstein, "Interview with Patrick McGilligan," 186.

33 **"the boys wrote the police stuff":** Robinson, "Interview with Joel Greenberg," 308.

33 **"It was set in Casablanca, Africa":** Ibid., 306–7.

33 **"I've got almost a mystical feeling":** Harmetz, *The Making of,* 13.

34 **"Remember we were not screenwriters":** Ibid., 330.

35 **"These characters are part of me":** Margolick, "The Creator of Rick's."

35 **"give, grant, bargain":** Ibid.

35 **"Plaintiffs may play it again":** Ibid.

35 **"We called it 'the curse of *Casablanca*'":** Adrienne Burnett, interview with the author, July 23, 2015.

35 **"You know the story":** Aljean Harmetz, "Murray Burnett, 86, Writer of Play Behind *Casablanca*," *New York Times*, September 29, 1997.

36 **"Miss Dietrich read on":** Quoted in Amy Lawrence, "Marlene Dietrich: The Voice as Mask," in *Dietrich Icon,* ed. Gerd Gemünden and Mary R. Desjardins (Durham, N.C.: Duke University Press, 2007), 91.

36 **"she was a female version of Rick":** Burnett interview.

36 **"I'm very proud of the play":** Gritten, "You Must Remember This."

37 **In a letter to the editor:** Howard Koch, "Setting the Record Straight on 'Casablanca,'" *Los Angeles Times*, June 1, 1991.

38 **"an exercise in cinema cultdom":** Milton Shulman, review of *Rick's Bar Casablanca, Evening Standard*, April 11, 1991.

38 **"Would a Bulgarian Jew":** John Peter, review of *Rick's Bar Casablanca, The Sunday Times*, April 14, 1991.

38 **"What does come across":** Review of *Rick's Bar Casablanca, Variety*, April 22, 1991.

38 **"*Rick's Bar Casablanca* should have been left":** Charles Osborne, review of *Rick's Bar Casablanca, Daily Telegraph*, April 12, 1991.

39 **"*Casablanca* is an extraordinary film experience":** Syd Field, *Screenplay: The Foundations of Screenwriting*, rev. ed. (New York: Delta, 2005), 160–61.

39 **"We know characters better":** Robert McKee, *Story: Substance, Structure, Style and the Principles of Screenwriting* (New York: Harper Entertainment, 1997), 375.

40 **"He screened *Casablanca* over six hours":** Ian Parker, "The Real McKee," *The New Yorker,* October 20, 2003.

41 **"I strongly recommend":** Chuck Ross, "The Great Script Tease," *Film Comment,* November–December 1982, 17.

41 **"One of the most popular films of all time":** Howard Koch, "*Casa-*

blanca? They'll Play It Forever, Sam," *New York Times*, February 23, 1986.

41 **"The reason I rejected it":** Renee Cho, "*Casablanca* Postscript," *New York Times*, March 30, 1986.

CHAPTER 2. USUAL SUSPECTS

43 **"Ann Sheridan and Ronald Reagan":** *The Hollywood Reporter*, January 5, 1942; see also the studio's "Hollywood News" publicity announcement, "Sheridan, Reagan and Morgan to be Starred in 'Casablanca,'" January 7, 1942, box 1, folder 683, WBA.

44 **"using [George] Raft":** Jack L. Warner, memo of April 2, 1942, to Hal Wallis, box 1, folder 1881A ("Casablanca" Story Memos 4/22/42–5/21/42), WBA.

44 **"I have thought over very carefully":** Hal Wallis, memo of April 13, 1942, to Jack Warner, box 1, folder 1881A, WBA.

47 **"The war was great stuff":** Stefan Kanfer, *Tough Without a Gun: The Extraordinary Life and Afterlife of Humphrey Bogart* (New York: Knopf, 2011), 12.

47 **"rather trenchant example of bad acting":** Ibid., 19.

48 **"Most of them were standard products":** Ibid., 49.

48 **"I don't think he could have been":** Aljean Harmetz, *The Making of "Casablanca": Bogart, Bergman, and World War II* (New York: Hyperion, 2002), 86.

48 **"practically perfect":** Kanfer, *Tough Without*, 71.

48 **"every considered drag":** Ibid., 115.

48 **"Bogart became the thinking man's patriot":** Andrew Sarris, *"You Ain't Heard Nothin' Yet": The American Talking Film, History and Memory, 1927–1949* (New York: Oxford University Press, 1998), 402.

49 **"I remember, years ago":** Sam Jaffe, Academy Oral History 109, p. 239, Margaret Herrick Library, Academy of Motion Picture Arts and Sciences, Beverly Hills, Calif.

50 **"Who would want to kiss":** Ibid.

50 **"It was a difficult movie for my father":** Stephen Bogart with Gary Provost, *Bogart: In Search of My Father* (New York: Penguin, 1995), 88.

51 **"No one would ever refer":** Kanfer, *Tough Without*, 84–85.

51 **"I wanted Ingrid Bergman":** Hal Wallis with Charles Higham, *Starmaker: The Autobiography of Hal Wallis* (New York: Simon & Schuster, 1985), 86.

53 **"I had already seen the Swedish version":** Charlotte Chandler, *Ingrid: Ingrid Bergman, A Personal Biography* (New York: Applause, 2008), 70.

53 **"She was natural":** James Harvey, *Watching Them Be: Star Presence on the Screen from Garbo to Balthazar* (New York: Faber & Faber, 2014), 76.

54 **"Tell him anything":** Laurence Leamer, *As Time Goes By: The Life of Ingrid Bergman* (New York: Harper & Row, 1986), 83.

54 **"a feat of verbal hocus-pocus":** Howard Koch, *"Casablanca": Script and Legend* (Woodstock, N.Y.: Overlook, 1973), 18.

54 **"I said *Casablanca* is going":** Leamer, *As Time Goes By*, 83.

55 **"David O. Selznick liked it":** Ingrid Bergman and Alan Burgess, *Ingrid Bergman: My Story* (New York: Delacorte, 1980), 114–15.

55 **"The picture is called":** Ibid., 114.

55 **"From the very start":** Ibid., 115.

56 **"We don't know yet":** Ibid.

56 **"I don't want any roots":** Bergman, interview with Merv Griffin, 1980, www.youtube.com/watch?v=wT4BvqjXpC8.

56 **"a horrible example of womanhood":** B. James Goldstone, *The Man Who Seduced Hollywood: The Life and Loves of Greg Bautzer, Tinseltown's Most Powerful Lawyer* (Chicago: Chicago Review, 2013), 116.

57 **"Probably the most iconic performances":** William Friedkin in *"Casablanca": An Unlikely Classic*, short documentary directed by Gary Leva for the 2012 Warner Home Video DVD release of *Casablanca*.

57 **"In *Casablanca*, I kissed Bogart":** Donald Spoto, *Notorious: The Life of Ingrid Bergman* (New York: HarperCollins, 1987), 127.

58 **"She was a healthy":** Rudy Behlmer, *America's Favorite Movies: Behind the Scenes* (New York: Ungar, 1982), p. 160.

58 **"I made so many films":** David Parkinson, "Ingrid Bergman," *Moviemail*, February 7, 2015.

58 **"Ingrid Bergman, you're so perty":** Woody Guthrie, "Ingrid Bergman," unrecorded song, Warner/Chappell Music Inc., Sony/ATV Music Publishing LLC, Universal Music Publishing Group.

59 **"It is a fantastically beautiful climate":** Lisl Henreid to Eleonora Mendelssohn, June 23, 1941, Eleonora Mendelssohn Papers, box 2, Paul and Lisl Henreid Folder, New York Public Library, Rare Books and Manuscripts Division, New York City.

59 **"considered a number of degrees":** Paul Henreid with Julius Fast, *Ladies Man* (New York: St. Martin's, 1984), 93.

59 **"Perhaps I saw filmmaking":** Ibid., 93–94.

59 **"the suave ladies' man":** Ibid., 96.

60 **"How about a roll in the hay":** Ibid., 101.

60 **"It was an intimate":** Ibid., 115.

60 **"It's something that's going":** Ibid., 116.

60 **"Paul Henreid achieves":** Ibid., 117.

61 **"the second lover in a film":** Ibid., 120.

61 **"I thought Maltz and Koch":** Ibid., 121.

61 **"I'm supposed to be a leader":** Ibid., 122.

62 **"polished and even-tempered performance":** David Skal with Jessica Rains, *Claude Rains: An Actor's Voice* (Lexington: University Press of Kentucky, 2008), 115.

62 **"Rains avoided the fray":** Ibid., 117.

64 **"Paul Hemorrhoid":** Ibid., 118.

64 **"a big baby":** Henreid, *Ladies Man*, 124.

64 **"Mr. Rains is properly slippery":** Skal, *Claude Rains*, 118.

65 **"I am stealing money":** Leonid Kinskey, "It Lingers Deliciously in Memory as Time Goes By," *Movie Digest*, September 1972, 129.

65 **"Now the European actors driven out":** Alfred Polgar, "Life on the Pacific" (1942), in Mark Anderson, ed., *Hitler's Exiles: Personal Stories of the Flight from Nazi Germany to America* (New York: New Press, 1998), 271.

66 **"I know this man well":** John T. Soister, *Conrad Veidt on Screen: A Comprehensive Illustrated Filmography* (Jefferson, N.C.: McFarland, 2002), 312.

67 **"swapping skins":** Stephen D. Youngkin, *The Lost One: A Life of Peter Lorre* (Lexington: University Press of Kentucky, 2005), 18.

67 **"The modern psychopath, through Peter Lorre's acting":** Ibid., 65.

67 **"Europe's greatest actor":** Ibid., 99.

68 **"rococo cherub gone slightly astray":** Ibid., 109.

68 **"We cannot approve":** Ibid., 180.

68 **"Like a blanched weasel":** Ibid., 204.

68 **"Lorre is in and out":** Review of *Casablanca*, *The Hollywood Reporter*, December 8, 1942.

69 **"Oh yes, yes—oh, God, yes":** Henreid, *Ladies Man*, 126.

70 **"It has always been":** David Thomson, *The New Biographical Dictionary of Film*, 6th ed. (New York: Knopf, 2014), 357.

72 **"In one of our proposed":** Hal Wallis, memo of February 5, 1942, to Steve Trilling, box 1, folder 1881A, WBA.

73 **"It wasn't hard":** Dorothy Kilgallen, "Here Comes Mr. Dooley," *Collier's*, February 12, 1944, 63; see also Elliot Carpenter, Personal Papers, box 1, Elliot Carpenter Papers, Schomburg Center for Research in Black Culture, New York.

73 **"He didn't pay":** Kilgallen, "Here Comes Mr. Dooley."

75 **"As much as I hate":** Johnny Depp, "Peeing on the Lilacs," *The Hollywood Reporter*, December 5–7, 1997.

75 **"begin looking immediately for a Negro":** Peter Wegele, *Max Steiner: Composing, "Casablanca," and the Golden Age of Film Music* (Lanham, Md.: Rowman & Littlefield, 2014), 103.

76 **"*Casablanca* the much-talked-about film":** Dan Burley, "Wilson's Role in *Casablanca* Tops for Hollywood," *New York Amsterdam News*, February 6, 1943.

76 **"he seemed too much":** Wallis, *Starmaker*, 87.

77 **"Mr. Wilson's performance":** Bosley Crowther, "*Casablanca*, with Humphrey Bogart and Ingrid Bergman," *New York Times*, November 27, 1942.

77 **"In the jungle":** Thomas Doherty, *Projections of War: Hollywood, American Culture, and World War II* (New York: Columbia University Press, 1993), 210.

79 **"who isn't at three":** Kanfer, *Tough Without*, 144.

79 **"Bogart's a hell of":** Ibid.

79 **"One does not go to see":** James Baldwin, *The Devil Finds Work* (New York: Vintage, 1976), 30.

79 **"I hated Humphrey Bogart":** Harmetz, *The Making of*, 55.

80 **"I examine your":** Kanfer, *Tough Without*, 191.

80 **"I feel sometimes":** Chandler, *Ingrid*, 14 and 81.

80 **"I really thought it was":** Interview with Michael Parkinson, 1973. Bergman told the same story in her interview with Richard Anobile a year later; see Richard J. Anobile, ed., *Casablanca* (New York: Avon, 1974), 6.

81 **"Ingrid, come in":** Bergman and Burgess, *Ingrid Bergman*, 483.

81 **"I feel about *Casablanca*":** Chandler, *Ingrid*, 88.

81 **"I think because":** Anobile, *Casablanca*, 7.

82 **"People think he is French":** Robert Marquand, "*Casablanca* Star Lives in the Shadow of His Character," *Christian Science Monitor*, February 25, 2008.

82 **"if Henreid hadn't done the movie":** Ibid.

83 **"More than one film critic":** Dana Polan, "*Casablanca*," in Jeffrey Geiger and R. L. Rutsky, eds., *Film Analysis* (New York: W. W. Norton, 2005), 368–69.

83 **"It was one of those":** Kiron K. Skinner et al., eds., *Reagan: A Life in Letters* (New York: Free Press, 2003), 128.

CHAPTER 3. I STICK MY NECK OUT FOR NOBODY

85 **"Hitler and Hitlerism will pass":** Michael E. Birdwell, *Celluloid Soldiers: Warner Bros.'s Campaign Against Nazism* (New York: New York University Press, 1999), 16.

86 **"Fascism tipped":** Helen Zigmond, "Hollywood and the European Apple Cart," *Jewish Telegraphic Agency*, December 25, 1938, quoted in ibid., 19.

86 **"I immediately closed":** Jack Warner with Dean Jennings, *My First Hundred Years in Hollywood* (New York: Random House, 1964), 249.

87 **"He had the toughness":** Birdwell, *Celluloid Soldiers*, 7.

87 **"While no one":** Neil Gabler, *An Empire of Their Own: How the Jews Invented Hollywood* (New York: Anchor, 1989), 131.

87 **"Every worthwhile contribution":** Ibid., 131–32.

87 **"to expose Hitler":** Birdwell, *Celluloid Soldiers*, 19.

88 **"the first time a studio head":** "Jack Warner's Dinner to Exiled Thos. Mann May Touch Off a Militant Anti-Hitler Campaign in Hollywood," *Variety*, March 23, 1938.

88 **"In their zeal":** Birdwell, *Celluloid Soldiers*, 11.

88 **"Excellent melodrama":** Rudy Behlmer, *America's Favorite Movies: Behind the Scenes* (New York: Ungar, 1982), 155.

89 **"Behind the action and its background":** Rudy Behlmer, *Inside Warner Bros., 1935–1951* (New York: Simon & Schuster, 1985), 197.

89 **"Frank Capra went to Washington":** Julius Epstein, "Interview with Patrick McGilligan" (1983), in Patrick McGilligan, ed., *Backstory: Interviews with Screenwriters of Hollywood's Golden Age* (Berkeley: University of California Press, 1986), 185.

90 **"One of Hitler's chief secret weapons":** Thomas Doherty, *Projections of War: Hollywood, American Culture, and World War II* (New York: Columbia University Press, 1993), 74.

90 **"Mike [Curtiz] leaned strongly":** Howard Koch, *"Casablanca": Script and Legend* (Woodstock, N.Y.: Overlook, 1973), 24.

93 **"an investigation":** U.S. Senate, 77th Cong., 1st sess., *Propaganda in Motion Pictures*, Hearing Before a Subcommittee of the Committee on Interstate Commerce, on S. Res. 152, 9-26-1941 (Washington, D.C.: GPO, 1941). See also Clayton R. Koppes and Gregory D. Black, *Hollywood Goes to War: How Politics, Profits, and Propaganda Shaped World War II Movies* (New York: Free Press, 1987).

93 **"Go to Hollywood":** Saverio Giovacchini, *Hollywood Modernism: Film and Politics in the Age of the New Deal* (Philadelphia: Temple University Press, 2001), 114.

93 **"Merchants of Death":** Birdwell, *Celluloid Soldiers,* 156.

93 **"were the work in part":** Ibid., 160.

94 **"He has two major interests":** "Warner Brothers," *Fortune*, December 1937.

94 **"We're not newcomers":** Steven Carr, *Hollywood and Anti-Semitism: A Cultural History up to World War II* (New York: Cambridge University Press, 2001), 273.

94 **"a factual portrait":** Birdwell, *Celluloid Soldiers,* 167.

94 **"intention of making":** Giovacchini, *Hollywood Modernism*, 94.

94 **"to educate, to stimulate":** Harry Warner, "Hollywood Obligations in a Producer's Eyes," *Christian Science Monitor*, March 16, 1939. See also Betty Warner Sheinbam, "Obligations Above and Beyond: Remembering Harry Warner," in *Warners' War: Politics, Pop Culture and*

Propaganda in Wartime Hollywood, ed. Martin Kaplan and Johanna Blakley (Los Angeles: Norman Lear Center Press, 2004), 11–13.

95 **"filmic embodiment of Harry Warner":** Birdwell, *Celluloid Soldiers*, 60.

96 **"America's first anti-Nazi film":** "Amerikas erster Antinazi-Film," *Aufbau*, May 1, 1939.

96 **"The world is faced":** Mark Harris, *Five Came Back: A Story of Hollywood and the Second World War* (New York: Penguin Press, 2014), 38.

97 **"scores of actors":** Giovacchini, *Hollywood Modernism*, 95.

97 **"propose a toast":** Doherty, *Projections of War*, 40. See also Thomas Doherty, *Hollywood and Hitler, 1933–1939* (New York: Columbia University Press, 2013).

98 **"Our fathers came to America":** Birdwell, *Celluloid Soldiers*, 72.

99 **"THE PICTURE IS EXCEEDINGLY GOOD":** Carr, *Hollywood and Anti-Semitism*, 275.

100 **"It will be to Hollywood's credit":** Leo Rosten, *Hollywood: The Movie Colony, the Movie Makers* (New York: Harcourt, 1941), 154.

102 **"The Warner Boys in Africa":** Manny Farber, "The Warner Boys in Africa," *The New Republic*, December 14, 1942, reprinted in Robert Polito, ed., *Farber on Film: The Complete Film Writings of Manny Farber* (New York: Library of America, 2009), 38–40.

102 **"It's got a lot to do with the timing":** Leslie Epstein, interview with the author, June 18, 2012.

103 **"established the figure of the rebellious hero":** Pauline Kael, *5001 Nights at the Movies*, rev. ed. (New York: Henry Holt, 1991), 122.

104 **"a counterculture hero":** Kent Jones, interview with the author, March 30, 2015.

104 **"the products of a deep crisis":** Barbara Deming, *Running Away from Myself: A Dream Portrait of America Drawn from the Films of the Forties* (New York: Grossman, 1969), 11.

105 **"recasts propaganda as a romantic act":** Karina Longworth, interview with the author, January 22, 2015.

107 **"The film needs Rick":** Doherty, *Projections of War*, 38.

109 **"I have never contributed":** Stefan Kanfer, *Tough Without a Gun: The Extraordinary Life and Afterlife of Humphrey Bogart* (New York: Knopf, 2011), 54.

111 **"one of the most stirring":** Steven Spielberg in *"Casablanca": An Unlikely Classic*, short documentary directed by Gary Leva for the 2012 Warner Home Video DVD release of *Casablanca*.

111 **"If you know the movie":** Jones interview.

112 **"Everybody in Casablanca":** Stephen D. Youngkin, *The Lost One: A Life of Peter Lorre* (Lexington: University Press of Kentucky), 202.

112 **"This made a huge impression":** J. Hoberman, interview with the author, May 12, 2015.

112 **"On the 'Marseillaise,' when it is played":** Hal B. Wallis, "Music Notes *Casablanca*," September 2, 1942, box 1, folder 1881A ("Casablanca" Story Memos 6/12/42–8/4/43), WBA.

112 **"I am described by the Germans":** Paul Henreid with Julius Fast, *Ladies Man* (New York: St. Martin's, 1984), 121–22.

113 **"You've got an easy day today":** Nathaniel Benchley, *Humphrey Bogart* (Boston: Little, Brown, 1975), 105.

113 **"the first women's picture made for men":** David Thomson, *The Big Sleep* (London: British Film Institute, 1997), 28.

113 **"If It's So Schmaltzy":** Harvey R. Greenberg, "*Casablanca*—If It's So Schmaltzy, Why Am I Weeping?" in *The Movies on Your Mind: Film Classics on the Couch, from Fellini to Frankenstein* (New York: E. P. Dutton, 1975), 79–105.

113 **"*Casablanca* reassured its male audience":** Robert B. Ray, "The Culmination of Classic Hollywood: *Casablanca*," in *A Certain Tendency of the Hollywood Cinema, 1930–1980* (Princeton, N.J.: Princeton University Press, 1985), 111.

114 **"Perhaps the essential reason":** Ingrid Bergman and Alan Burgess, *Ingrid Bergman: My Story* (New York: Delacorte, 1980), 116.

114 **"There are better movies":** Aljean Harmetz, *The Making of "Casablanca": Bogart, Bergman, and World War II* (New York: Hyperion, 2002), 6.

115 **"Remember that it was completed":** Doherty, *Projections of War*, 200.

116 **"Now, Rick Blaine":** Kanfer, *Tough Without*, 87.

117 **"BOOK CALLED HOLY BIBLE":** Birdwell, *Celluloid Soldiers*, 164.

117 **"I know your farms":** Jean Edward Smith, *FDR* (New York: Random House, 2007), 564.

118 **"The film's message was clear":** Warren F. Kimball, *The Juggler: Franklin Roosevelt as Wartime Statesman* (Princeton, N.J.: Princeton University Press, 1991), 81.

118 **"in part a private joke":** Richard Raskin, "*Casablanca* and United States Foreign Policy," *Film History* 4 (1990): 161.

118 **"They may feel that General Eisenhower":** John Lardner, "Pre-Eisenhower," *The New Yorker*, November 28, 1942.

118 **the Warners publicity department:** "De Gaulle Asks Warner Bros. for Special Screening," press release of December 18, 1942, box 1, folder 683, WBA.

119 **"When the 'treat 'em nice":** Kanfer, *Tough Without*, 106–7.

120 **"Americans don't like":** Chris Matthews, "There's a Little Rick in All of Us," *Newsweek*, October 28, 2002, 44.

121 **"Continuing to serve":** Kathy Kriger, *Rick's Café: Bringing the Film Legend to Life in Casablanca* (Guilford, Conn.: Lyons Press, 2012), 8.

121 **"an expression of solidarity":** Michael Cooper, "After Paris Attacks, 'La Marseillaise' Echoes Around the World in Solidarity," *New York Times*, November 16, 2015.

122 **"a revolutionary tune":** Ibid.

122 **"It's just a movie":** David Shipman, "Howard Koch," *The Independent*, August 18, 1995.

CHAPTER 4. SUCH MUCH?

125 **"one of the most beautiful pieces":** R. W. Fassbinder, "Michael Curtiz—Anarchist in Hollywood? Unorganized Thoughts on a Seemingly Paradoxical Idea" (1980), in *Anarchy of the Imagination: Interviews, Essays, Notes*, ed. Michael Töteberg and Leo A. Lensing (Baltimore: Johns Hopkins University Press, 1992), 104.

125 **"on accents in *Casablanca*":** Doris Berger, *Light and Noir: Exiles and Émigrés in Hollywood, 1933–1950* (Los Angeles: Skirball Cultural Center, 2015), 33.

126 **"Don't you guys know":** Anthony Heilbut, *Exiled in Paradise: German Refugee Artists and Intellectuals in America from the 1930s to*

the Present (1983; repr., Berkeley: University of California Press, 1997), 236.

126 **"[my] German at the time":** Leonid Kinskey, "It Lingers Deliciously in Memory as Time Goes By," *Movie Digest,* September 1972, 129.

127 **"Efficiency is still":** Hans Kafka, *Hollywood Calling: Die "Aufbau"—Kolumne zum Film-Exil* (Hamburg: ConferencePoint, 2002), 52.

127 **"it's a grotesque":** Ibid., 84.

127 **"The cast and crew":** "All Nationalities Included in Film," *Casablanca* press kit, n.d., box 1, folder 683, WBA.

127 **"Foreign Stars Enjoy a Boom in Hollywood":** Berger, *Light and Noir,* 61.

128 **"special appealingly schlocky romanticism":** Pauline Kael, *5001 Nights at the Movies,* rev. ed. (New York: Henry Holt, 1991), 122.

128 **"If you think of *Casablanca*":** Quoted in Aljean Harmetz, *The Making of "Casablanca": Bogart, Bergman, and World War II* (New York: Hyperion, 2002), 212.

129 **"I suddenly realized":** Ibid., 213.

129 **"It would be exciting":** Ibid., 225.

131 **"For the opening of the picture":** Hal Wallis, memo of August 1, 1942, to Don Siegel, box 1, folder 1881A, WBA.

132 **"Jewish persecution in Europe":** Joachim Schlör, *Victor Laszlo—ein Wunsch-Bild aus der Emigration* (Graz: Leykam, 2015), 28.

133 **"I felt at the time":** Stephen D. Youngkin, *The Lost One: A Life of Peter Lorre* (Lexington: University Press of Kentucky), 201–2.

133 **"absence of the Jewish question":** André Aciman, interview with the author, May 4, 2015.

135 **"The [Warner Bros.'] commissary":** David Denby, "Everybody Comes to Rick's: *Casablanca* on the Big Screen," *The New Yorker,* March 19, 2012.

136 **"I can assure you":** Alfred Polgar, "Life on the Pacific" (1942), in Mark Anderson, ed., *Hitler's Exiles: Personal Stories of the Flight from Nazi Germany to America* (New York: New Press, 1998), 271.

136 **"If for instance someone":** Ibid., 272.

137 **"I saw many friends":** Gerd Gemünden, "From 'Mr. M' to 'Mr. Murder': Peter Lorre and the Actor in Exile," in *Light Moves: German Pop-*

ular Film in Perspective, ed. Randall Halle and Margaret McCarthy (Detroit: Wayne State University Press, 2003), 103.

137 **"Every day, to earn my daily bread":** Erhard Bahr, *Weimar on the Pacific: German Exile Culture in Los Angeles and the Crisis of Modernism* (Berkeley: University of California Press, 2007), 80.

137 **"Wherever I go":** Heilbut, *Exiled in Paradise*, 177.

137 **"The poor refugees had a hard time":** S. Z. Sakall, *The Story of Cuddles: My Life Under the Emperor Francis Joseph, Adolf Hitler, and the Warner Brothers*, trans. Paul Tabori (London: Cassell, 1954), 208.

138 **"America is a 'melting pot'":** Lotte Andor, *Memoirs of an Unknown Actress: Or, I Never Was a Genuine St. Bernard*, in Erich Leyens and Lotte Andor, *Years of Estrangement*, trans. Brigitte Goldstein (Evanston, Ill.: Northwestern University Press, 1996), 87.

139 **"I would work a day or two,":** Ibid., 100.

140 **"Goethe's language":** Sakall, *Story of Cuddles*, 190.

141 **"MR. YANI SAKALL, FILM STAR":** Ibid., 191.

141 **"Once I arrived in Hollywood":** Ibid.

141 **"So many times I have":** Ronald Haver, "Finally, the Truth About *Casablanca*," *American Film*, June 1976, 16.

141 **"Don't worry vat is rough":** Ibid., 13.

141 **"separate together in a bunch":** Ibid., 12.

141 **"send a silly fool":** Kinskey, "It Lingers Deliciously," 126.

141 **"Those who tell tales":** Sakall, *Story of Cuddles*, 191.

142 **"my Yani is very depressed":** Ibid., 192.

142 **"Yesterday we went to a cinema":** Ibid., 195.

142 **"a club for disenchanted Europeans":** Heilbut, *Exiled in Paradise*, 236.

143 **"at least I had star billing":** Julian Jackson, *La Grande Illusion* (London: British Film Institute, 2009), 72.

143 **"*Casablanca* has a roll call":** Leslie Epstein, interview with the author, June 18, 2012.

143 **"I'M VERY MISERABLE AND UNHAPPY":** Hans von Twardowski, to Eleonora Mendelssohn, telegram, March 8, 1943, Eleonora Mendelssohn Papers, box 3, Hans von Twardowski Folder, New York Public Library, Rare Books and Manuscripts, New York City.

144 **"Paul Panzer":** Brigitte Mayr and Michael Omasta, "Homeless in Hollywood: Casting *Casablanca*, Warner Bros., and the European Film Exile," in Werner Hanak-Lettner, ed., *Bigger Than Life: 100 Years of Hollywood—A Jewish Experience* (Berlin: Bertz & Fischer, 2011), 105–6.

144 **"I have such a small part":** Harmetz, *The Making of*, 214.

145 **"the refugee glance":** Erich Maria Remarque, *The Night in Lisbon*, trans. Ralph Manheim (New York: Harcourt, Brace & World, 1964), 86.

146 **"Curtiz's recent problems":** Haver, "Finally, the Truth About *Casablanca*," 14. See also Kati Marton, *The Great Escape: Nine Jews Who Fled Hitler and Changed the World* (New York: Simon & Schuster, 2006), 147.

146 **"I am very sorry":** "Refugees Re-Live Invasion," press release, November 30–December 7, 1942, box 1, folder 683, WBA.

147 **"When I went back to Germany":** J. C. Allen, *Conrad Veidt: From "Caligari" to "Casablanca"* (Pacific Grove, Calif.: Boxwood Press, 1987), 120.

147 **"novelists Lion Feuchtwanger":** Paul Henreid with Julius Fast, *Ladies Man* (New York: St. Martin's, 1984), 104.

148 **"I love the water":** Youngkin, *The Lost One*, 106.

148 **"Jews and Dogs Not Permitted":** Henreid, *Ladies Man*, 100.

149 **"we don't like to be called":** Hannah Arendt, "We Refugees" (1943), in Anderson, *Hitler's Exiles*, 253.

149 **"We lost our homes":** Ibid., 253–54.

149 **"We were expelled from Germany":** Ibid., 258.

149 **"Refugees driven from country to country":** Ibid., 262.

150 **"to Rick's Café for social purposes":** Hal Wallis, memo of June 3, 1942, to Mike Curtiz, box 1, folder 1881A ("Casablanca" Story Memos 5/22/42–6/11/42), WBA.

150 **"central casting's idea of the kind of refugee":** Mark Rappaport, "The Double Life of Paul Henreid," www.fandor.com/blog/the-double-life-of-paul-henreid (entry of September 25, 2012).

150 **"The atmosphere of *Casablanca*":** Aciman interview.

151 **"The American forces landed":** Jim Herron Zamora, "Congregation Remembers *Casablanca*," *Los Angeles Times*, December 5, 1992.

151 **"coincidence, fate, intrigue":** *"Casablanca:* Hollywood," *Aufbau,* December 4, 1942.

151 **"Can the average American moviegoer":** Ibid.

152 **"There are so many former German":** Ibid.

153 **"he subsisted on very small":** Gerold Ducke, *"Der Humor kommt aus der Trauer": Curt Bois* (Berlin: Bostelmann & Siebenhaar, 2001), 137.

154 **"A Berliner comic has returned":** Ibid., 246–47.

154 **"Curt Bois can play Gogol":** Ibid., 248.

155 **"Not only was our joy":** Lotte Andor, "Ich war nie ein Bernhardiner" (unpublished manuscript), Leo Baeck Institute, New York City.

155 **"a critical touchstone":** Alexander Horwath, interview with the author, September 29, 2015.

156 **"Michael Curtiz's *Casablanca*":** Brigitte Mayr and Michael Omasta, "Fluchtpunkt Rick's Café," http://kinountersternen.at/fluchtpunkt-ricks-cafe/.

157 **"*the* Hollywood classic":** Stefan Volk, interview with the author, December 7, 2015. See also Stefan Volk, "Politische Filmzensur: Verkürzt, verfremdet, verfälscht," *Der Spiegel,* November 30, 2015.

157 **"He'd heard of the legend":** Peter Härtling, *Hubert oder Die Rückkehr nach Casablanca* (Hamburg: Luchterhand, 1978), 251–52.

157 **"He encountered himself":** Ibid., 253.

158 **"Who are you really?":** Ibid., 255.

158 **"another 'Marseillaise'":** Marc Augé, *"Casablanca": Movies and Memory,* trans. Tom Conley (Minneapolis: University of Minnesota Press, 2009), 4.

159 **"The movies give us":** Ibid., 39 and 42.

159 **"the essential scenes":** Ibid., 12.

159 **"the actor/myth":** André Bazin, "The Death of Humphrey Bogart," in Jim Hillier, ed., *Cahiers du Cinéma, the 1950s: Neo-Realism, Hollywood, New Wave* (Cambridge, Mass.: Harvard University Press, 1985), 99.

159 **"December 25":** Gyula Gazdag, interview with the author, August 6, 2015.

161 **"Then it struck me":** Mårten Blomkvist, interview with the author, May 9, 2016.

161 **“everyone’s favorite émigré film”:** Thomas Elsaesser, “Ethnicity, Authenticity, and Exile: A Counterfeit Trade?” in Hamid Naficy, ed., *Home, Exile, Homeland: Film, Media, and the Politics of Place* (New York and London: Routledge, 1999), 100.

161 **“the best refugee film of the war years”:** Mark Yost, review of *Light and Noir: Exiles and Émigrés in Hollywood, 1933–1950, Wall Street Journal*, October 28, 2015.

CHAPTER 5. WE’LL ALWAYS HAVE PARIS

167 **“No picture shall be produced”:** “The Production Code,” in John Belton, ed., *Movies and Mass Culture* (New Brunswick, N.J.: Rutgers University Press, 2000), 138–39.

167 **“The sanctity of the institution”:** Ibid., 139.

167 **“The main thing that affected our work”:** Harlan Lebo, “A Conversation with Julius Epstein,” in *“Casablanca”: Behind the Scenes* (New York: Simon & Schuster), 10.

168 **“must not be explicitly treated”:** “The Production Code,” 139.

168 **“maintain the continued flow”:** Quoted in Thomas Doherty, *Hollywood’s Censor: Joseph I. Breen and the Production Code Administration* (New York: Columbia University Press, 2007), 154.

168 **“The war simply does not affect”:** Ibid., 155.

169 **“prop”**: Production Notes, Production Code Administration Files, Margaret Herrick Library, Academy of Motion Picture Arts and Sciences, Beverly Hills, Calif.

171 **“Hitler or no Hitler, kiss me”:** Lebo, *“Casablanca”: Behind the Scenes*, 116.

172 **“We have read Part I”:** Joseph I. Breen to J. L. Warner, May 19, 1942, Production Code Administration Files, Margaret Herrick Library.

172 **“unacceptably sex suggestive”:** Ibid.

173 **“The present material contains certain elements”:** Joseph I. Breen to J. L. Warner, May 21, 1942, Production Code Administration Files, Margaret Herrick Library.

175 **“The film implied a great deal more”:** Roger Ebert in *“Casablanca”: An Unlikely Classic*, short documentary directed by Gary Leva for the 2012 Warner Home Video DVD release of *Casablanca*.

175 **"charming scoundrels":** Umberto Eco, "*Casablanca*: Cult Movies and Intertextual Collage" (1984), in *Travels in Hyperreality: Essays* (New York: Harcourt, 1986), 205.

176 **"After a meeting between Breen":** Aljean Harmetz, *The Making of "Casablanca": Bogart, Bergman, and World War II* (New York: Hyperion, 2002), 164.

176 **"keeping scenes moving":** Hal Wallis with Charles Higham, *Starmaker: The Autobiography of Hal Wallis* (New York: Macmillan, 1980), 85.

177 **"a masterpiece of light entertainment":** Charles Higham and Joel Greenberg, *Hollywood in the Forties* (New York: A.S. Barnes, 1968), 101.

177 **"'Look, the sin is punished'":** Casey Robinson, "Interview with Joel Greenberg," in Patrick McGilligan, ed., *Backstory: Interviews with Screenwriters of Hollywood's Golden Age* (Berkeley: University of California Press, 1986), 306.

178 **"as good a way for a new":** Ibid., 296.

179 **"'This is no love story,' he said":** Ibid., 308.

179 **"Play up very strongly":** Robinson, "Notes on Screenplay *Casablanca*," quoted in Harmetz, *The Making of*, 176.

180 **"much along the lines":** Casey Robinson, memo of May 20, 1942 ["Notes on Screenplay 'Casablanca'"], to Hal Wallis, box 1, folder 1881A, WBA.

180 **"She comes, as she tells Rick":** Ibid.

181 **"I would play the beginning of the next scene":** Ibid.

182 **"The present material":** Joseph I. Breen to Jack L. Warner, June 18, 1942, Production Code Administration Files, Margaret Herrick Library.

183 **"Bogart is smoking":** Richard Maltby, "'A Brief Romantic Interlude': Dick and Jane Go to 3½ Seconds of the Classical Hollywood Cinema," in *Post-Theory: Reconstructing Film Studies*, ed. David Bordwell and Noël Carroll (Madison: University of Wisconsin Press, 1996), 437.

183 **"the intricate and intimate relationship":** Ibid., 434–35.

184 **"A pale, rational, dead-gray":** Parker Tyler, *The Hollywood Hallucination* (New York: Creative Age, 1944), 37.

184 **"At all times, at all moments":** Maltby, "'Brief Romantic Interlude,'" 442.

186 **"He is not just solving":** Casey Robinson, memo of May 20, 1942 ["Notes on Screenplay 'Casablanca'"], to Hal Wallis, box 1, folder 1881A, WBA.

186 **"Given the restrictive morals":** Lebo, *"Casablanca": Behind the Scenes*, p. 110.

187 **"five reels of transgression followed":** Maltby, "'Brief Romantic Interlude,'" 455.

187 **"The suggestion that Ilsa":** Joseph I. Breen to J. L. Warner, June 21, 1942, Production Code Administration Files, Margaret Herrick Library.

187 **"Joe Breen called me yesterday":** Hal Wallis, memo to Charles Einfeld, August 28, 1942, box 1, folder 1881A, WBA.

188 **"All right, Major":** Hal Wallis, memo to Michael Curtiz, July 22, 1942, box 1, folder 1881A, ibid.

188 **"This should be delivered":** Ibid.

188 **"'Holy Shit' he wheezes":** Robert Coover, "You Must Remember This" (1987), in *A Night at the Movies, or, You Must Remember This* (Rochester, N.Y.: Dalkey Archive, 1992), 161.

189 **"easing him into her":** Ibid., 162.

189 **"own buttocks bouncing up":** Ibid., 163.

189 **"Gott in Himmel, *this is fonn*!":** Ibid., 162.

189 **"This is not Victor inside her":** Ibid.

189 **"It was the best fokk I effer haff":** Ibid., 164.

190 **"She fits two cigarettes in her lips":** Ibid., 171–72.

190 **"He raises his glass":** Ibid., 182.

190 **"Wouldn't you rather be with Humphrey Bogart":** Nora Ephron, *When Harry Met Sally* (New York: Knopf, 2012), 8.

191 **"happier with Victor Laszlo":** Ibid., 38.

192 **"How many times can you see it?":** Nora Ephron, "Nora Ephron's Favorite Love Stories," *The Daily Beast*, February 14, 2012.

192 **"They have the lousiest tune":** Peter Wegele, *Max Steiner: Composing, "Casablanca," and the Golden Age of Film Music* (Lanham, Md.: Rowman & Littlefield, 2014), 94.

192 **"None of us likes having to use":** Harmetz, *The Making of*, 254.

192 **"Even before he started work":** Wallis, *Starmaker*, 90.

193 **"In the best Wagnerian manner":** Wegele, *Max Steiner*, 164.

193 **"'As Time Goes By' must have":** Lebo, *"Casablanca": Behind the Scenes*, 182.

193 **"There's only one explanation":** Dorothy Kilgallen, "Here Comes Mr. Dooley," *Collier's*, February 12, 1944, 63.

194 **"rolls, strides, bounces":** Ronald Haver, "Finally, the Truth About *Casablanca*," *American Film*, June 1976, 16.

194 **"The thing about that song":** Jody Rosen, interview with the author, January 27, 2016.

195 **"Love is being able":** David Thomson, *Moments That Made the Movies* (New York: Thames & Hudson, 2013), 71.

195 **"Two clichés make":** Eco, "*Casablanca*: Cult Movies," 209.

197 **"the national anthem":** Johnny Depp, "Peeing on the Lilacs," *The Hollywood Reporter*, December 5–7, 1997.

198 **"It's such a great song":** Esther Zuckerman, "Director John Carney on the *Casablanca* Moment in *Begin Again*," *The Wire*, June 27, 2014.

198 **"The piano is a star of the film":** Joe Sterling and Gabriel Falcon, "*Casablanca* Piano Will Be Played Again," CNN.com, December 17, 2012.

198 **"How can anything say":** "Piano from *Casablanca* Could Sell for $1 Million at N.Y. Auction," *New York Times*, November 27, 2012.

199 **"Fifteen minutes into the movie":** James Barron, "*Casablanca* Piano Sells for $3.4 Million at Bonhams," *New York Times*, November 24, 2014.

CHAPTER 6. PLAY IT AGAIN

201 **"one of the year's most exciting and trenchant films":** Bosley Crowther, "*Casablanca*, with Humphrey Bogart and Ingrid Bergman," *New York Times*, November 27, 1942.

201 **"impressively topical":** Howard Barnes, "On the Screen," in Howard Koch, *"Casablanca": Script and Legend* (Woodstock, N.Y.: Overlook, 1973), 274.

201 **"Academy Award caliber":** Review of *Casablanca*, *The Hollywood Reporter*, December 8, 1942.

201 **"a film with as many top":** Review of *Casablanca*, *Daily Variety*, December 8, 1942.

202 **"Before Allied troops":** Manny Farber, "The Warner Boys in Africa," *The New Republic*, December 14, 1942, reprinted in Robert Polito, ed., *Farber on Film: The Complete Film Writings of Manny Farber* (New York: Library of America, 2009), 39.

202 **"Oh, Victor, please don't go":** James Agee, *Film Writing and Selected Journalism*, ed. Michael Sragow (New York: Library of America, 2005), 42.

202 **"*Casablanca* is still reverently":** Ibid., 82.

202 **"One's tender sentiments":** Pauline Kael, *Kiss Kiss Bang Bang* (Boston: Little, Brown, 1965), 245.

203 **"some consideration is being given":** Hal B. Wallis to Verne Chute, April 29, 1943, box 1, folder 1881A, WBA.

203 **"There is no necessity":** Frederick Faust, "Report on 'Sequel to *Casablanca*' by Frederick Stephani," circa spring 1943, box 1, folder 2456A ("Casablanca"—Story—Sequel—Correspondence & Summary), WBA.

204 **"Good sequels":** Ibid., 220.

204 **"Popularity of North African pictures":** Publicity announcement, n.d., box 1, folder 683, WBA.

206 **"a mishmash of leftovers":** Stephen D. Youngkin, *The Lost One: A Life of Peter Lorre* (Lexington: University Press of Kentucky, 2005), 221.

206 **"Every film is a preview":** Max Horkheimer and Theodor W. Adorno, *Dialectic of Enlightenment*, trans. Edmund Jephcott (Stanford, Calif.: Stanford University Press, 2002), 132.

206 **"the kind of tinny romantic melodrama":** Agee, *Film Writing*, 404.

208 **"swapped assignments with Michael Curtiz":** Dave Clayton, "Shooting Down the *Sergeant York–Casablanca* Swap," *Los Angeles Times*, September 24, 2000.

209 **"*the* major musical hit of the next season":** Personal correspondence in Leland Hayward Papers, box 168, folder 10, Billy Rose Theatre Division, New York Public Library for Performing Arts, New York City.

210 **"I think *Casablanca* was the first":** Aljean Harmetz, "Film; . . . And His Favorite Movie for All Seasons," *New York Times*, November 29, 1992.

211 **"Final exams were coming":** Stefan Kanfer, *Tough Without a Gun: The Extraordinary Life and Afterlife of Humphrey Bogart* (New York: Knopf, 2011), 229.

211 **"Sometime in the sixties":** David Denby, "Everybody Comes to Rick's: *Casablanca* on the Big Screen," *The New Yorker*, March 19, 2012.

212 **"To be at the Brattle":** Aljean Harmetz, *The Making of "Casablanca": Bogart, Bergman, and World War II* (New York: Hyperion, 2002), 6.

212 **"Our whole little crowd":** Harmetz, "Film."

212 **"If you were to diagram":** Todd Gitlin, interview with the author, February 18, 2016.

212 **"Everybody would pile":** Honor Moore, interview with the author, May 20, 2016.

213 **"When Captain Renault":** Howard Koch, "In Conclusion: What Happened to Story in the Contemporary Film?" in Koch, *"Casablanca": Script and Legend*, 211.

214 **"Art is the recreation":** Ibid., 221.

214 **"The thing that bothered me":** Ibid., 222–23.

215 **"Maybe it's an emotion":** Ibid., 221.

215 **"*Casablanca* is the kind of film":** Ibid., 222.

215 **"Like pilgrims, they go back":** Ibid., 223.

216 **"unoriginal and lots of cornball":** Nick Macdonald, interview with the author, June 14, 2016.

216 **"Though not the best movie":** Carrie Rickey, "As Time Goes By: After Decades of *Casablanca* on TV, It's Returning to the Big Screen," *Philadelphia Inquirer*, April 9, 1992.

216 **"the most decisive exception":** Andrew Sarris, *The American Cinema: Directors and Directions, 1929–1968* (New York: E. P. Dutton, 1968), 176.

217 **"*Casablanca* achieved its cult status":** Peter Wollen, "The Auteur Theory, Michael Curtiz, and *Casablanca*," in *Authorship and Film*, ed. David A. Gerstner and Janet Staiger (New York: Routledge, 2003), 62–63.

217 **"It's not my favorite Humphrey Bogart film":** Antoine de Baecque and Serge Toubiana, *Truffaut*, trans. Catherine Temerson (Berkeley: University of California Press, 2000), 307–8.

218 **"the city of my childhood dreams":** Marc Augé, *"Casablanca":*

Movies and Memory, trans. Tom Conley (Minneapolis: University of Minnesota Press, 2009) 8.

219 **"It's because we need to believe":** Ibid., 30.

219 **"To see a film again":** Ibid., 42.

219 **"Bogart is a man":** Peter Bogdanovich, *Who the Hell's in It?* (New York: Random House, 2010), 47.

220 **"Here is an 'impossible'":** James Monaco, *Alain Resnais* (New York: Oxford University Press, 1979), 52.

221 **"The spectators quote the best lines":** Umberto Eco, "*Casablanca*: Cult Movies and Intertextual Collage" (1984), in *Travels in Hyperreality: Essays* (New York: Harcourt, 1986), 197–98.

221 **"*Casablanca* is a cult movie":** Ibid., 208.

222 **"to remember one film":** Augé, *"Casablanca": Movies and Memory,* 10.

222 **"one of life's great watchers":** Woody Allen, *Play It Again, Sam: A Romantic Comedy in Three Acts* (New York: Samuel French, 1968), 8 and 5–6.

223 **"a cringingly miserable":** Brendan Gill, "Son of Walter Mitty," *The New Yorker*, February 22, 1969.

223 **"There's no secret, kid":** Allen, *Play It Again, Sam*, 7 and 19.

224 **"There's a new Godard":** Ibid., 40 and 55.

226 **"The best compliment":** Kevin Kelly, "*Play It Again, Sam* Clicks," *Boston Globe*, January 28, 1969.

227 **"Perhaps the biggest error":** Peter Buckley, review of *Play It Again, Sam, Films and Filming*, February 1973.

228 **"It works as nostalgia":** Leo Braudy, *The World in a Frame: What We See in Films* (New York: Doubleday, 1976), 205.

228 **"It's one of thousands":** Harmetz, *The Making of*, 347.

228 **"a junky play":** Ralph Gardner Jr., "Writers Annotate Their Classics to Benefit PEN American Center," *Wall Street Journal*, November 30, 2014.

229 **"a movie that demonstrates":** Kael, *Kiss Kiss Bang Bang*, 245.

229 **"Like those cynical heroes":** Pauline Kael, "Trash, Art, and the Movies," *Harper's Magazine,* February 1969, 65.

231 **"It was during the second semester":** Stan Brooks, interview with the author, December 10, 2015.

231 **"I think it's a mistake":** Lou Lumenick, "With Seventy Years Gone,

Is Hollywood Finally Prepared for a *Casablanca* Sequel?" *New York Post*, November 4, 2012.

233 **"It is film criticism and movie history":** David Thomson, *Suspects* (New York: Knopf, 1985), epigraph page.

233 **"In truth, she never warmed":** Ibid., 8.

234 **"The affair with Ilsa":** Ibid., 168.

234 **"Apparently he took one long look":** Ibid.

235 **"*Suspects* is a book":** Scott Eyman, "*Suspects* a Bleak Rip-Off of Film Suspects, *Sun-Sentinel*, June 23, 1985.

235 **"Part of the reason":** Lou Lumenick, "Outtake: David Thomson on That *Casablanca* Sequel," *New York Post*, November 5, 2012.

235 **"After leaving Casablanca":** Lumenick, "With Seventy Years Gone."

236 **"he grew up to be":** Ibid.

236 **"*Casablanca* is art":** Susan Linfield, "The Color of Money," *American Film*, January–February 1987, 32.

236 **"We're doing everything except":** Jack Mathews, "Colorization: Beginning to See Possibilities, As Time Goes By," *New York Times*, November 9, 1988.

237 **"In today's popular culture":** Martin Arnold, "After That Night at the Airport," *New York Times*, October 22, 1998.

238 **"It's a great story":** Ibid.

238 **"Letting a German author write an update":** Cornelius Fischer, "Play It Again," *The Hollywood Reporter*, November 24–30, 1998.

238 **"It's a tough business":** Arnold, "After That Night."

238 **"I don't want anybody":** Lumenick, "With Seventy Years Gone."

239 **"Did anyone want to imagine":** Jeanine Basinger, *I Do and I Don't: A History of Marriage in the Movies* (New York: Knopf, 2013), xxi.

CHAPTER 7. A BEAUTIFUL FRIENDSHIP

241 **"one of those rare films":** Roger Ebert, audio commentary for the 2002 Warner Home Video DVD release of *Casablanca*.

242 **"My first response":** Howard Koch, "In Conclusion: What Happened to Story in the Contemporary Film?" in *"Casablanca": Script and Legend* (Woodstock, N.Y.: Overlook, 1973), 209–10.

242 **"One more reward":** Stanley Kauffmann, "Out of the Past," *The New Republic*, May 4, 1992.

242 **"When I think of it":** Koch, *"Casablanca": Script and Legend*, 222.

242 **"At age twelve":** James Card, "Confessions of a *Casablanca* Cultist: An Enthusiast Meets the Myth and Its Flaws," in *The Cult Film Experience*, ed. J. P. Tellotte (Austin: University of Texas Press, 1991), 66.

243 **"This is a film from my parents' generation":** Todd Gitlin, interview with the author, February 18, 2016.

244 **"Like Jay Gatsby":** Robert B. Ray, "The Culmination of Classic Hollywood: *Casablanca*," in *A Certain Tendency of the Hollywood Cinema, 1930–1980* (Princeton, N.J.: Princeton University Press, 1985), 100.

244 **"It provides tangible evidence":** Ronald Haver, "Finally, the Truth About *Casablanca*," *American Film*, June 1976, 16.

244 **"in a darkened theater":** Leonard Maltin, interview with the author, April 12, 2016.

245 **"When asked what is":** Ebert, audio commentary, 2002 Warner Home Video DVD.

245 **"*Casablanca* is the most sociable":** David Denby, "Everybody Comes to Rick's: *Casablanca* on the Big Screen," *The New Yorker*, March 19, 2012.

245 **"one of the best-told narratives":** Steven Spielberg in *"Casablanca": An Unlikely Classic*, short documentary directed by Gary Leva for the 2012 Warner Home Video DVD release of *Casablanca*.

246 **"People who have never seen":** Jeanine Basinger, interview with the author, March 16, 2016.

246 **"The finished film manages":** Kenneth Turan, *Not to Be Missed: Fifty-Four Favorites from a Lifetime of Film* (New York: Public Affairs, 2014), 81.

246 **"sticks to you forever":** Ibid., xiv.

247 **"To a young boy":** Leslie Epstein, "Duel in the Sun," *The American Prospect*, November 16, 2001.

247 **"It was more of a deterrent":** Anya Epstein, interview with the author, March 22, 2016.

247 **"it tells a very noble story":** Monika Henreid, interview with the author, February 24, 2016.

247 **"Ask the man on the street":** David Thomson, *The Big Screen: The Story of the Movies—and What They Have Done to Us* (New York: Farrar Straus Giroux, 2012), 202.

248 **"One of the first things":** Henreid interview.

249 **"movies were dead!":** Mike Fitelson, introduction to *Casablanca* screening, United Palace of Cultural Arts, New York City, November 17, 2013.

249 **"I've seen *Casablanca* projected":** Lou Lumenick, interview with the author, March 17, 2016.

251 **"Of all the portraits":** Lloyd Clark, "Stamp Fails to Portray 'Real' Bogey," *Sun City* (Ariz.) *Daily News-Sun*, August 19, 1997.

252 **"The inclusion of more quotes":** Lloyd Clark, "AFI Omits One Key Line from *Casablanca*," *Sun City* (Ariz.) *Daily News-Sun*, March 16, 2010.

252 **"I'm an African-American":** Tom Hennessy, "He'll Always Have *Casablanca*," *Long Beach Press-Telegram*, August 17, 1999.

253 **"Doing the right thing":** Ibid.

253 **"boundaries of cinema culture":** Andrew Kingsford-Smith, "Bringing *Casablanca* Back to Life: Future Cinema's Immersive Experience," TheCultureTrip.com, n.d.

253 **"These are movies which you'd want":** Aljean Harmetz, interview with the author, March 17, 2016.

254 **"I chose not to go public":** Bernard Weinraub, "Anthony Perkins's Wife Tells of Two Years of Secrecy," *New York Times*, September 16, 1992.

254 **"simulation of the black market":** Nenad Dukic, "Yugoslavia Plays *Casablanca* One More Time," *The Hollywood Reporter*, November 17, 1992.

254 **"The idea of other actors":** "*Casablanca* the Musical Premiered in Beijing," *China Daily*, March 28, 2005.

255 **"A film is different than a performance":** Ibid.

255 **"I hope the Chinese audiences":** Ibid.

256 **"the Takarazuka romantic dream":** "A Kiss Is Just a (Fake) Kiss," *The Lobster Dance*, January 11, 2010.

256 **"They say that one is the greatest":** Adam Johnson, *The Orphan Master's Son* (New York: Random House, 2012), 126, 305, 306, and 429–30.

257 **"Some of my fondest memories":** Kathy Kriger, *Rick's Café: Bringing the Film Legend to Life in Casablanca* (Guilford, Conn.: Lyons Press, 2012), 56.

257 **"I'm Madame Rick":** Ibid., 173.

257 **"We're known all over the world":** Samantha North, "'As Time Goes By': Defining Casablanca's Modern City Brand," *Middle East Eye*, June 7, 2016.

260 **"According to Colonel Levinson":** Jack Warner to Roy Obringer, January 28, 1946, box 1, folder 2870, WBA.

261 **"Apparently there is more than one way":** Groucho Marx, *The Groucho Letters* (New York: Simon & Schuster, 2007), 14.

262 **"Professionally, we were brothers long before":** Ibid., 14 and 16.

263 **"Paul Hangover, our hero":** Ibid., 17–18.

267 **"A show like ours":** Matt Selman, interview with the author, April 5, 2016.

268 **"A bris is still a bris":** Corey Kilgannon, "Lower East Side Troubadour," *New York Times*, June 2, 2013.

268 **"Xerox of a Xerox":** Selman interview.

270 **"a prototype for a virtual cineplex":** Matthew Mirapaul, "They'll Always Have Paris (And a Scholarly Web Site)," *New York Times*, March 18, 2002.

271 **"it's remarkable how shocked":** Paul Krugman, "Twilight of the Apparatchiks," *New York Times*, February 26, 2016.

272 **"You might consider them romantics":** John McCain, "The Good Soldier," *New York Times*, March 24, 2016.

272 **"Humphrey's fifteen minutes":** Tim Cockey, "Don't Bogart Those Cultural Touchstones," *Boston Globe*, August 10, 2015.

273 **"If watching old movies":** Leon Wieseltier, "Letter of Recommendation: Turner Classic Movies," *New York Times Magazine*, February 27, 2015.

273 **"Bruce and I will be celebrating":** Elizabeth Warren, Facebook post, December 31, 2015.

Illustration Credits

iv–v Courtesy of the Museum of Modern Art Film Stills Archive.

xv Courtesy of Photofest.

13 Courtesy of Saul Nirenberg.

21 Courtesy of Leslie Epstein.

32 Courtesy of Academy of Motion Picture Arts and Sciences.

46 Courtesy of the Museum of Modern Art Film Stills Archive.

49 Courtesy of the Margaret Herrick Library, Academy of Motion Picture Arts and Sciences.

57 Courtesy of Photofest.

70 Courtesy of the Kobal Collection at Art Resource, NY.

75 Courtesy of the Margaret Herrick Library, Academy of Motion Picture Arts and Sciences.

92 Courtesy of Photofest.

111 Courtesy of Photofest.

124 Courtesy of Photofest.

130 Courtesy of Warnes Bros. Entertainment Inc.

132 (left) Courtesy of Art Resource, NY; (right) Courtesy of Photofest.

138 Courtesy of Photofest.

140 Courtesy of Photofest.

166 Courtesy of Photofest.

171 Courtesy of the Museum of Modern Art Film Stills Archive.

196 Courtesy of Photofest.

224 Photo by Friedman-Abeles, courtesy of New York Public Library of the Performing Arts.

230 Courtesy of Stan and Tanya Brooks.

232 Courtesy of Photofest.

259 Courtesy of Photofest.

261 Courtesy of Photofest.

266 Courtesy of Photofest.

270 Courtesy of *The New Yorker* Collection/The Cartoon Bank.

Index

Note: Italic page numbers refer to photos and figures, and accompanying captions.

INDEX